This book is based on y...   ...many architects and administrato...   ..., thank you for your support over the ye...   ...ne. Thank you to everyone who has provided fe...   ...y the cadre of reviewers who read every chapter! Thank ...   ...who have given me projects to learn and develop my career, and ... trusting in my follow-through. This book is dedicated to all those furthering the art of infrastructure design and mentoring others. A very special dedication goes to my family Amy, Catherine, Sofi, Lila, Dorine, Harun, George, Judy, whose love and support was there throughout my many projects and startup adventures! Thank you for being there for me. I love you. – *John Yani Arrasjid*

* * *

To my family and friends for enabling and encouraging me to grow personally and professionally over the years, and for all the help they will provide in the future. My special thanks to Bridget, who gave up many nights and weekends with me so I could work on this project. Thank you to everyone who I have worked with for the past 20 years in the IT field. You have all provided me encouragement, challenges, and inspirations to continue to give back to you all these years. – *Mark Gabryjelski*

* * *

Every day I get to engage with folks who are elite minds in the world of information technology in the enterprise. These people can be found in my colleagues at work, former students, and counterparts at partner, parent, and competing companies. To all of these folks I say thank you for helping me become a better architect with every interaction. Most importantly to my wife, Stacy, and our kids, Hayden and Hudson. The three of you deserve significant recognition for the amount of technical neediness you endure by living with me. Though it's hard for me to travel and be away from you, know that I do it for you. You are my motivation and my inspiration to continue to get better and expand my horizons in my professional life as much as in my personal life. Thank you. I love you. – *Chris H. McCain*

IT ARCHITECT:

Foundation in the Art of

Infrastructure Design

A Practical Guide for
IT Architects

John Yani Arrasjid, VCDX-001

Mark Gabryjelski, VCDX-023

Chris McCain, VCDX-079

 IT ARCHITECT SERIES

Upper Saddle River, NJ • Boston • Indianapolis • San Francisco
New York • Toronto • Montreal • London • Munich • Paris • Madrid
Cape Town • Sydney • Tokyo • Singapore • Mexico City

IT Architect: Foundation in the Art of Infrastructure
Design, A practical guide for IT architects

Published by IT Architect Resource, LLC
14 Ansel Street, Salem, New Hampshire 03079
Itar.com

Warning and Disclaimer
Every effort has been made to make this book as complete and as accurate as possible,
but no warranty or fitness is implied. The information provided is on an "as is" basis.
The authors and the publisher shall have neither liability nor responsibility to any
person or entity with respect to any loss or damages arising from the information
contained in this book or from the use of the CD or programs accompanying it.

ISBN: 978-0-9966-4770-0 (sc)
ISBN: 978-0-9966-4771-7 (hc)
ISBN: 978-0-9966-4772-4 (e)

Library of Congress Control Number: 2016901105

Rev. date: 3/18/2016

CONTENTS

TABLES

FIGURES

FOREWORD

"Knowing the behavior of a system and its intrinsic architectural structure is far more valuable than just having deep expertise in a specific component."

I have been fortunate to spend my career involved in the radical transformation of numerous technology industries. I began my career as the networking industry recreated itself into the IP and Internet era. I then participated in the transformation of the real time communications industry from circuit to packet/IP switching and software, then helped accelerate the cellular industry to become broadband in the air (4G) and now am fortunate to be in the center of the transformation of the data center IT stack from segmented and hardware based to software defined. In all of these transformations, the difference between success and failure was based on understanding the goals and desired behavior of the system and architecture and using that vision as the litmus test for the numerous technical decisions that would be made.

Today, the IT industry is in a period of unprecedented transformation at every layer. We are adopting cloud automation models, hybridizing our topologies, leveraging external services in new ways, changing the way we develop original applications, creating technology via community development, virtualizing everything in many ways, and even rethinking the definition of what a user is. Each of these changes is challenging but the fact that they are all happening simultaneously can be overwhelming.

In order to deal with this rapid acceleration of technical change, the best tool at our disposal is a greater investment in system and architectural level thinking. The purpose of your IT environment is still clear even with all of these technical changes. Your goals of speed, agility, efficiency, security, reliability and most critically business relevance are still valid. However the scale of technical changes has distracted us from keeping our system level thinking fresh. For this reason, I am personally excited with this work, "The Art of Infrastructure Design, A Practical Guide for IT Architects". It's focus on IT system design and the holistic approach as the most important skill we can cultivate as the technical churn continues is critical.

The emphasis on simplicity of the system via an architectural approach based on the real business goals of technology adoption sets a framework for the dialog. The discussion of the IT stack layering, and how they must interwork, helps decompose a complex system into something manageable. And finally the detailed dialog on how the individual layers are evolving helps build a strong modern technical foundation.

It is clear that we will live times of even more technology churn at the component level for the foreseeable future so investing in a top down system level view of the IT stack will be critical. For that reason I highly recommend this book both for those seeking to expand their industry certifications but also for the IT practitioner simply trying to make sense of the complex and changing layers of the IT stack.

John Roese
Global Chief Technology Officer, EMC
Chairman, Cloud Foundry Foundation

FOREWORD

Over the last few years I have been travelling the world meeting with customers and partners who have come to depend on VMware technology. Many build complex infrastructures including virtualization and cloud solutions to support their business objectives and use cases. As VMware continues to play a central role in helping these companies move to a software-defined enterprise, we've recognized the need to provide deep technical guidance that helps our customers and partners realize success. Our comprehensive certification programs best support this objective.

During my visits, I've had the opportunity to meet with many VMware Certified Design Experts (VCDXs). VCDX holders are part of an elite group of architects leading virtualization and cloud implementations around the world. Being a VCDX is not just about technical expertise; many, if not all, are leaders in their respective companies. I see them as "Field Generals" helping their companies and customers achieve business objectives, overcome challenges, and create transformative solutions.

This new book, "The Art of Infrastructure Design, A Practical Guide for IT Architects" will support experienced IT infrastructure architects who want to pursue their VMware Certified Advanced Professional (VCAP) design or VCDX certification, and will help infrastructure administrators who are interested in learning more about design. This book complements the VMware Press book "vCloud Architecture Toolkit (vCAT)" and is an extension to the "VCDX Boot Camp, Preparing for the VCDX Boot Camp" book.

VCDX Certification is achieved through the Design Defense where all candidates must submit and successfully defend a production-ready VMware Solution before a panel of veteran VCDX-holders. This unique testing process ensures that those who achieve VCDX are peer-vetted and ready to join an elite group of world-class consulting architects. Included in this book is an in-depth look into the full methodology and design process and includes a case study to help both new and experienced architects develop a solution that can be submitted for the VCDX defense. Examples of infrastructure design documents that benefit both experienced and aspiring architects are provided as a reference. The methodology can be applied for use in other training for infrastructure architects, and has proven success in the field.

I highly recommend this book for anyone pursuing design level certifications such as the VCAP and VCDX certifications. I believe this book will be an indispensable reference in their day-to-day activities as an architect. Certified VCDX holders are role models for their peers and inspire those who seek to achieve a higher degree of technical excellence. Once you have joined the elite community of VCDXs, I hope you will continue to grow your leadership skills and to give back to the community that supported you in achieving your goal.

Pat Gelsinger
VCDX Alpha
VMware CEO

PREFACE

"Infrastructure Design, at its core, is about the seamless reflection of the business upon the canvas of the company cloud. When done right, the information technology team is seen as a powerful enabler of strategy and vision. When dysfunctional, IT is deadweight that inhibits growth and innovation. How does your business view your design?"
— *Andrew Hald, VCDX-004*

This is the first in a series of books for IT architects.

There are several outcomes of this book. One is to educate the reader on the design methodology for an IT infrastructure. The second is to support architecture design courses. A third is to provide a set of reference architectures and tools for an IT infrastructure covering conceptual, logical, and physical design examples.

This book complements the VMware Press Book "VCDX Boot Camp, Preparing for the VCDX Panel Defense" which provides details on the process for the defense of the VCDX certification, including preparation and handling the different phases of the VCDX defense. This book expands significantly on the area of architecture design and provides templates, in the form of Tables of Content and design examples that will help candidates with a starting point for what certification teams call the Minimally Qualified Candidate (MQC).

This book also complements the VMware Press Book "vCloud Architecture Toolkit (vCAT)" that provides a suite of tools for use with a vCloud solution. It includes design patterns, operational guidelines, and more.

This book educates the reader on the full design process. It covers server and desktop virtualization in a solution to the case study in Chapter 3.

The current dearth of examples prompted us to build a book to educate, and to help both new and experienced architects develop a solution. It can be used to help prepare a design by structuring design strategies around requirements and available technology. This can be used as a reference guide for those wishing to review an infrastructure design utilizing VMware technology for the physical design solution.

This book provides the blueprints for constructing an infrastructure solution that will support production workloads. We use a vendor agnostic approach in developing the conceptual and logical design areas.

Readers will be presented with a case study, workflow for developing and submitting a design, analysis of design decisions, and a blueprint based design review checklist. Where multiple options exist for a design area, alternatives are included with discussion on the advantages and disadvantages of each choice. Supporting information and potential impacts, positive and negative, beyond their original intent are included. Readers will be better prepared for understanding the criteria used for development and providing supporting evidence.

We will focus on design methodologies for virtualization (server and desktop), provide case studies and exercises, and provide reference architectures in support of the case study. It is important that an architect balance requirements, budget, schedules, and skill sets to provide the optimal design for a particular customer. There are typically several options that can be applied. We take the approach of choosing one option for each of the major decisions and provide a more general reference architecture based on the result of these choices. We provide decision trees to assist in understanding the typical workflow an architect may choose to follow to discover all the design requirements and architect the final solution. Although a design choice may be justified based on design choice criteria, there may be other impacts to the project, both positive and negative. We choose to provide a set of exercises that can be adapted to your environment to help you craft your own design.

Understanding the phases of design, the workflows for success, and addressing challenges are all important. We hope this book will help more aspiring architects be successful and drive others to develop solid design skills. We provide you with guidance, but getting the experience is up to you.

WHO SHOULD READ THIS BOOK

Aspiring and experienced IT infrastructure architects can benefit from this book. This book takes a vendor agnostic approach until the physical architecture. It then uses VMware technologies as the example reference architecture basis. We provide three IT infrastructure solution designs. The methods included within this book can be used with other technologies. The examples have to include real technologies to demonstrate the approach from start to finish.

Our audience is that of infrastructure administrators interested in learning more about design to help them in both current operations work and future work as a team member working with architects.

Our other audience includes those pursuing infrastructure design certifications, like the VCDX certification. VCDX certification is for virtualization and cloud architects and has demonstrated a large value proposition. It includes a vendor agnostic approach for conceptual and logical design, and considers products from a primary vendor, VMware, and integrated technologies from other vendors for the physical design. If you are currently working with VMware technologies and solutions as an architect, the VCDX certification can be a valuable certification. For many, this book will support them in achieving their certifications, and in their day-to-day activities as an architect. As an extension to the "VCDX Boot Camp" book (VMware Press), this book provides details on the design methodology and the documentation created for customer success.

GOALS AND METHODS

The primary goal of this book is to increase the number of architects developing successful and scalable IT infrastructure solutions.

To aid you in understanding both the methodology and the requirements for successful infrastructure design solutions, this book includes the following components:

Overview of a Design: Throughout the book we provide guidance on what is necessary for a successful design. The minimal design examples presented can be expanded and enhanced to provide more value. We provide discourse on the design decisions made. We include suggestions on selecting and developing a design.

Infrastructure Design Methodology & Documentation: Chapter 2 provides an overview of the design methodology we have used in infrastructure design. It overlaps with that used by a majority of successful candidates for a VCDX design submission. This section also discusses the creation of a document set, providing an example Table of Contents for each of the documents for a full design.

Example Design Documents: Chapters 3 through 6 include a case study and a set of documents matching the submission of a minimally qualified candidate. The case study covers desktop and server virtualization in support of the business needs. The documents include architecture, installation, validation, operations, and risk management.

Design Analysis: Chapter 7 includes analysis of both the design and operational patterns presented in the example design documents. This section provides extra information to explore the details beyond the example designs presented, and shows the tradeoffs of alternate design choices. This is also valuable to learn how an architect evaluates design choices within each document.

Presenting and Defending the Design: Chapter 8 provides guidance on creating a design presentation and conducting a review, defending decisions made as part of the process. Included is an example design presentation based on the first example for virtualization design. This helps prepares an architect for presenting a design to a customer, or to a VCDX panel.

Tools: The appendices include various tools for use by architects. (A) The Discovery Phase Survey Questions covers the types of questions used to gather information for a project. (B) The Design Decision Workbook helps document the decisions that are made for the project along with the justification, impact, and risk. (C) The Design Review Readiness Assessment provides an example way of determining if a design and the architect are ready for a review. (D) Building a Design Lab provides guidance on creating a lab to use for developing a design.

HOW TO USE THIS BOOK

This book was written in the order that the authors believe is best for learning the methodology and completing a solution-based architecture for an enterprise. For details on the VCDX defense process, please see the complementary books mentioned earlier. This book is a teaching tool and a reference for architects and for VCDX candidates.

The core chapters and appendices cover the following topics:

Chapter 1, "Introduction" This chapter provides an overview of what we will cover in the book and how it aligns with design methodologies, such as that practiced by a VCDX individual. It includes the goals of the book, the target audience, and insight from a large number of the existing VCDX around the world.

Chapter 2, "Infrastructure Design Methodology" This chapter focuses on the methodology for developing infrastructure designs. This methodology can be used by infrastructure design architects and is used as a teaching tool.

Chapter 3, "Case Study" This chapter covers the case study used to create the example documents that are presented in the following chapters.

Chapter 4, "Server Virtualization – Architecture Design Example" This chapter provides an example document covering the architecture design that support the Case Study presented in Chapter 3 for server virtualization. This is a starting point, beyond templates, that a candidate can use as a reference in developing a design to submit. The same starting point is given for desktop virtualization in Chapter 6. This chapter provides an additional value to those interested in setting up a virtual lab that can be used for training lessons.

Chapter 5, "Server Virtualization – Installation, Validation, and Operation Examples" This chapter provides an example set of documents for installation, validation, and operations of the design that support the Case Study presented in Chapter 3 for server virtualization.

Chapter 6, "Desktop Virtualization – Architecture Design Example" This chapter provides an example set of documents that support the Case Study presented in Chapter 3 for desktop virtualization.

Chapter 7, "Analysis" This chapter provides analysis of both design and operational patterns used in Chapters 4 through 6 to provide context beyond what is included in the base documentation. It is also an area where we provide alternative design choices that might be chosen with the potential increase or decrease to the design quality.

Chapter 8, "Presenting and Defending the Design" This chapter provides an approach to developing a presentation and using it to describe the design to a customer, or to defend the design in a VCDX defense. The presentation describes the design and also provides additional supporting information in defense of design decisions and design patterns used. Techniques for presenting as an Infrastructure Architect are provided. Example presentations are provided with recommendations on the organization and use of hyperlinks to strengthen the presentation.

Appendix A, "Discovery Phase Survey Questions" This provides example questions asked by an architect working on gathering the business requirements and aspects of the current workload use cases, current infrastructure, and business/project requirements.

Appendix B, "Design Decision Workbook" This includes tables that we have found useful in tracking design decisions. Traceability and accountability are both important. If an assumption is confirmed, then this should be tracked, including how and who confirmed it.

Appendix C, "Design Review Readiness Assessment" This is used to determine how closely an architect aligns their design documents in preparation for delivering a solution based on VMware technologies, but it can also be modified for use as a tool to assess an individual's readiness to present and defend a design when complete. This includes material to determine the completeness of the design. These checklists are designed to be adapted for use in non-VMware solutions. Items in Italics are VMware vendor specific.

Appendix D, "Building a Design Lab" This is used to describe building a lab that can be used for developing a design for a customer and evaluating the functional and operational aspects.

ABOUT THE AUTHORS

 **John Yani Arrasjid, VCDX-001**, is a Senior Consultant Technologist in the EMC Office of the CTO. His current work is focused on converged infrastructure strategy and engineering tools. John previously worked at VMware for almost 12 years. There he developed solutions and software as a Consulting Architect, A Principal Architect, and as a VMware Ambassador in the Field Office of the CTO. John holds VMware vExpert and EMC Elect status. John regularly speaks at conferences and related workshops and industry events including VMworld, VMware Partner Exchange, VMware vForum, VMware User Groups (VMUG), Cloud Expo, and the USENIX LISA, ATC and HotCloud conferences.

John was lead architect and chief product owner for the VMware vCloud Architecture Toolkit (vCAT) from 2011 to 2014, and launched this in book form through VMware Press in 2013. The online electronic version is accessible for free at http://www.vmware.com/go/vcat.

John's first early books in the USENIX Association Short Topics in System Administration series include Deploying the VMware Infrastructure, Foundation for Cloud Computing with VMware vSphere 4, and Cloud Computing with VMware vCloud Director. John has also co-authored the VCDX Boot Camp book that is complementary to this book.

During his time at VMware, John has developed multiple consulting engagements and conference tutorials that focused on security, performance, and availability of virtualized and cloud infrastructures. John's earlier work at VMware included development of free backup (vmsnap) and recovery (vmres) tools for virtual machines using snapshot technology, and development of virtual infrastructure workshops on Performance Management, Virtual Security, Disaster Recovery, and Infrastructure Design.

John participated in the initial development of the VCDX program and continues his support with online and onsite workshops (VCDX Tips, VCDX Boot Camp, #vBrownbag Boot Camp Live Online). John also developed and released the VCAP Admin and VCAP Design boot camps.

John is active in supporting projects outside of VMware to better the world we live in. These include work with non-profits like the Ocean Futures Society, led by Jean-Michel Cousteau. John has also supported the Wounded Warriors with other VCDX through fundraising activities. John is vice president of the USENIX Association Board of Directors. John was co-founder of the VMware "Elastic Sky" band, which has been billed at VMware events with Foreigner, INXS, The Killers, Jon Bon Jovi, and The Black Keys. He can be followed on Twitter as @vcdx001 and can be seen playing guitar and ukulele at The Strawberry Music Festival.

Mark Gabryjelski, VCDX-023, has been involved in design and integration of solutions for clients in all markets since 1996. With focus on datacenter optimization, he has worked with companies across all aspects of business. Mark brings his expertise to his client's teams and is expanding their teams' capabilities with provided Professional Services, Managed Foundation Services, Virtualization Services, Disaster Recovery Services, as well as Architecture and Design Services while consistently providing additional efficiencies in the datacenter.

Leading the virtualization trend since 2002 nationally, with a focus in the Northeast corridor, he has been on the bleeding edge of solutions involving network, storage, server, operating system, and application virtualization. Mark was the 46th to receive his VCP (VMware Certified Professional) Certification, and 23rd person in the world to receive his VCDX (VMware Certified Design Expert) certification, which requires a review by your peers prior to being awarded this title.

Mark's leadership at Worldcom Exchange, his current employer, has been extending by offering his mentoring and sharing his vast array of technical capabilities with the Professional Services and leadership teams. Combinations of the technical skills proven over time, he has been able to architect solutions and lead projects for datacenters from concept to complete forklift upgrades, with minimal business impact.

Mark has been involved in the Users' Groups in the New England area for 8 years, and he strives to find ways to encourage others to think outside the box, find ways to better themselves & their organization, and bring their collaborative results back to the User Groups to share with others.

Disaster Recovery, Business Continuance, Virtual Infrastructure, Virtual Desktop Infrastructure, server consolidation, server containment, migrations, SAN solutions, network architecture, integration of solutions, education, knowledge transfer, and best of breed solutions are brought to the table when engaging this Virtualization Practice Manager who brings 18 years of experience to an IT infrastructure.

Delivering solutions that focus on simplicity and proven technologies, with guaranteed results, the persistence of Virtualization Practice Manager can bring his love of delivering solutions, acting as Trusted Advisor, and empowering IT organizations nationally to optimize their datacenters. You may have to bring him into YOUR organization as he discovers additional cost savings across your datacenter practices, just waiting to drive down recurring costs and finding solutions to simplify the operation of your datacenter.

Over the years, Mark has held IT certifications from vendors like BEA, CompTIA, Cisco, Compaq, EMC, Hewlett-Packard, IBM, Microsoft,

Novell, Nutanix, Polyserve, Sun, Veeam, and VMware. You can follow him on Twitter as @MarkGabbs.

Chris McCain, VCDX-079, has worked in the enterprise information technology space for over 14 years as a consultant, trainer, and author. In 2008, Chris authored the first book on VMware technologies, Mastering VMware Infrastructure 3 opening the doors for thousands of folks to begin their journey during VMware's first period of IT disruption with compute virtualization. Chris is now a director in the networking and security business unit at VMware where he is helping to once again change the landscape of data centers and IT organizations around the world with network virtualization. In addition to being a dual VCDX in Data Center Virtualization (DCV) and Network Virtualization (NV), Chris holds enterprise certifications from Microsoft and Cisco as well as the status of VMware Certified Instructor (VCI). Chris lives in St Petersburg, FL with his wife, two sons, and a dog. You can follow Chris on Twitter as @hcmccain.

ACKNOWLEDGMENTS

The authors would like to thank the following people for their support in developing and reviewing the material included. Thank you to our family and friends who supported our efforts in creating this work.

Deploying a product is like building a house. Deploying an infrastructure is like building a city. The latter requires greater planning and a higher level of governance due to the complexity of multiple technologies and services.

Thank you to the following. They have contributed to the creation of this book with their ideas, feedback, and critical insight. Doug Baer, Michael Webster, Ben Lin, Steve Kaplan, Mark Ewert, Christian Mohn, Martijn Baecke, Rupen Sheth, Benjamin Troch, and Raman Veeramraju. Thank you to Raman Veeramraju for contributing to image development. Thank you to Gary Baker for getting me started on my journey as an architect and working as project manager with many of the larger consulting projects. Thank you to Amy Arrasjid for the cover art.

Thank you to reviewers including the above individuals and Tim Antonowicz, Daemon Behr, Steven Bochinski, Linus Bourque, James Bowling, Mark Brunstad, Jonathan Copeland, Brandon Hahn, Paul McSharry, Manish Patel, Iwan Rahabok, Daniel Rethmeier, Greg Robertson, Christian Strijbos, Matt Vandenbeld, Rene Van Den Bedem, and Raman Veeramraju.

John Yani Arrasjid, VCDX-001
Senior Consulting Technologist, EMC Office of the CTO
Vice President, USENIX Association Board of Directors

.

PLEASE SHARE YOUR FEEDBACK!

As authors we recognize and value your feedback on what we're doing well, areas to improve, and new content that you feel would benefit those pursuing a role as an infrastructure design architect. If there are other topic areas that you believe would be valuable in the IT Architect Series, we are here to listen. We are working with additional authors to continue the series with material tied to infrastructure design such as software-defined networking, software-defined storage, applications, and cloud.

When you share your feedback, please be sure to include this book's title, along with your name, e-mail address, and phone number. We will carefully review your comments but may not be able to provide a direct response to all submissions. Thank you for sharing with us.

Mail: IT Architect Resource, LLC, Salem, NH 03079
Website: www.itaseries.com

READER SERVICES

Visit the book website

http://itaseries.com
or
http://www.itarchitectseries.com

Register this book for convenient access to any updates, downloads, or errata that might be available for this book.

CHAPTER 1

INTRODUCTION

"Infrastructure design is about careful discussion, planning, and development of a technical and operational solution to meet the needs of the business now, while also being open to future enhancements. Infrastructure design, in terms of scope, is comparable to designing a city versus designing a house."
— *John Yani Arrasjid, VCDX-001*

The material included in this book provides the design methodology for building IT Infrastructures. For this book we have included example infrastructure design material for server virtualization and desktop virtualization. In this millennium, computing infrastructure is touching everything. Look at the Internet of Things (IoT) to get an idea of how quickly things are growing and how valuable infrastructure design has become.

Consider the following. Designing for a product is like designing a house. Designing for an infrastructure is like designing a city. The infrastructure has many moving parts, including disparate technologies and complicated procedures, which need to be integrated for a successful solution. The design must be validated, structured, tested, and maintained. We are including a methodology used by many virtualization and cloud architects. This is not the only way, but it is one that is proven to work for many successful customers.

This book is designed to help both aspiring and established architects understand a structured approach to IT Infrastructure design. This methodology is a superset of what is practiced by individuals holding advanced design certifications. It includes additional suggestions for developing quality designs with examples to illustrate how the design documents are put together, how they are evaluated (design analysis), and how they are presented to a customer.

VCDX NOTE: A VCDX is an enterprise architect specializing in VMware design solutions and technologies. Although this is a vendor certification, the skills applied by the VCDX can be used with different vendor solutions with slight adjustments to the tools provided.

This book is intended both as a teaching tool and reference work that spans multiple infrastructure types supporting a variety of applications and operating systems. Our goal is to strengthen the IT Infrastructure design community through knowledgeable architects and eventually design certification holders. Broadening skills and showing examples of what is expected in a set of design documents is what we believe can help architects and their customers. The end state is for customers to receive better and more complete documentation when the architect follows the process we have defined.

Where the VCDX Boot Camp book covers the process for a VCDX candidate, with a heavy focus on the actual panel defense, this book provides a deep dive on infrastructure design methodology as practiced by a typical infrastructure design architect.

Audience

There are several groups that will benefit from the material in this work:

- Current and aspiring infrastructure design architects
- Design certification candidates
- Businesses looking to develop a Software Defined Data Center (SDDC)-based infrastructure)
- Those requiring a reference architecture that spans multiple disciplines
  - Server Virtualization
  - Desktop Virtualization
- Project managers
- Infrastructure support teams
- Infrastructure administrators

This work draws from the experience of enterprise architects, existing VCDXes, instructors, and administrators. It teaches through example infrastructure design documents, analysis of select design decisions and design patterns, reference material, and tools created for practicing architects.

One of the fundamental considerations that an architect makes is the appropriate match of a solution to a project. This includes both core and ancillary technologies. In many cases the design will integrate multiple vendor technologies and must ensure supportability, expandability, and adaptability. The designs must support business critical applications, take into consideration capacity planning for future expansion, and have the flexibility to adapt to changing business needs. The designs must be current but the flexibility provided is very valuable to the customer. You may not be able to predict everything, but you should plan for the most common cases that would require a contingency plan.

We are presenting a documentation set that is minimal in design and may include strengths and weaknesses. In chapter 7, Analysis, we examine these areas and provide insight into the pros and cons, and where appropriate, alternative choices. The goal of our examples is to provide a foundation that can be extended based on your design requirements. In chapter 8, Presenting and Defending the Design, we provide guidance on how to develop and present a design presentation with example slides included. These slides are based on the Chapter 4 design.

Architecture vs. Design

When we use the term architect we are talking about an individual acting as an Enterprise Architect, defined as a practitioner of enterprise architecture which is "a well-defined practice for conducting enterprise analysis, design, planning, and implementation, using a holistic approach at all times, for the successful development and execution of strategy."[1]

In our experience we have seen many combine two terms that are related to what we cover in this book. The design phase is where we create a solution. The architecture phase is a component of design that focuses on specific technologies that alone do not provide a complete solution. The goal of an architect is to do both. When we see the term 'Architecture Design', we look at this as a design that includes the physical architecture components of specific products.

---

[1]   http://en.wikipedia.org/wiki/Enterprise_architecture

The first macro step is to develop the design solution that is the conceptual model of what a customer or project requires and a supporting logical architecture that describes the high-level solution areas.

The second macro step is to develop the physical architecture that includes the components supporting the design. These components include vendors, product technologies, and configurations. The components together may be architectures that have specific purposes within the greater design.

These are further broken down into more granular steps.

As you read this book and work on designing solutions, remember that they will include architecture.

Phases of Designing a Solution (D4)

There are four major phases for designing a solution. We have covered several already. Here are the phases in order with details and comparisons.

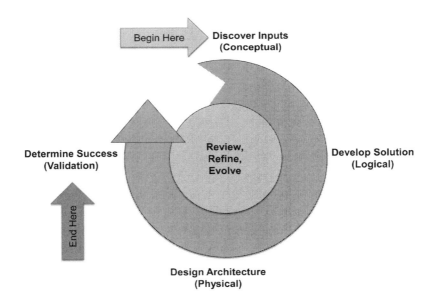

Figure 1 - Phases of Designing a Solution (©2014 John Yani Arrasjid)

Phase 1: Discover the Inputs

This phase provides what we consider the conceptual model. Identifying requirements, constraints and risks, as well as confirming assumptions, are all part of this phase. These items are elements used to justify the design decisions made and the design patterns chosen.

Phase 2: Develop the Solution

This phase develops the logical architecture showing the high level design without specific technology, versions, or configurations. It shows the big picture view of the design. During this phase the architect creates a solution. This logical design represents a solution that will be useable longer than a physical architecture. This phase also shows the relationships between the inputs to the design.

Phase 3: Design the Architecture and Operations

This phase produces the physical architecture and the details to operate the infrastructure. This is where the implementation details of the selected technology and configuration are specified. It is also where operation guides drive the activities to ensure successful operations and management. Once this phase has been completed there is a limited window of time to implement the design before the specific technology becomes outdated.

Phase 4: Determine Success

This phase is the validation of the design. The final phase ensures all requirements are met and that constraints and risks are validated. This phase ensures success of the project by validating critical components and procedures.

Review/Refine/Evolve

This is not listed as a phase. It is an overlay to each of the four phases. This typically occurs once a project is completed, after a period of time, as business needs evolve and workloads change within the infrastructure. Review in this context is not the same as the validation of the design. This review is done to determine if the current infrastructure matches current business needs. If not, the design can be refined and/or evolved to meet the changed requirements. You may find, however, that the review, refine, and evolve process could take place in the middle of a project, as enterprises don't come to a halt as new designs are being created. It is not uncommon for business needs to shift midstream.

Perspectives on IT Infrastructure Design

The following quotes have been provided by existing Enterprise Architects, including existing VCDX certified individuals. We thought this would be valuable to hear from those holding this valued certification about their experience and recommendations. These quotes are in response to the question "What is infrastructure design about?"

"Infrastructure design is about careful discussion, planning, and development of a technical and operational solution to meet the needs of the business now, while also being open to future enhancements. Infrastructure design, in terms of scope, is comparable to designing a city versus designing a house." **John Yani Arrasjid**, VCDX-001

"Infrastructure design is the process of preventing problems before they happen." **Mostafa Khalil**, VCDX-002

"When I think of infrastructure, I think of the underlying technology that makes software work. So when it comes to Infrastructure design, I have to consider not just the hardware bits that will make up the infrastructure and how they are interconnected, but also the software that will be run on top of it. As such there is no generic infrastructure design, just an application of good architectural principles with the goal of accommodating a specific class of software needs." **Kamau Wanguhu**, VCDX-003

"Infrastructure Design, at its core, is about the seamless reflection of the business upon the canvas of the company cloud. When done right, the information technology team is seen as a powerful enabler of strategy and vision. When dysfunctional, IT is deadweight that inhibits growth and innovation. How does your business view your design?" **Andrew Hald**, VCDX-004

"A good, well laid out design is simply good for business." **Mahesh Rajani**, VCDX-005

"Infrastructure design is defining an infrastructure system that will meet the customer's goals for Functionality, Availability, Manageability, Performance, Efficiency, Recoverability, and Security." **Craig Risinger**, VCDX-006

"Designing infrastructure considers business requirements and dependencies, and makes assumptions to come up with a platform supporting your business services with agreed service levels. With the industry standardizing on hyper-converged and software defined, infrastructure design will become a commodity play. Focus and efforts will shift from physical design to tighter OSS/BSS integration." **Richard Damoser,** VCDX-008

"The creation of specifications typically in the form of conceptual, logical and physical designs for a technology solution. The specification should fulfill a defined set of requirements, that ensure the solution will enable end users to achieve their goals." **Aidan Dalgleish**, VCDX-010

"It's about creating an infrastructure that is effectively invisible to those consuming it providing effortless business agility with managed risk." **Paul Nothard**, VCDX-011

"Infrastructure design is an iterative process to converge on an IT solution that immediately meets the needs of the business and that is also future proof." **Shridhar Deuskar**, VCDX-012

"IT infrastructure design involves defining and describing all the entities and their relationships and dependencies that comprise an environment, with sufficient detail and clarity so that the environment can be implemented repeatedly in a consistent manner." **Pang Chen**, VCDX-013

"Infrastructure Design is the design of technology based systems and processes to support the business needs of the application and data aimed at providing service to the user." **Rupen Sheth**, VCDX-014

"Infrastructure design is about the actualization of targeted business requirements through alignment with the architectural capabilities of an IT solution. This actualization should occur through a top-down approach to design, ensuring business requirements drive architectural infrastructure design decisions within each layer of a design as you move through the creation of conceptual, logical and physical design elements." **Wade Holmes,** VCDX-015

"Infrastructure design is about creating a solution that not only meets the stated requirements but anticipates the unstated current and future requirements through flexibility and scalability. The well designed infrastructure enables business as it is now and as it changes in the future in a cost effective and efficient manner." **Matt Theurer**, VCDX-018

"Infrastructure design involves applying experience and knowledge, in a combination of art and science, to produce efficient solutions that meet requirements while mitigating risks and accounting for constraints. An infrastructure architect must be able to effectively communicate and justify the decisions that affect each aspect of the work while instilling confidence that the proposed solution will succeed." **Doug Baer**, VCDX-019

"Today, the best performing organization will leverage information technologies to achieve their business objectives. Technologies will help the organization to establish a solid competitive advantage. The organization relies on the expertise of architects to understand the business objectives to design the right solution that will transform and increase the business performance." **Jean-Francois Richard**, VCDX-022

"Infrastructure design should keep in mind that the ongoing consumption, maintenance, and scaling out of the design is kept as simple as possible, while addressing all business requirements, to make the ongoing day to day routines as simple as possible." **Mark Gabryjelski**, VCDX-023

"Infrastructure design and the architect should articulate the vision, design and end goals to a number of audiences both technical and non-technical." **Kev James**, VCDX-24

"I like to compare it to house building. Every house needs a proper foundation that fits. Same for infrastructure – it needs to provide the foundation build to the requirements of the use case. Or you cannot build Skyscrapers on a minimalistic foundation." **Alexander Thoma**, VCDX-026

"Good architects are difficult to find. Why? Because to work well the architecture must cover a bigger scope, linking across more domains, yet still remain hidden in the closeness of everyday activities." **Bruno Bedette,** VCDX-031

"For me infrastructure design is about providing a resilient and performant foundation for software solutions. The first and possibly most important element required for creating this design is an effective and accurate understanding of the customers' requirements and constraints." **Thomas Kraus**, VCDX-032

"Datacenters come in many shapes and sizes. Many of them share common attributes but each is unique in detail. A consultative approach is the key to successful infrastructure design, deployment, and operation. Listen to the goals and requirements. Understand the environment and constraints. Mitigate assumptions and communicate risks." **Jason Boche**, VCDX-034

"Infrastructure design is a process and a project flow in order to match customer requirements to a working solution that can guarantee not only the customer needs but also the technical choices according to the specific use cases, the service level agreements, and the recommended and suggested industry practices." **Andrea Mauro**, VCDX-035

"The world of IT has been driven by the need to meet all needs and expectations of not just the business owners but also of the end users. To design the perfect infrastructure is a combination of technological prowess, business acumen and a psychology understanding of the people that will consume this technology. This is how great Infrastructures are designed."
Brad Maltz, VCDX-036

"Infrastructure design is the art of balancing features, specifications, objectives, security, recoverability in a manner that allows one to mitigate risks and problems whilst at the same time being cognizant of a platform that is easily operable and most importantly manageable in its simplest way without the overhead of complexity." **Sachin Bhowan**, VCDX-038

"Infrastructure design is a balancing act, working with opposing forces like complexity versus simplicity and uniqueness versus standardization. The architect has to factor in all the design boundaries, crafting a solution that is a custom fit for the customer's requirements but that can be implemented with consistent results." **Scott Lowe**, VCDX-039

"Infrastructure Design is about creating the most robust infrastructure solution while taking into account all customer requirements and (technical) constraints." **Kenneth van Ditmarsch**, VCDX-040

"Infrastructure Design should be like any other design exercise; understand the requirements (the conceptual), translate into Logical (which should be timeless within the bounds of requirements, assumptions and constraints) and develop physical specification to support the logical. Leverage concepts of modularity, reuse and the KISS principal to promote elegance." **Michael Francis**, VCDX-042

"The art of translating business and technical inputs into an adaptable solution that efficiently achieves stakeholder goals while minimizing risk and complexity." **Ben Lin**, VCDX-045

"Infrastructure design is about having enough familiarity with the environment (applications, equipment, etc.) to know your constraints in relation to your design goals. The ability to work within those constraints to achieve design goals is what separates infrastructure design from infrastructure building." **Harley Stagner**, VCDX-046

"The key to infrastructure design is in understanding the business and technical requirements to then create a design that makes the least amount of compromise and risk to more closely meet the scope and budget." **Chris Kranz**, VCDX-047

"Design is about building an infrastructure that meets the current and future needs of the end users, while simultaneously trying to accommodate both technical and business demands." **Kyle Husted**, VCDX-048

"Infrastructure Design is an art in which you create a highly flexible solution for today, with the best information and technology available, knowing it will need to evolve tomorrow into something more." **Mark Achtemichuk**, VCDX–050

"The difference between an infrastructure designer and a infrastructure admin or builder is not the ability to meet and exceed the requirements for the project. The difference is the ability to effectively communicate the 'why' to both technical and non-technical audiences. It is as much art, experience, psychology, and writing, as it is technical understanding." **Matt Cowger**, VCDX-052

"At the heart, infrastructure design is the building of a home for dynamic and static applications and data to live and function. Similar to building a home, infrastructure design helps to provide the foundation, structure, and flow for applications and data throughout their lifecycle based on business requirements, constraints, and assumptions (when lacking data or insight). Like a home, an infrastructure design should allow for current and future needs in a manner that is efficient, minimizes risk, and manages initial cost, and cost over time. And to help meet those goals the overall infrastructure design should be kept as simple as possible, while still meeting the requirements of the business." **Lane Leverett**, VCDX-053

"…understanding an organization's requirements while providing guidance on possibilities that may not have yet been considered." **Jason Langone**, VCDX-054

"Infrastructure design is art applied to technology and driven by business requirements. Its guiding principle is defined by fundamental qualities like availability and resiliency within specific cost boundaries. It must be elegant, intelligent, and consistent across technical areas while providing flexibility and scalability over time." **Nicolas Vermande**, VCDX-055

"Infrastructure design is about creating en environment that meets the customers business & technical requirements. The environment must respect the customers constraints and the conditions, clearly identify any risks and outline the assumptions made during the design process." **Magnus Andersson**, VCDX-056

"Infrastructure design is about planning, about making decisions upfront. It's about achieving efficiency in implementation, function and operation in a way that allows those leveraging the platform you build, to do the same." **Johannes "Jannie" Hanekom**, VCDX-057

"Design is about providing the customer with a clean and future ready solution that meets the customer's requirements within the given constraints." **Kees van Vloten**, VCDX-059

"Design is about aligning infrastructure capabilities to deliver cost efficient IT services that are reliable and improve business agility." **David Noonon**, VCDX-061

"A design includes the needs, which are important for a customer to set up their Virtualization Environment. The design should include, as applicable for the customer need, the VMware Best Practices and guidelines for a good and stable environment." **Christian Strijbos**, VCDX-064

"Designing information technology infrastructure is about creating a plan for a system which addresses requirements, constraints, risks, budgets, and operations in meeting the purpose for its development." **Ryan Grendahl**, VCDX-065

"IT Infrastructure Design is the process of solving problems by marrying customer requirements and constraints to infrastructure components in a way that forms an integrated business solution, while minimizing risk, complexity and cost. If your customer wants a horse and you design a solution that specifies a pig, no matter if you put lipstick on it or not, it's still a pig, and it doesn't meet the customers requirements." **Michael Webster**, VCDX-066

"An IT infrastructure design is just like a building architecture blueprint, it defines the magnificent. Without it, the Empire State will never stand tall." **Benham Chia**, VCDX-067

"Infrastructure design is a formal description of a system at component level to guide implementation. The design is to provide business value or to solve business problem." **Gang Zhang**, VCDX-068

"The process of planning and forming a blueprint that is constrained by a body of rules which creates a foundation for business services to operate reliability with predictive results." **Matthew Meyer**, VCDX-069

"Infrastructure design is simply working with the customer to understand their business requirements and guiding them through accomplishing those requirements in the face of any risks and constraints. The design should meet the defined requirements without introducing any unneeded complexity allowing for ease of management and accounting for the lifecycle of the solution." **Mike Brown**, VCDX-071

"Consider customer requirements, keep all dependencies in mind, think about simplicity and manageability and build an infrastructure that scales and can be run in a secure way." **Peter Oberacher**, VCDX-073

"Infrastructure design is about taking and documenting informative decisions that are agreed with the stakeholders, satisfy the client requirements and help in achieving their business goals." **Stanimir Markov**, VCDX-074

"Infrastructure design includes the gathering of critical business requirements at every level of the overall architecture. It is not simply applying cookie cutter 'best practices' but molding the design decisions around what will make the customer environment as optimal as possible." **Michael Marzotto**, VCDX-078

"Infrastructure Design is about designing a manageable solution for your customer that meets their requirements while conforming to the constraints present in their environment." **Harold Simon**, VCDX-080

"Infrastructure design is about creating a stable and secure foundation for organizations to store their valuable information and to operate the applications that run their business. Well planned infrastructure allows a company to spend more time focusing on on their products and services rather than the technology that enables them." **William Huber**, VCDX-081

"Modern infrastructure should be designed to meet the intense demands from organizations such as agility, predictable levels of performance, self-healing and non-disruptive scaling and upgrades. The end state of a great design should be one that is simple to operate while providing a great experience to its users." **Michael Berthiaume**, VCDX-084

"Infrastructure design involves providing a supportable and scalable foundational architecture that meets the requirements of your customer, fits within their budget, and supports future growth." **Nathan Raper**, VCDX-085

"Infrastructure designs should be based on problem solving solutions for critical and non-critical business requirements. The designed solutions should be agnostic from products and proprietary technology perspectives and focused around currently available capabilities for solving the presented problems. This design approach would allow the design of all architectures the ability to stand the test of time and evolve as the requirements evolve over time. Enterprise infrastructure designs should never be dictated by any one particular proprietary technology or capability as it can become outdated and obsolete in a short period of time." **Rawlinson Rivera**, VCDX-086

"Infrastructure design is about the balance between requirements and beauty. An excellent design has a minimalist feel that not only satisfies the needs of the business and stakeholders, but does so in a way that is the most reduced, simplistic version of all possible designs. Any very well thought out design needs to be both functional and elegant to be truly brilliant."
Greg Herzog, VCDX-087

"It is documenting a workable solution that meets defined requirements while staying within acceptable risk and budget." **Eiad Al-Aqqad**, VCDX-089

"Producing a detailed design for a datacenter solution is a balancing act between meeting the customers requirements, working within the constraints such as technology or budget and minimizing risk. The next challenge is making the solution as simple as possible to implement while reducing operational complexity and cost. The design should be documented to a point where it can be picked up by an engineer to implement without involvement from the architect. To achieve this the architecture must have clearly documented all design decisions with requirements, justifications, alternatives and implications. Supporting documentation such as Implementation Guide, Operational Verification & Operational Procedures are critical to ensure the success of not only the implementation phase but the ongoing management & support of the solution." **Josh Odgers**, VCDX-090

"To meet and exceed expectations by creating a platform design that will empower your company to reach it's goals today and tomorrow." **Brian Smith**, VCDX-091

"Sometimes there is a difference between what the customer wants and what they actually need to accomplish the purpose of the project. Infrastructure Design is about understanding the customer's requirements (both current and short- to medium-term future needs), taking into consideration any technological and/or business or organization limitations and presenting a solution that uniquely fits the actual business requirements in a cost effective manner." **Shane White**, VCDX-095

"Infrastructure design is the art of delivering a solution that meets requirements within constraints, whilst minimizing assumptions and risks." **Travis Wood**, VCDX-097

"The Infrastructure Design is a blueprint that balances customer requirements and constraints against industry best practices and generates a unique, yet optimal solution for the customer." **Mohan Potheri**, VCDX-098

John Yani Arrasjid, Mark Gabryjelski, Chris McCain

"Plumbing for applications – nothing more, but nothing less!" **Tomas Fojta**, VCDX-099

"Infrastructure Design is all about managing business expectations to prevent technical debt and aligning IT infrastructure with business requirements." **Joep Piscaer**, VCDX-101

"Antoine de Saint-Exupery provides the gist of infrastructure design when he says 'A designer knows he has achieved perfection not when there is nothing left to add, but when there is nothing left to take away.' This applies to design of everything, especially when considering complex infrastructures, to minimize risk while meeting requirements." **Chris Slater**, VCDX-102

"All things are created twice; first mentally, then physically. The art of IT infrastructure design is to do it in those steps: first think then build." **Martijn Baecke**, VCDX-103

"Design is the process of meeting the requirements of the business, while operating within its constraints, to deliver a supportable and effective solution." **Matt Vandenbeld**, VCDX-107

"Design is a creative endeavor shaped by resources, requirements, and an imperfect view of the future. With a powerful influence on the health and culture of business, an architect must make strides to remain holistic throughout the design process to consider the impact of all decisions." **Ethan Rowe**, VCDX-109

"Design is about looking at goals and objectives with an open mind and creating not only a solution, but one that is uniquely fit for their project." **Tim Antonowicz**, VCDX-112

"Infrastructure design is about the journey, not the destination. It is a process of continuous evolution and improvement. Clarity, simplicity, and value are achieved through thoughtful consensus." **Tim Curless**, VCDX-114

"Infrastructure Design is the art of being able to craft elegant IT solutions that have the ability to truly deliver value to an organization. In many cases, this is no easy task, as these solutions need to meet a business' diverse set of requirements, while adhering to a sometimes vast array of constraints and while striving to mitigate risk." **Jonathan Kohler**, VCDX-116

"Infrastructure design is the art of designing for customers objectives while managing constraints and risks." **Brian Suhr**, VCDX-118

"To me, infrastructure design is about building a robust, scalable and secure platform on which applications and services can be delivered most optimally to the business with the flexibility to respond to changing business needs and seasonal demands." **James Galdes**, VCDX-119

"Infrastructure design is creating the best infrastructure solution for a customer based on his requirements, while making optimal use of available technology options." **Viktor van den Berg**, VCDX-121

"A customer executive should be able to read your design up to and including the conceptual design. If it doesn't translate to their high-level strategy and goals then how can you be sure that the logical and physical design meets their needs? It is expected that a final design can be picked up by a qualified administrator or consultant and the proposed solution be implemented from the logical and physical design with little or no need for clarification. The IT design is a blueprint for a proposed system that follows a methodological approach from the initial idea to the final specification." **Ray Heffer**, VCDX-122

"Infrastructure design is understanding business and technical requirements (both current and future) to produce a solution that mitigates risk and minimises unnecessary complexity." **Steve Wenban**, VCDX-123

"Infrastructure Design is an art of providing simple solution to the most complex looking infrastructure problems and a science which enables the solution to be technically viable given the Business Requirements, Constraints and Risks." **Samir Roshan**, VCDX-124

"Infrastructure design is art of blending business requirements, design constraints, assumptions and risks into a holistic architecture that addresses security, manageability, performance, recoverability and availability. It is a fine balancing act which requires expertise in a number of areas, all while ensuring business objectives are met in an efficient manner. It is not about throwing every technical solution in your arsenal at a problem just because it's 'cool'." **Derek Seaman**, VCDX-125

"Design is about identifying the unique challenges, strategic drivers and technical requirements of an organisation in order to piece together the individual infrastructure components; thus supporting the businesses end goals." **Richard Arsenian**, VCDX-126

"Infrastructure design is matching technology to the requirements and the constraints. The true art of Infrastructure design is often identifying those requirements and constraints." **Hersey Cartwright**, VCDX-128

"Design is the easy part, relatively speaking. Coming up with (and executing) the proper methodology that will lead you to a solid design is the hard part." **Josh Coen**, VCDX-129

"Infrastructure design in itself is a tightrope act. A design is the balance that is achieved by taking all stakeholders needs and the business function into consideration and proposing a solution that benefits the business while mitigating risks and failure wherever possible." **Kalen Arndt**, VCDX-132

"Infrastructure design is about simple, elegant, enterprise-level solutions for mission critical applications, where you do more with less and clearly link the Customer Requirements to the Solution Architecture and the Engineering Specifications." **Rene Van Den Bedem**, VCDX-133

"The ideal design is the design which satisfies the business requirements where at the same time complies with the design constraints and provides the highest design quality aspects." **Safouh Kharrat**, VCDX-136

"Infrastructure design is more than just designing the solution to work, but also preventing risk of failure. You must really consider all of the scenarios in which a solution can fail, understand the impact, then mitigate or solve them within the constraints of the design." **Joseph Silvagi**, VCDX-174

"If you fail to design an infrastructure with redundancy, availability, manageability, performance, and security, your infrastructure design will fail." **Todd Simmons**, VCDX-184

"The next generation of data centers and the applications that will run atop them require that we become not storage, compute, networking or virtualization people but data center people. We must understand how the illities of design impact the adoption and integration of technology within the architecture as a whole, accept that change will come and plan accordingly." **Jayson Block,** VCDX-186

"Infrastructure design at the X-level is an incredibly demanding art. It requires a superbly skilled technologist who can capture the essence of a business enterprise and create the foundation for its success. If you aspire to be a world-class Enterprise Architect this should always be your primary goal." **Mark Brunstad**, Manager, Nutanix nu.school, former VCDX Program Manager

"Successful infrastructure architects have two things in common. They understand their design clients' business goals, not just their technical goals. This understanding allows them to remain calm in the face of client politics and requirements churn. They also have a well-developed "sixth sense" for risks, honed by experience and technical depth. This sense allows them to perceive single points of failure and problematic dependencies, so that they can be mitigated early on." **Brian Rice**, Technical Course Developer, former VCDX Program Manager

"IT Infrastructure design is critical in communications and computing infrastructure in this digital age. Considerations must be given to securing, protecting and maintaining the integrity of these infrastructures while meeting specific business needs. Today, solutions must protect, scale, and evolve with industry needs for virtual, physical, and mixed-mode environments." **Melissa Tuite**, Board of Directors, The Performance Testing Council, VCDX "M" (Former VCDX Program Manager)

Exercises Included in Chapters

We have included exercises in each chapter to provide you an opportunity to learn more by practicing each phase of design. The subjective nature of design means there are multiple paths one can take and no single correct answer. The final choice will be based on your experience, your skills, and the requirements and constraints of the project. We hope you find them educational. If you have suggestions for exercises to include in our next edition, we look forward to you feedback.

We recommend you use the exercises provided to help develop your skills in design and fully benefit from the material presented.

## CHAPTER 2

DESIGN METHODOLOGY
AND DOCUMENTATION

*"IT infrastructure design involves defining and describing all the
entities and their relationships and dependencies that comprise
an environment, with sufficient detail and clarity so that the
environment can be implemented repeatedly in a consistent manner."*
— *Pang Chen, VCDX-013*

Methodology includes both the "what" and the "how" in principles, tools,
and practices used in achieving a goal. It includes the methods applied to
reach a solution.

A framework is a loose but incomplete structure that allows flexibility of
alternative choices for tools and process. In many cases an architect uses
both an enterprise architecture framework and a technology framework. For
examples of other design frameworks, see The Open Group Architecture
Framework (TOGAF[2]) or the Zachmann Framework[3].

We will talk about infrastructure design methodology and the creation of
the supporting documentation. This provides a framework for architecture
design, while allowing flexibility within the framework based on skills,
technology, and other influencing factors.

---

[2]   TOGAF® is an Open Group standard that includes proven enterprise
architecture methodology and framework used by organizations to improve
business efficiency. It is an enterprise architecture standard that ensures
consistent standards, methods, and communication among enterprise
architecture professionals.

[3]   The Zachman Framework is an enterprise architecture framework providing
a formal and highly structured way of viewing and defining an enterprise. It
consists of a two- dimensional classification matrix based on the intersection
of six communication questions (what, where, when, why, who and how) with
five levels of reification to move from abstract to concrete ideas.

Architecture vs. Design

Architecture is the art of designing and creating infrastructure components. To reiterate what we covered in the introduction, design is the creation of a solution that uses architecture components.

- Why are these definitions important?
- Because there are multiple ways that these two words are used.

For the sake of the examples in this book, we are focused on designing a solution for an IT infrastructure, which utilizes architecture for each of the relevant pieces.

Enterprise Architecture

The methodology we describe applies to enterprise architecture, comprised of business, data, application, and technology architectures.

Methodology and Framework

Infrastructure architects, including VCDX, practice a methodology with roots in enterprise architecture. These architects work on both large and small infrastructures using software and hardware technologies but must consider operational aspects for a complete solution. If what appears to be a great design cannot be implemented and operated, the architect has failed. The methodology presented here focuses on three design areas (conceptual, logical, and physical) that span multiple domains.

Infrastructure architects must demonstrate mastery of both design considerations and operational considerations, including the rationales, in the following areas:

- Understanding different architecture design strategies
- Identifying and understanding business requirements
- Validating assumptions

- Identifying constraints and risks
- Translating business requirements into technical requirements
- Making and justifying decisions
- Understanding the impact of design choices
- Understanding how to determine best path for design quality

As an architect presents a design, considerations for the participants present in the meeting must be made. The participants could be project stakeholders and coworkers, or they could be panelists for a design certification defense. They review the material presented and evaluate if there is a complete solution that addresses all requirements and constraints, and mitigates identified risks. They also evaluate how the architect answers questions on the design, and whether they can defend the design decisions made. In this case, design decisions encompass all documentation, including the business, technical, and operational aspects.

VCDX Note
In the VCDX program these areas are evaluated by panelists, as described in the VCDX Boot Camp book. The next aspect evaluated is the ability of the candidate to demonstrate an ability to work effectively in design meetings, which are tested in the design scenario phase. The final aspect evaluated is the ability of the candidate to work through issues that may be present in a design, implementation, or operations. This is tested in the troubleshooting scenario phase.

When developing a design, there are three important design rules that an architect must follow.

- Use business requirements to drive both the design and implementation decisions.
- Ensure the design is suited for mission-critical applications as well as other applications that are not mission critical but still important to the business.
- Ensure the design supports a managed environment and includes operational guidelines.

Assessment Criteria and Use Cases

What is needed to formulate a good design?

Prior to design there are several things that must be completed.

First is creation of the conceptual model, an abstraction of the business requirements and their relationships.

Second is development of the logical design. This is a layout of the architecture to support the conceptual model. It includes the components without reference to specific vendors, products, versions or configurations. This ensures that the design is scalable and will not require change unless the business requirements change. The logical design has a longer life than the physical design.

Third is architecting of the physical design. This is derived from the logical design using the physical components (vendor, product, version, configuration information) and the connectivity between them. The physical design may change over time as newer technologies are introduced and older technologies are phased out.

Supporting each of these design areas requires some form of discovery or assessment to be performed. These assessments are based on a combination of the business requirements and the technology features that are used to support the requirements.

When we look at the conceptual model we are also creating use cases for the design solution. These use cases should be validated at the completion of the project. Use cases may be tied to one or more industries, may include a business scenario, may have a deployment model, and will include a set of application types. Use cases help drive the design characteristics. The following are the components that can benefit a use case: identifying label (numeric or alphanumeric), use case title, description, primary and supporting actors (those with a goal and/or role in the use case), stakeholders, success criteria, and special requirements. Other components can be added as appropriate based on the architect.

Virtualization Assessment

One example of a tool used during the discovery phase is a virtualization assessment. This analyzes the systems that are candidates for virtualization, be this for server/desktop virtualization or for cloud. It identifies resource requirements for the systems and can provide models for a virtual infrastructure based on specified hardware platforms. This assessment can be done on physical systems or existing virtual systems to provide an input for sizing the physical design components.

A virtualization assessment for servers does not specifically identify the application requirements to determine if the applications running on the servers being analyzed can run on a virtualized infrastructure. An application assessment may be required as an extension to the virtualization assessment to understand dependencies, functionality, and interoperability requirements.

A virtualization security assessment for servers will help identify the security posture of the virtual infrastructure and establish optimal measures and controls through various governance and compliance standards to mitigate any identified risks.

A virtualization assessment for desktops in a VDI (virtual desktop infrastructure) project does not specifically identify how the applications can be brought into the VDI solution, though some guidelines are presented. While providing the ability to size the VDI Infrastructure, deeper analysis of the applications is required if there is a need to define a solution that provides users with a desktop experience that is better than what they run today on physical computers. In this instance, an applications assessment *is* required to understand the dependencies, interoperability, and strategies available for delivering applications to the end users through the many available options. Examples of the options to consider include the base image, the mechanism used to deliver applications to users, published applications, and use of separate desktop pools for specific user groups or applications.

Health Check

Another example of a tool used during the discovery phase is a health check. This provides a baseline analysis of an existing environment. The health check compares a current infrastructure with best practices. These best practices are based on both the technology and field experience of customers, vendors, and consultants. Best practices are applicable to a majority of situations, but these "best practices" may not fit every scenario.

Contingency theory[4] can apply in regards to best practice, as there are internal and external situations that can drive a specific best practice for use in a solution. Most health checks are based on baseline reference architectures for comparison.

Reference architectures provide details on how a fully featured technology can be implemented. In some cases, the reference architecture is provided by a vendor and can be modified to suit the business requirements provided. In other cases, the reference architecture is created to meet a specific set of business requirements and acts as both a baseline for future deployments and as a checkpoint during the life of a virtual infrastructure deployment. A similar approach for cloud solutions applies because we are designing an infrastructure service level that is based on warranties tied to compute, storage, and network utility.

Phases for Developing an Architecture Design

Most architects will go through four phases in the development of their architecture design as shown in the Introduction, figure 1. The "Review/

---

[4]   http://www.businessmate.org/Article.php?ArtikelId=11 and http://en.wikipedia.org/wiki/Contingency_theory - discuss from the standpoint of organizational leadership but can be applied to design decisions and risk management.

Refine/Evolve" defines what is done between major design projects to adjust for changes in business requirements affecting the original infrastructure design.

An architect starts with discovering the inputs to develop the conceptual architecture. Once this is done they will develop the solution, or the logical architecture, that goes into technology areas and relationships but are not providing specific details such as vendors, products, versions, or configurations. Once approved to proceed based on the logical architecture, the design architecture (physical architecture) is created.

A conceptual model, the architect provides the logical model, and the implementer or builder uses the physical model (created by the architect). This Design Architecture phase is where we lock in specific details. When developing vendor-based architectures, we know that specific technologies will be included and may integrate with other vendor technologies. The final phase is validation of the design including testing of project requirements. Although we call out four phases, most IT Infrastructures have a lifecycle. A design implemented today may be updated and expanded in the future; therefore each project is complete but may evolve in the future to meet changing business needs.

VCDX NOTE
In this situation, the VCDX will typically take a hybrid approach. If there is a required technology that is a constraint for the design, such as a VMware View environment based on a VMware vSphere foundation, we may use the vendor product without versioning in the Logical Architecture. Why do we break from the "don't include the vendor or product" rule of enterprise architecture? It is because the constraints mandate that the technology is not up for debate. Should you do this? That is up to you but there should be clear demarcations between the logical and physical aspects of the design. In most cases, a VCDX provides the conceptual model followed by the logical design, then the physical design. It should not be a difficult task to separate product details from a logical design.

VCDX NOTE
For those pursuing the VCDX certification, if you make a choice and document your approach you will have met the VCDX design expectations.

Conceptual Architecture (The Owner Perspective)

Conceptual architecture is used to show the components of a system related to the requirements provided, but in an abstract form. This form does not provide details of the components or how interfaces are configured between components. This means there are no technology specifications or vendor/product information included. The components and relationships that will influence the logical design are included. The goal of conceptual architecture is to convey the solution so that non-technical team members can understand the approach to the design that will be taken.

We recommend reading the paper 'Conceptual, Logical, Physical, It Is Simple' by Zachman, listed in the References section of this book. This provides examples to help clarify the phases and components using a non-IT related example.

The conceptual architecture abstracts the requirements and the environment into ideas with relationships. These ideas and the relationships are the primary focus of the conceptual architecture. This architecture is formalized in diagrams and text that convey the abstract, initial, non-technical representation. It includes decisions that will influence the design's composition including key architectural constructs.

An example of conceptual architecture for a business requiring a datacenter infrastructure to run their business would look something like the following.

Requirements:

- The owner wants an infrastructure to support both mission critical business applications as well as those with lower priority.
- The owner wants to support both server and desktop virtualization with a hybrid cloud solution to reduce TCO, increase ROI, and to support business agility.
- The solution architecture must meet governance requirements.
- The infrastructure requires specific resources to support application workloads such as compute, networking, and storage.

The infrastructure must provide security mechanisms.

The infrastructure must provide recoverability mechanisms such as backup/recovery of workloads, and site failover capabilities.

At this stage we are providing general information, not specific details. The Logical Architecture will include generic components and specifications such as use of native virtualization technologies, and the Physical Architecture will include specific components and specifications such as "VMware vSphere 5.5" and "VMware vSphere DRS" configured for default settings.

Another way to look at this is that the business owner provides requirements for the concepts

We will provide conceptual architecture reference material in the subsequent case study and design examples. The following illustrates an example of building an architecture model going through conceptual, logical, and physical.

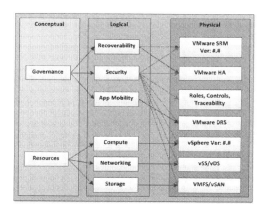

**Figure 2 - Relationship from Conceptual to
Logical to Physical design models**

The example shown in this figure shows the progression from conceptual to logical to physical. We start with the highest-level concepts, develop a vendor agnostic solution, and then finally develop the details of technology and configuration.

Let's use one example to show this evolution of the design.

1. **Conceptual Model** – The business follows internal and external governance. External regulations require compliance with laws covering credit card transactions and patient data in a healthcare business.
2. **Logical Design** - The regulations that must be met specify details for recoverability, security, availability, access controls, and traceability.
3. **Physical Design** – The chosen technologies to address the logical design specifications include the following technologies. In addition, details for configuration and operations are included.
   a. VMware Site Recovery Manager (SRM) version X.Y will be used to address recoverability of major datacenter failure.
   b. VMware HA (vSphere version X.Y) will be used to address component failure within the infrastructure, specifically that of one or more compute servers.
   c. VMware DRS (vSphere version X.Y) will be used to address availability of resources through balancing workload access to available resources.
   d. Roles and controls are defined and configured using VMware vSphere version X.Y. Traceability utilizes change control procedures defined for the customer, roles and controls for access, and logging for traceability.

Logical Architecture (The Architect Perspective)

The Logical Architecture is based on the conceptual model and provides a more detailed view of the components and relationships that will be necessary to functionally work and achieve the requirements specified.

The following figure illustrates an example of a logical architecture. In it we show the relationships between the business requirements, identified in the conceptual architecture, and the infrastructure components proposed to support them.

If we were to break this down to show a simple example of a single item, such as an VMware ESXi host, we could see how these items are nested inside each other. Refer to following figure as an example.

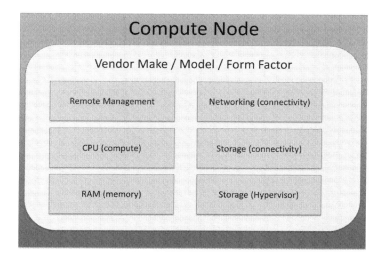

Figure 3 - Sample Logical Architecture Component

Creating this logical architecture sample can show how the server block can be presented initially, with the components included to create a finished product. In a later diagram, you could call out a cluster of servers as a single block, without including all the details shown here in Figure 3. You are essentially creating a reference architecture of components that can be modified as requirements or constraints change, without changing the **entire** logical architecture.

Each architect may have a different approach to presenting this information, and each project will have different logical components that are required in the architecture. In a VMware vSphere infrastructure design, there are other specific items to discuss, such as VMware vCenter, storage arrays, storage presentation, network presentation/segmentation, or additional external components such as backup solutions.

Additional items that can be included, depending on the solution, are listed here:

- Business Objectives or Business Scenarios
  - Server Consolidation
  - Business Continuity
  - Virtual Lab Automation
  - Desktop Management
- Lifecycle Objectives
  - Build
  - Deploy
  - Update
  - Monitor
  - Recover
  - Retire
- Business Continuity and Compliance
  - Data Protection
  - High Availability
  - Disaster recovery
  - Compliance
- Data Center Locations
  - Enterprise In-house
  - Enterprise Extranet
  - Service Provider
  - Remote and Branch Office
- Operations
  - Provisioning
  - Consumption
  - Issue Resolution

You should include the items appropriate for your design.

Physical Architecture (The Builder Perspective)

Physical Architecture provides the detailed specifications of the components and interfaces. At this stage we can specify down to the vendor, model, and version of components; 1Gbps Ethernet connection utilizing Intel™ networking cards (I350-T4), across CAT-6 cabling, and connecting to a Cisco 6513 switch.

The following figure, again focused on an ESXi host, shows one way of presenting this information and details the components required to build the solution being proposed.

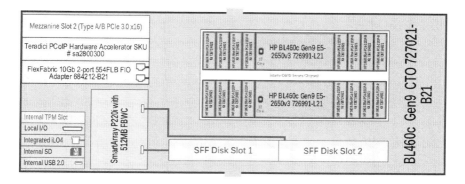

Figure 4 - Physical Architecture - Example Server

When selecting the specific hardware, consider the whole solution, including business requirements and the constraints of the project. Creating a physical design is not only about meeting the requirements of the project, but should also consider how ongoing maintenance will be performed. This should include, as much as possible, elimination of single points of failure. Be sure to have considered how to maintain all the items you have included in your design.

Validation

Validation is required and includes tests of design decisions, design patterns, operational characteristics, and technical functionality.

Design Considerations

The following are examples of design considerations faced in a typical design. These provide perspective on the questions an architect needs to answer to determine the physical architecture.

- Will the network switches that servers connect to be separate physical switches or are the switches stacked as a single logical unit? If they are stacked, is there a situation that would arise where the whole switch stack is rebooted, causing an outage for network communications?
- Is there 10 Gb Ethernet available today, or can it be acquired as part of this solution? Will you be limited to 1 GbE connectivity? Perhaps cost per port is part of this 1 GbE vs. 10 GbE decision, or perhaps the physical separation of network traffic makes 10 GbE an unrealistic choice for this implementation.
- Does the storage you plan to use for the infrastructure utilize Fiber Channel or Ethernet to present storage to hosts? Does it already exist, or will it be purchased? Is there more than one type of storage being used in this infrastructure?
- What is the connection speed of the storage array? Can the array provide the throughput required for the workloads that you plan to run? What is the IOPS capability of the back end storage array that has been selected? What is the IOPS required by the application.
- **Vendor Example**: When selecting physical servers, are you selecting two (2) or four (4) socket systems to create your solution? Would there be a reason to mix server types (example: across VMware vSphere clusters) to run different types of workloads? Would you select four (4) socket servers if there were only a need for twelve (12) CPUs total in your VMware vSphere Infrastructure? How do you choose quantity of CPU sockets, number of cores, and cache?
- Will this include software defined networking (SDN) or software defined storage (SDS) components? How does this impact the design as compared to the use of traditional network & storage design?

- What would be the largest virtual machine you would run in the infrastructure? If there is a need to run a virtual machine with 16 processors, selecting a two (2) socket server with six (6) cores per socket may not meet this requirement.
- Will a blade-based solution be appropriate, or are traditional rack mount servers selected? If using a chassis-based solution, are you required to consider the loss of a whole chassis as part of the availability strategy?
- Would a converged infrastructure solution be appropriate? If so, why?
- **Vendor Example**: When building VMware vSphere clusters, will you account for VMware High Availability, by adding the number of hosts needed to run the workload, and then adding host(s) to provide additional capacity required to meet the VMware High Availability requirements of the solution? For example, is there a need to have two hosts for VMware High Availability, to help minimize the potential for a cluster running with degraded performance or to maintain the required level of availability even during maintenance activities?
- Are you providing or calling out redundancy for infrastructure components? Will racks have power from different UPS systems? Will redundant power circuits be available within the racks? What type of redundancy is in place for the UPS used? Will the UPS capacity fulfill the RPO/RTO for particular mission critical applications? Are you required to design the solution to account for the loss of a whole rack of physical components?

Assessment Methodology

"What is needed to formulate a good design?"

This is a common question asked of architects.

Information on the past, present, and future state of the infrastructure is important. The future state is tied to capacity planning to ensure what is implemented today will be supported as the environment changes. Identify the current environment and related details. What has and has not worked with the technology solutions that are supporting the needs of the business. The more information gathered, the better, but you will need to manage the time and questions during this discovery phase. You will need to sort through this data, apply priorities, and align them to support the design.

Identify the use cases and problems addressed by the solution you are designing. Is the customer looking to consolidate servers and take advantage of workflow automation for disaster recovery or provisioning? Would you like to cover both server and desktop virtualization utilizing a hybrid cloud?

Cost savings (equipment, software, operations, and maintenance), single management pane (VMware vSphere for consolidation, deployment, and updates), disaster recovery capabilities (VMware vCenter SRM), and desktop operations management (VMware Horizon View) all provide compelling reasons to virtualize.

In formulating a design we take the information initially provided and add in interviews, assessments, and the business requirements provided. The interviews allow us to delve deeper into the requirements and better understand the existing infrastructure components, application workloads, and pain points or gaps in the current solution. When using disaster recovery technologies such as VMware vCenter SRM, an architect will spend time with the application owners to determine the requirements for recovery, including the manual steps required, sequencing, application dependencies, and application recovery and validation processes.

We will now cover the inputs used for the virtualization assessment and for the health check. If an architect does not have access to the vendor-specific utilities, other methods, including scripting, can be used to gather the appropriate inputs that will influence the design. Many of the vendor tools are available for a fee or for free. For example, if you are the end user architect for an enterprise and would like to use VMware's health check tools, your VMware Partner will be happy to assist you, and provide information on what these tools can gather.

Current State Analysis Assessment

A current state analysis or assessment is a review of the current infrastructure with analysis of the hardware and software. The existing infrastructure can be physical, virtual, or cloud based for running workloads. The physical systems, the operating system, and the applications are all taken into consideration for the design and may influence which design patterns to utilize. The analysis will have feedback on components, systems, and the complete infrastructure.

The infrastructure assessment should examine the network and storage topology, components, and issues with the current infrastructure deployment. Understanding the current capacity and performance abilities and requirements allows a comparison between the current design and the new design capabilities. It should include a 'gap analysis' to determine what changes are required in the form of hardware, software, and process to meet the project guidelines. It will also identify major issues that may prevent a successful virtualization deployment.

Timeframe

Data points for analysis must be taken over a continuous timeframe. A typical analysis can be completed in thirty days of resource utilization statistics. Some sites may require more than 30 days to support specific application workload analysis, such as end-of-year financial analysis. Experience has shown that 30-90 days of data points provides sufficient details on resource utilization and infrastructure activities that are necessary for a successful design.

Data Points

The data points collected for analysis are broken down into inventory of hardware and software, and other resource utilization.

Physical hardware inventory data points should be grouped by physical machine name and include processor information (vendor, model, family, cache, cores, processor speed), memory (RAM vendor, model, size), storage (vendor, model, type, size of disks, size of disk cache, speed), network (vendor, model, number, speed), and other devices (USB, serial devices, parallel devices) attached and used by the system. This information is used to determine the resource requirements of the virtual machine that would be created to host each workload.

Although one approach may be to mimic the original machine with the exact same configuration, a virtual machine typically is configured with some changes from the original physical machine specifications. One example is to look at the peak resource requirements for CPU and RAM of the original machine and provide a maximum for the virtual machine that is matched with the peak CPU and RAM loads expected. Storage and network requirements may be reduced or expanded as needed for the new virtual machine.

Software inventory includes both applications and services that are running. If possible, dependencies external to the physical machine should be identified.

Guidance on best practices and configuration details for specific technologies can be found in product documentation or other resources that are listed in the references section of this book. We recommend the same approach for any vendor used within the design of an infrastructure.

Analysis

The following provides recommendations for analyzing the data points that have been gathered and the interviews that were conducted.

Recommendations

Recommendations for the resource related components are typically provided as a 'best case' and a 'second choice'. If the 'best case' option cannot be used, the 'second choice' option should be able to fit within the specified requirements and budgets. Projects are driven by the budget permitted, or negotiated, and understanding this early is a good way to save work and constrain a design. Example: Don't design a full multi-site DR solution for a customer that has no budget to build out or acquire another site. We provide more detail on dealing with the financial aspects shortly.

Recommendations should be based on the business requirements, constraints, best practices, and experience. Remember that best practices may need to be modified for a project where appropriate.

Financials

No assessment is complete without a financial assessment. This is where we align with budget and determine what will be used to fit within the financial boundaries.

In some cases, a budget may be predetermined for the initiative, and the design plan will need to conform. In others, the organization may be more open to a flexible budget depending upon the potential benefits, such as cost reductions, it can realize as a result of implementing the project.

Architects will sometimes need to help an organization identify and quantify the expected benefits and any projected cost reductions. This will provide them justification for necessary funding for a successful project and also help them adopt a big picture perspective for the project. This in turn helps ensure success in the face of unexpected obstacles such as people and politics.

The financial assessment should also identify the budget source today and any potential risks. For example, if the organization is looking to immediately or eventually implement a private cloud, a project-based budgeting model can create significant challenges. As resources reach capacity, a service requestor may be forced to bear the burden of large expansions to the infrastructure. Switching to a chargeback or showback funding process can help alleviate the bottlenecks frequently resulting from a project-based budgeting model.

Regardless of the funding source or corporate strategy for capital or operational expenditures, be sure to understand the financial impact that a decision will have on a project.

Health Check

Any current state analysis will utilize a health check. We call out the VMware Health Check tool as a vendor specific example. This will provide perspective on what could be covered if you need to analyze an existing infrastructure.

The VMware Health Check evaluates a comprehensive checklist of best practices and identifies potential bottlenecks within an infrastructure. The tool is used on an existing virtualization deployment by connecting to a management server and analyzing the collected data.

Considerations for a health check.

1. WORKLOAD ASSESSMENT: For a set of physical machines, resource utilization metrics including CPU, memory, disk I/O and network I/O. Capture metrics using OS tools such as perfmon, sar, etc. Note the time related to the metrics or create a baseline. If possible collect the metrics for replay. Do you notice changes over time or periods of the week or month?

2. WORKLOAD ASSESSMENT: Using a load generation tool such as IOmeter, generate loads on the same physical systems. We recommend running IOmeter on a physical, not virtual, platform based to ensure the results are accurate. Capture metrics again. How different are peak resource loads from average resource loads on the systems?

3. ARCHITECTURE: Create some business requirements. Then create a conceptual model to show relationships between requirements. Identify areas of overlap. Why is there overlap?

4. ARCHITECTURE: Using the conceptual architecture, create a **logical** topology of the technology areas and the procedures that define the relationships within the architecture. Within this detailed view of components and relationships do NOT include specific

vendor technologies. For example, define a network relationship without defining a specified vendor or defined configuration such as VLANs, port-trunking, or network speed and bandwidth.

5. HEALTH CHECK: Using technology documents such as reference architectures and knowledge base (KB) articles, compare the implementation with best practices, maximums, KB articles, and white papers related to the current release of technologies used. Are you within parameters? Is the site following general best practices? Do they have site-specific best practices adapted for their requirements and constraints? Is the site following a best practice based on the specific environment?

Design Characteristics

The design characteristics are the areas that all infrastructures running mission critical applications take into consideration. The design includes solutions for these areas that are compatible with the other areas. The requirements, constraints, and assumptions are mapped into one or more of the following qualities. A good design will meet the requirements and constraints, with the appropriate technology and operational guidance while meeting the schedule, staffing skills, and budget provided.

Availability

This characteristic is influenced by a design decision to support the uptime of the infrastructure components and workloads. The design should deliver highly available operation, as measured by percent uptime of relevant components.

Manageability

This characteristic is the effect a design decision will have on how well the infrastructure will run and the operational considerations required for success. The design should provide ease of managing the environment and maintaining normal operations. Sub-qualities may include scalability and flexibility. Scalability affects support of expanded workloads within the infrastructure while maintaining or increasing performance of the workloads.

Manageability also includes operational considerations such as automation and workflow orchestration. There may be vendor specific and vendor agnostic tools used together to manage the entire infrastructure.

Performance

This characteristic is the effect a design decision will have on performance of applications, operating systems, and infrastructure components. Performance measures the amount of useful **work accomplished** within a **specified time** with the **available resources**. The design should deliver the standards of responsiveness of components of the desired environment to meet the application workloads deployed and SLAs specified.

Recoverability

This characteristic is the effect of a design decision on the ability of the infrastructure, workloads, and data to be recovered in the event of an unexpected incident that affects availability of an environment.

Security

This characteristic is the effect a design decision will have on the infrastructure and workloads, including components and systems, to meet the project security requirements. The design should provide overall data control, confidentiality, integrity, accessibility, governance, and risk management, often including the capability to demonstrate or achieve compliance with regulation.

Considerations for Design

During the discovery phase with a customer, the architect will draw out requirements, constraints, and risks and will look to validate any assumptions.

Requirements

The requirements are from the customer, directly or indirectly. A direct requirement could be related to a service level agreement (SLA). An indirect requirement might be derived from governance such as a regulatory compliance related requirement.

Constraints

Constraints are items that are not easily changed. An example could be a budget constraint or a single-vendor choice by the customer.

Risks

Risks are related to the business or the infrastructure supporting the business. These can be technical or non-technical. The technical risk of a device failure would be addressed by fault tolerance and redundancy. The non-technical risk of an earthquake may be high for one location but low for another and may be addressed through data center redundancy. It is important to identify risks related to any design, and provide the impact of this risk, as well as a potential mitigation strategy of that risk.

A simple vendor example showing risk, impact, and mitigation follows.

- Risk – A single VMware ESXi host failure can have virtual machines unavailable
- Impact – High

- Mitigation – VMware High Availability will recover virtual machines within 15 minutes, in accordance with the SLA's defined. If zero downtime is required as part of an SLA, VMware Fault Tolerance can be used, though this may require a VMware Cluster dedicated for this resiliency.

Assumptions

Assumptions are derived items that should be validated. An example of an assumption could be that the organization running the infrastructure you design has the appropriate training and skills. Don't let an unconfirmed assumption result in failure of the solution you create!

Another common example of an assumption is that time service or DNS infrastructure is currently available and running correctly in the infrastructure.

Validation of these services should be included in the design or installation guide. They provide the foundation for the components you will be integrating to create the infrastructure and services detailed in your architecture.

VCDX NOTE: The VCDX program looks at these items from your submitted design to evaluate how you utilize and/or address each one. As you develop the conceptual model you will need to validate the relationships between the components for this and the other phases of design.

Guidelines to Develop a Document Set

There are multiple document areas that can be included for a design. It is up to the architect to determine how these documents are created and whether some are combined before submitting.

The following provides an overview of one approach starting with the discovery phase and ending with a review of the final document set.

Thank you to Martijn Baecke for providing the basis for this diagram and permission for inclusion with minor modifications.

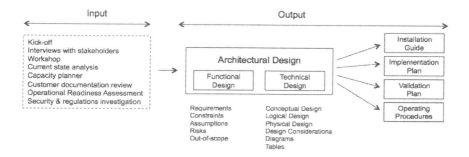

Figure 5 - Guidelines to develop a document set

Design Input

When developing a design, most architects will hold a kick-off meeting. This meeting is typically the starting point where the architect meets the sponsors, stakeholders, and project team to gather the initial conceptual model components. The next aspect is detailed interviews with stakeholders. This is sometimes done as part of a workshop, or even in the initial meetings with your potential client, where core concepts are developed, assumptions are confirmed, and conflicts in requirements and constraints are resolved.

Figure 6 - Design Input Activities

A current state analysis is typically performed to understand the current environment. This includes the current infrastructure technologies and operations from the IT team. It also includes an understanding of the workloads that will be run and the various dependencies in the environment. These dependencies may be technical or operational.

Analysis of capacity is also done to determine current capabilities and scalability to support the design being created.

Vendor example: VMware and VMware Partners typically use a tool called Capacity Planner. Organizations that do not have access to this tool can still conduct an analysis using their existing toolsets, or work with their VMware Partners to use the Capacity Planner tool in their environment.

Vendor example: Virtustream Advisor is a performance and capacity assessment tool designed to measure resource and application workloads across thousands of servers simultaneously. Advisor creates a true apples-to-apples comparison of different resources regardless of type, size, service tier, or OS by converting performance measurements (CPU, memory, network, and disk activity) into MicroVMs (μVMs) and modeling the activity for application, environment, or business category.

Vendor example: The EMC Adaptivity Business Intelligence Platform is a design tool that can help infrastructure architects. It delivers automated and intelligent optimization of mission-critical application and infrastructure life-cycle management. The Adaptivity solution actively analyzes, aligns, and integrates current and future state IT efficiencies with an organization's unique business drivers and priorities. This accelerates business agility and operational efficiency, allowing organizations to keep pace with the speed of today's competitive and ever-changing landscape.

The outcome of this analysis helps drive design patterns and technology choices to support the project.

An architect will review existing documentation to further understand the environment and the business processes and applications supported by the current infrastructure.

An understanding of the operational readiness is important for the architect. He or she will use the level of readiness (technology and operations) to develop a matching installation guide, implementation plan, operating procedures, and identify any training that may be required to support the proposed infrastructure being designed.

All organizations have some form of governance, typically driven by regulatory compliance guidelines. The architect must investigate this, as it is another area that will drive the design. Compliance may be for internal or external reasons.

Example: Consider a hospital that requires data-at-rest-encryption for their SAN. This will drive a SAN selection to meet their requirement. This might require that two separate SANs are included in the design, one to meet this data-at-rest-encryption requirement, and another that is cost effective storage for data that does not need data at rest encryption.

All of these inputs drive the design and are considered inputs. Reference architectures may be used to determine design pattern choices. Most companies develop reference architectures based on use cases.

Vendor Example: VMware vCloud Architecture Toolkit (vCAT) is an example of a reference architecture that includes design patterns and operational recommendations. Most reference architectures are tied to specific use cases. This toolkit supports many use cases with supporting information such as justification, impact, and risk.

If you are utilizing a technology as part of your design, check with the vendor to see if they have reference architectures you can review for ideas to ensure your design meets the vendor guidelines.

Design Output

The architectural design includes multiple components that will be created. There is the architectural design, the installation guide, the implementation plan, the validation plan, and the operating procedures at a minimum. The architectural design includes both the functional design and the technical design.

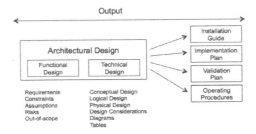

Figure 7 - Design Outputs

The Architecture Design includes the functional and technical design components that provide the bulk of the material that drives a solution. The functional design includes requirements, constraints, assumptions (that must be validated), risks, and a list of out-of-scope items. The technical design includes the conceptual design, logical design, physical design, various design considerations, diagrams, and tables that support the solution. Justifications and implications of design considerations are valuable for inclusion in the documentation for the owner, architect, and builder of the solution. Consider this the keystone or foundation for your design documentation set.

The **Installation Guide** provides details on the installation and configuration of the design solution customized for the project or customer. This means it goes beyond what is included in the product documentation, training guides, and any design templates that are used as a starting point.

The **Implementation Plan** provides details on the project schedule and required training for the customer or project team to utilize the solution. It includes the roles, responsibilities, timelines, and deployment guidance.

The **Validation Plan** considers the entire design and provides the testing that must be performed in order to ensure a successful solution. Many architects include this by technology or functional areas and also include a checklist to support the instructions. The Validation Plan may include unit-level testing (ULT), system-level testing (SLT), integration-level testing (ILT), performance/stress testing, and other tests as appropriate for the solution. These tests should be customized for the project or customer.

The **Standard Operating Procedures** provide the regular activities required by the supporting IT team. This includes recurring, regularly scheduled activities. It should also include special activities that are documented for consistency and supportability.

VCDX NOTE: If you are developing this solution for a customer and plan to use it for your VCDX design submission, consider 'sanitizing' the documents by removing any information that would be considered confidential or NDA type material. Also remember that the quality of the design in meeting the business requirements is more important than the length of the material included.

Design Decisions

Design Decisions will support the project requirements directly or indirectly. Project and implementation requirements provide the justification for a design decision. The same applies for operational decisions. When a specific technology is required to meet a design goal, justification is important and should be provided. With each design decision there is a direct, intended impact, but there are also other areas that may be affected in positive, negative, or neutral manners. With each design decision there are advantages and disadvantages, the net result typically making one option a better choice for the design. These options and their respective value can add quality to the design you make and provide insight into why you took a specific path. In each of these design decisions, the disadvantages can be identified as potential risk items. Major risk areas should be summarized at the beginning or end of the design. The minor risks may be introduced in the area where the design decision is presented.

Justification

Justification is what provides the supporting information for the design choice made. In some cases there may be more than one item that provides support.

Impact

Impact describes how the design decision will affect one or more areas of the design. Each of these may be positive, negative, or neutral in effect. For example, choice of a slower network may affect availability of an application. Inclusion of areas that are not impacted (neutral) may be included to address potential questions. Anticipating questions on the design helps an architect develop more comprehensive design documentation.

Risk

*"Complexity can guarantee resilience. Because they consist of complex webs of relationships, and because a lot of control is distributed rather than centralized, complex systems can adapt to a changing world. They can survive in the world thanks to this ability to adapt. So how can it be that complexity contributes to failure, to accidents? What is the relationship between complexity and drift? Complexity opens up a way for a particular kind of brittleness. Their openness means unpredictable behavior. ....
Complexity and systems theory gives us a language, and some metaphors, to characterize what may happen during the journey into failure, during the trajectory toward an accident." – Sidney Dekker, Drift into Failure, p. 153*

Risk Management is an art based on analysis, design, and operations. It includes identification of risks, an assessment on their likelihood, and prioritization with other risks identified. Risk Management then focuses on minimizing the impact through monitoring and control. Success means identifying, understanding, and mitigating risks.

When we look at Risk Management of infrastructure we look at single points of failure, system level failure, and site failure. The mitigation can include redundancy of hardware and software, systems, and facilities. In many cases we see the design of multiple datacenters with redundant but divergent links.

Decision-Making Skills

An infrastructure architect must have both strategic and tactical decision making skills. The foundation of education, experience, and certification, added to practicing the relevant skills, will lead to success.

Some decisions are made when creating the conceptual model and are typically strategic in nature. Other decisions are more tactical as you move to the logical and then physical architectures. At the physical architecture level there are significant levels of technical details.

When developing solutions, the architect uses pattern recognition skills to rapidly develop solutions. When available, reference architectures and best practices documentation will help. Many vendors provide these reference architectures, best practices, or white papers that provide a set of baseline configuration parameters to deliver the logical and physical requirements. Keep a collection of these supporting documents as part of your project, and include them as part of the design documentation to show justification of design choices made.

As an architect develops their decision making skills he or she will use both analytical and intuitive activities. The analytical activities are based on multiple design patterns that are evaluated for the best choice in a design. The intuitive activities are based on the experience where the architect recognizes a design pattern match.

For decision-making skills there is an excellent PDF available online and developed by the National Wildfire Coordinating Group titled "Design and Delivery of Tactical Decision Games, TDGS/STEX Workbook, PMS 468," released September, 2011. The following is a summary of key points. We recommend reviewing the article and consider how to apply their process to yours.

"The classical model of decision making is a rational and systematic process of analysis based on a comparison of multiple options. If all information is accurate and all pertinent information is known, the analytical decision-making process guarantees the best possible decision is made.

This analytical decision-making model should work well if the facts are not variable, the decision-making environment is held constant, there are no time constraints, and human factors are limited to our personal values. In the fire environment this perfect analytical decision-making process is challenged by a constantly changing environment where not all the information is available, fatigue and other stress is normal, and time is always limited.

The essential factor in intuitive decision-making is experience. Experience allows recognition of similarities to previous situations. A pattern of typical cause and effect develops to allow a decision that does not require analysis or reason. The more experience gained in applying a variety of patterns, the more likely you'll know what to do."[5]

The workbook above was developed for leaders in the fire fighting profession. The five activities for Tactical Decision Games (TDGS) mirror approaches described in the "VCDX Boot Camp" book. Role-play activities, limited information, limited time, and scenarios are all included in both with one exception. The TDGS "After Action Review (AAR)" is where the players as architects would analyze the solution for correctness and to add new design patterns to the pool of existing known ones. The approach used is something that many enterprise architects follow. Examples can be found on blogs and community forums discussing design decisions and design patterns.

Software Defined Data Center considerations

As we see more discussions around the software defined data center, we need to differentiate between definitions. As an example there is Software Defined Networking (SDN) and Software Defined Storage (SDS), where the networking and storage are virtualized.

---

[5]   Design and Delivery of Tactical Decision Games, Wildland Fire Lessons Learned Center, TDGS/STEX Workbook, PMS 468, September 2011, National Wildfire Coordinating Group.

There are many companies that show products with 'software-defined' labeling. Richard McDougall has written, *"The best way to think about this space is that hardware-based storage can be software-defined if it has a fully software-controllable API that allows simplification of provisioning and management. The other, arguably more important part of software-defined storage is emerging as we speak – storage implemented as scale-out software on servers."*[6] The same considerations apply to software defined networking.

Why is it important to understand this?

It is because there are different design considerations based on how the networking and storage is used and integrated. Different characteristics can be added to a software-defined solution that can provide additional benefits that may not be available in a hardware only solution.

Converged Infrastructure Considerations

Multiple vendors are now offering solutions in the Converged Infrastructure platform space. When considering implementation within an infrastructure design, use cases will demonstrate the value of the platforms used. When looking at the Converged Infrastructure landscape, there are some types that address specific use cases, and there are others that support general use.

Additionally, considerations for integration with existing infrastructure components must be considered. A basis for converged infrastructure is the management and orchestration of the platform. This must be integrated with legacy management and orchestration products in the datacenter. Even a green-field datacenter deployment with converged infrastructure platforms must consider the other components of the datacenter such as physical networking components such as routers and switches (hardware), monitoring and management (software), and the operational considerations for the staff.

---

[6]   http://cto.vmware.com/storage-big-data-2014/

Example Table of Contents for Design Documents

To provide a starting point for an architect, we are including several table of contents for the documents for an infrastructure design project.

1. Architecture Design Document
2. Installation Guide
3. Implementation Plan
4. Validation Plan
5. Operational Procedures
6. Risk Management
7. Extra: Business Continuity and Disaster Recovery Design

These examples can cover most infrastructure design projects using different vendors. We use the following terms to support a vendor agnostic terminology where possible.

Table 1 - Terms used in example tables of contents

Term	Description	Example
Host	Workload platform for resources	VMware ESXi host
Management Server	Primary server(s) that handle management and operations, including resources	VMware vCenter Server
Tech Feature #	Items specified to a vendor or product	VMware DRS
Virtual Infrastructure	Virtual components supporting the design	VMware vSphere

If there are assumptions that have not been validated they should also be called out. We recommend all assumptions be validated to minimize risk to the design. These can be listed under the title "Validated Assumptions". An assumption without validation should be listed under the risks section.

Architecture Design Document – Tables of Content

This document provides both the functional design and the technical design. The functional design includes the requirements, constraints, assumptions, risks, and items that are out of scope. This is where the conceptual design model is presented. The technical design includes the logical design and the physical design. These provide design and operational considerations, diagrams, and tables.

Note: In these tables of content we use *Italic* text to convey vendor specific examples.

Project Overview

1. Project Description
   a. Requirements
   b. Constraints
   c. Assumptions
   d. Risks
2. Conceptual Design
   a. Cluster Design
   b. Overview
   c. Logical Cluster Design
   d. Cluster Configurations
3. Host Hardware Design
   a. Overview
   b. Logical Hardware Design
   c. Physical Hardware Configuration
4. Network Design
   a. Overview
   b. Logical Network Design
   c. Physical Network Configuration
5. Storage Design
   a. Overview
   b. Logical Storage Design
   c. Physical Storage Configuration
   d. VMFS Design / Configuration
6. Virtual Machine Design
   a. Overview
   b. VMware vSphere Infrastructure Virtual Machines
   c. Template Virtual Machines

7. HA / FT / BC / DR and Recovery Design
   a. Overview
   b. VMware HA / VMware FT / Business Continuity
      i. Host Protection
      ii. Network Protection
      iii. Storage Protection
      iv. vSphere Infrastructure Protection
      v. Infrastructure Protection
      vi. Site Protection
   c. Disaster Recovery
      i. Host Protection
      ii. Network Protection
      iii. Storage Protection
      iv. VMware vSphere Infrastructure Protection
      v. Infrastructure Protection
   d. Recovery
      i. Host Recovery
      ii. Network Recovery
      iii. Storage Recovery
      iv. VMware vSphere Infrastructure Recovery
      v. Infrastructure Recovery

Installation Guide – Table of Contents

The installation procedures will include project specific guidance. In some cases, architects may include additional details.

1. Installation Procedures
   a. Outline of components for Installation Procedures
   b. Detail high level overview of components to install, prepare, and integrate in a 1-page synopsis
   c. Details not included other than some examples
   d. Host installation procedure
2. Integration Procedures
   a. Third Party Software
   b. Third Party Hardware

     c.   Compatibility Considerations

     d.   Special Considerations

Implementation Plan – Table of Contents

The implementation plan provides the project plan and schedule for deployment of the design.

1. A Bill of Materials (BoM) listing all required components. This includes hardware, software, training, and other items that are part of the total cost. (In some cases the BoM may be provided in a separate document included with the design documents and referenced by the Implementation plan.
2. Plan detailing the process from the hardware and software components to a deployed system
3. Training Plan
4. Project Plan Schedule for Implementation
5. Special Considerations

Validation Plan – Table of Contents

The validation plan provides details on ensuring the design patterns and operational patterns function as defined. Validation plans can include unit testing, system testing, integration testing, and others tests. Additionally, this is where governance can be evaluated in the categories of security and disaster recovery.

1. Overview
2. Unit Level Tests
   a. Products
   b. Primary components (example: VMware vSphere, VMware Horizon View, Cloud)
   c. Subcomponents
3. System Level Tests
   a. Availability

   b. Manageability
   c. Performance
   d. Recoverability
   e. Security
4. Integration Level Tests
   a. Hardware
   b. Software
   c. Operational Tests

Operational Procedures – Table of Contents

The operational procedures provide guidance on running the infrastructure that has been designed and deployed. These are typically customized to the customer project and may not include basics that are already covered in product documentation or in the customer's infrastructure operations documentation.

1. Routine Procedures
2. Infrequent Procedures
3. Special Case Procedures
   a. Backup/Restore
   b. Product Failure
   c. System Failure
   d. Site Failure

Risk Management – Table of Contents

The risk management document provides the types of risks, the likelihood of them occurring, and the risk mitigation steps.

1. Risk Identification
2. Risk Mitigation
3. Validation of Risk Management

Extra: Availability and Recoverability (Business Continuity and Disaster Recovery) Design – Table of Contents

Exercises

The following exercises test your learning of key concepts and how they tie together. We have included some additional exercises that do not have an answer key and designed to be projects that you can work on based on your skills, environment, and project parameters.

Key Concepts

1. Match the items in LIST 1 with the items in LIST 2.
   a. LIST 1: Technique, Philosophy, Methodology
   b. LIST 2: What, How
   c. ANSWER: (See quote at start of chapter)
      i. Technique = How
      ii. Philosophy = What
      iii. Methodology = What & How
2. Identify the expectations of an architect
   a. Identifies and understand business requirements
   b. Focuses on the technologies used as the highest priority
   c. (technology choices are made in the 3rd phase)
   d. Identify constraints and risks affecting the design
   e. Understands different architecture strategies
   f. Only uses vendor architecture strategies
   g. (other strategies may be required especially when integrating)
   h. Identifies and understands the impact of each design choices
   i. Understands the impact of only their design choices (must look at alternate choices)
   j. Understands all areas of the design, including those completed by other team members
3. Which three of the following design rules used by an infrastructure architect?
   a. Use business requirements to drive design and implementation decisions
   b. Ensure the design is suited for mission-critical applications

60

      c. Deliver a design for a managed environment

      d. Ensure the design has the highest availability (this is determined by the project requirements and constraints)

      e. Ensure the design has the highest performance (this is determined by the project requirements and constraints)

4. Describe the conceptual model.

5. Describe the logical design.

6. Describe the physical design.

7. Are installation instructions standardized or customized for the project?

      a. Answer = Customized because there will typically be differences for all designs. An example would be installation instructions that include IP address information or fully qualified DNS naming for internal systems.

8. What is included in an implementation plan? (answer = f)

      a. Bill of Materials (BoM)

      b. Process to deploy the design components

      c. Training Plan

      d. Project Plan

      e. Special Considerations

      f. All of the above

9. What types of tests are included in a validation plan? (answer = e)

      a. System Tests

      b. Integration Tests

      c. Infrastructure tests

      d. Workload tests

      e. All of the above

10. Match the Characteristic items to the items in the Design categories.

      a. Characteristic

            i.   Governance

            ii.   Recoverability

           iii. Roles, Controls, Traceability

           iv. vSphere version X.Y

            v.   Application Mobility

      b. Design Categories

            i.   Conceptual Model (answer = i)

           ii.   Logical Design (answer = ii and v)

          iii. Physical Design (answer = iii and iv)

Self-paced exercises

1. Identify the attributes for the design that you will build based on the business requirements. How do they relate to the solution you are building and to each other? Are there overriding items that will determine how the attributes will be facilitated?

2. Review an existing infrastructure and reverse engineer the physical architecture.

    a. Identify a use case for the existing infrastructure and any known supporting requirements, constraints, assumptions, or risks.

    b. Using this supporting information, create a conceptual model of what is needed.

    c. Create a bill-of-materials for the infrastructure; hardware, software.

    d. Create a logical architecture that shows the relationship of components without describing the vendor, product, or configuration.

    e. Compare the conceptual model from (b) with the logical architecture from (d). Does the logical architecture meet, exceed, or fall short of the conceptual model?

CHAPTER 3

CASE STUDY

"Infrastructure design involves applying experience and knowledge, in a combination of art and science, to produce efficient solutions that meet requirements while mitigating risks and accounting for constraints. An infrastructure architect must be able to effectively communicate and justify the decisions that affect each aspect of the work while instilling confidence that the proposed solution will succeed."
— Doug Baer, VCDX-019

Let's begin with the first part of any project, the business situation driving the design. We need to understand what the actual goals of the project are, and to have an understanding of the company, the business scenarios tied to the design, and existing resources available to the business. For our purposes, this case study will be driving the designs shown in Chapter 4 and Chapter 6, (virtualization of servers and desktops). We will show the components of the design as phases in the next chapters; server virtualization first, followed by end user computing, or desktop virtualization.

We present a case study that will be used to drive the development of the solution architecture. We are taking a hybrid approach in that we will have a business use case for both server and desktop virtualization.

The goal of this chapter is to provide the reader with an overview of our fictitious company, ITAR, and their plans to implement Datacenter Virtualization, and take their first step into End User Computing with a Virtual Desktop Infrastructure. OK, so the company is not fictitious (it is the company behind the IT Architect Series...), but let us pretend it IS fictitious....

Company Overview

ITAR, a division of ITAR, is a company that focuses on providing online and instructor led training. ITAR provides training across both hardware and software products, in the IT realm, from multiple vendors, to many students each year.

ITAR has high standards, in regards to the content they provide education on, as well as in the satisfaction of those who attend the courses (the students). ITAR has therefore been certified by vendors as an authorized training center for all of its partners (the vendors that ITAR provides courses for).

ITAR upgrades the hardware in its datacenter often, to incorporate new products that drive courses required by the students. Software is updated frequently as well, for the same reasons, and is driving ITAR to requirements that dictate a Software Defined Data Center (SDDC) must be incorporated into any new implementations.

ITAR's leadership supports the SDDC, and realizes that this is an important factor in its evolution as technology changes, but more importantly, it will assist in retaining long-term customers, who expect to be able to work with physical and virtual IT infrastructures from anywhere, at any time.

ITAR currently has a single datacenter in Johnstown, PA. Support for the hardware and software must be available, as Principal Engineers for ITAR are not local to the Johnstown, PA datacenter.

Project Specification

ITAR currently uses Dell equipment for much of its infrastructure. ITAR has forged a stronger relationship with Dell and EMC as part of the SDDC initiative. Therefore, ITAR will use only Dell and EMC in the next generation of its offerings. There are plans to build two separate infrastructures: one for the internal IT staff, and another for the delivery of classes to students.

Having the ability to create a modular solution, where network, storage, or compute re-sources can be interchanged in the environment will simplify the ongoing operations for ITAR, as hardware required for the training environments is consistently changing.

ITAR would like to create this solution so that performance of the classes being held is not affected. With an understanding of shared resources in a virtualized datacenter, having the solution built in a manner in which priorities can be assigned, if contention occurs, would be considered important.

ITAR currently has support Service Level Agreements (SLAs) of 1 hour, for end user support requests. Support for the hardware in the datacenter is currently 4-hour response from the vendors themselves. ITAR would like to improve support Service Level Agreements.

ITAR would like to reiterate that hardware purchases are limited, and use of existing equipment is requested. It is an understanding that not all equipment can be repurposed, and that some hardware may need to be purchased to have successful projects.

Existing Networking Infrastructure

Dell PowerConnect switches are the standard at ITAR. A mix of Dell PowerEdge 6248 and 5448 switches exist in the network to provide connectivity for the data center, as well as for classroom connectivity. This infrastructure is at 1-Gbp/s.

Performance problems in the network today are perceived by the end users, and seen only in certain segments. Upgrading the entire network to 10-GbE is desired, though may be cost prohibitive for ITAR.

Maintaining separation of classroom networks to isolate traffic to the classroom itself is considered an important goal. This isolation will allow students into the ITAR network to access the classrooms, but prevent the students from accessing internal ITAR resources, or other classrooms.

Existing Storage Area Network

ITAR's storage area network today is primarily built on a Dell EqualLogic iSCSI platform. This is built upon the existing 1-Gbp/s network infrastructure that mentioned previously. The iSCSI network runs in its own subnet / VLAN, to isolate the traffic from all other types of network traffic. Use of the existing network switches to support the iSCSI network reduced the number of physical switches required in the infrastructure. This adds a layer of isolation, and security to the iSCSI network.

The iSCSI network runs on the Dell PowerConnect switch environment described earlier.

The balance of the Storage Area Network is comprised of Fiber Channel based EMC CLARiiON storage. This storage arrays provide the high performance tier of storage.

The Storage Area Network is comprised of Brocade FC switches, running at 4-Gbp/s. QLogic FC HBAs are the preferred FC HBA in ITAR's environment.

Performance in this environment has been adequate to support the existing infrastructure at this time. Some performance data is available from the Storage Teams at ITAR, if re-quested.

Existing Desktop Environment

Today, the desktop environments used by students are physical systems with remote desktop enabled and published to the Internet. Students use the Microsoft Remote Desktop Client to connect to the student system.

ITAR has been purchasing desktops as it expands its infrastructure, and as additional classes are required. This results in a mix of desktops in the environment, making management, imaging, maintenance, patching, and repair a challenge. Desktops in the infrastructure today are a mix of Windows XP, Windows 7, and Windows 8 variants.

Once a class is defined, it may run for up to a year without modifications. Many of the classes being offered are repeated each week. As additional classes are created, ITAR currently purchases additional desktops if required to support the class.

The use Microsoft Remote Desktop Protocol (RDP) to access the classrooms has caused issues, as this runs over a well know TCP/IP port that is blocked by many organizations. This remote access method has functioned well enough, when possible, for students to complete classes, though it is known that improvements can be made.

BC / HA / FT / DR and Recovery Initiatives

ITAR recognizes that a two-hour disruption to classes due to a failure is disruptive, and impacts the classes significantly. Developing a strategy to reduce the time to recovery should be considered part of any datacenter update project. ITAR has some experience with virtualization, and is aware that improvements can be made in the availability and recoverability of datacenters build upon virtualized infrastructures.

The ability to realize continued operations in the event of failed servers, switches, and desktops is required. Most workloads in ITAR's operations can survive an outage of fifteen minutes or less. There are some workloads, such as the infrastructure supporting the classrooms, which are less tolerant of outages. Improvements to the availability of these resources will be considered key to the success of this project.

The current solution for recovery is to restore from tape backups. While this solution functions as required, it does not meet the Service Level Agreements for all aspects of ITAR's operations. Improvements in this area are expected, within the scope of this project.

Currently, there is not protection for a complete site failure. Having the ability to simplify recovery, and resume operations will be key, if another site becomes available for ITAR to prepare for and run Disaster Recovery workloads. Financial calculations show that the cost of a second data center is greater than the cost of allowing students to regain access to their lab equipment at a later time, even if that is after the class has completed and in the event that students need more time than originally offered.

Virtualized Datacenter

ITAR has been using VMware vSphere in some of its operations, and has realized some of the benefits that this brings to the operations of a datacenter.

Virtualization has eliminated the need to purchase new servers to support each classroom, and has made ITAR capable of bringing the back end resources online quickly to support new classes, as well as to bring services online in their corporate IT infrastructure.

Today there is a mix of Dell PowerEdge servers in use, ranging from 2950 series to the R710 series of servers.

With all of the ITAR support staff being remote to the Johnstown, PA datacenter, supporting fewer physical components will simplify the requirements of the IT staff, as supporting a Virtualized Infrastructure has been proven easier at ITAR, as well as shortens the time required to maintain or repair virtualized services.

ITAR expects to improve its availability, recoverability, and simplify ongoing IT infrastructure purchases by creating a "Virtual First" initiative in how to deploy new applications, services, and classes in its environment.

Virtualized Desktops

ITAR has been exploring Virtual Desktop Infrastructures for some time, and believes that VDI can solve many of the problems it has in maintaining its classroom environments.

Simplification of the provisioning process, being capable of adding students to a classroom at any time (even at the last minutes before a class begins), and maintaining this infrastructure during the course of normal day to day operations is key, if a VDI solution is to be considered successful at ITAR.

Eliminating the need to purchase new desktop hardware when bringing a new class online is currently seen as an obstacle, and delays the offering of a new class. ITAR would like to eliminate this, and believes that a VDI solution is capable of meeting this goal.

When customers access the classroom environments, the experience must be as good as, if not better, than sitting at a local computer. Customer access must be over standard TCP/IP ports, so that firewall rules that could impact connectivity do not affect the ability to connect to the classroom environments. This will reduce the number of calls to the Support Teams at ITAR, and improve the experiences of the students who attend classes at ITAR.

Improving security for the classroom desktops is important, as each classroom should only be able to communicate with itself, and not have the potential to impact other classes being held at that time.

Today, desktops are imaged as required to support classes. This adds complexity and time to provision a class. Simplifying this setup and configuration would ease the ongoing management of the classroom desktop infrastructure.

Case Study Review

ITAR has provided an overview of their infrastructure, its goals, and some of the hardware it has in use. But, as you have finished this chapter, you may realize, "...there is a lot of information that is missing for me to design a solution for ITAR." You are correct.

Like any initial meeting you will find that not only are you missing information but that you might also have been given conflicting information as well as information that is irrelevant to the scope of the project. For example, during interviews with ITAR they could have mentioned a business critical financial application. At this first mention you took notes, asked more questions, and maybe even began to think of solutions to support the application only to later find out that the application is not in scope for the education services project you were brought in to do.

You may have spent 15-20 minutes reading this chapter. Equate this to having an initial meeting with a client (or business group). During the initial meeting, you are looking to identify the business requirements that are driving the project at hand, as well as starting to construct a logical design to meet those requirements. It is nearly impossible to identify all of the requirements, constraints, assumptions, and risks during an initial meeting / consultation. This chapter leaves many unanswered questions regarding the desired solution, just as it would in nearly all real world situations.

Now with your assumption that information pertinent to developing a solution for ITAR is not complete, how do you proceed? It is an architect's responsibility to dive further into ITAR's operations and discover all the unanswered (and unasked) questions. By diving deeper into ITAR's operations, you will discover new requirements, additional constraints to developing your solution, find and document assumptions regarding the environment, and identify risks that may not have been presented during the initial discovery meetings.

How can you do this exercise without having the ITAR representatives around to answer your additional questions?

Think about the things that affect you day to day in YOUR operations. What would happen if the SAN in the back-end was replaced? How would this affect you? What if the switches in the solution were not Dell PowerConnect, as stated in case study, but switches from another vendor? Would that affect the manner in which you configured network cards in ESXi hosts? What if power to the datacenter was not actually redundant? Only a single UPS was present in the datacenter, with only a single circuit providing that power?

Chapter 7, Design Analysis, will ask you to consider these mentioned, as well as additional, considerations that could impact your design. In the meantime, if you read Chapter 3 again, and this time, proceed to take notes as if you were leading a discussion with customers / business groups that you are providing this solution for. Ask yourself questions as you see information that is missing, unclear, or you perceive as incorrect. As you progress through the design chapters that follow, you may see some of these questions answered. If you do not see them answered, consider that your thoughts might be uncovering additional risks, assumptions, constraints, or that you may uncover an undocumented requirement that the business has.

SERVER VIRTUALIZATION: ARCHITECTURE DESIGN EXAMPLE

"People don't use a product because of the great design; great design helps them use the product."
— *Viran Anuradha Dayaratne*

Chapter 4 provides a server virtualization design. The other documents supporting this follow in Chapter 5.

This design presents a base design that will have strengths and weaknesses based on the requirements, constraints, and design decisions. The Table of Con-tents shown in this chapter is for the design included.

This design provides an extra value. It is a product design for teaching environment. This can be of benefit to training companies and training organizations develop their own virtual lab.

All references to company names, team member names, project names, and locations are for the benefit of this example and do not represent real people, companies, or projects. This design was developed and deployed for use by one of the co-authors and demonstrates a virtual-on-virtual environment.

IT Architect Resource Virtual Data Center Design Guide

This document has undergone revisions that include but are not limited to changes in hardware, software, and configuration. As agreed upon by IT Architect Resource (ITAR) the infrastructure documentation need only include the most recent infrastructure design, implementation, and management specifications and data.

The parties involved in this project include members from the IT Architect Re-source and the consulting team from ITAR.

The project specifications were defined by the management team of IT Architect Resource and communicated to the Partner through John Doe, the infrastructure manager for the ITAR Executive and Technical Education Center in Denver, CO.

The team of consultants from ITAR included multiple architects (names with-held for the book, but should be included in your actual documentation).

This document was created using the official VMware icon and diagram library. Copyright © 2010 VMware, Inc. All rights reserved. This product is protected by U.S. and international copyright and intellectual property laws. VMware products are covered by one or more patents listed at http://www.vmware.com/go/patents.

VMware does not endorse or make any representations about third party information included in this document, nor does the inclusion of any VMware icon or diagram in this document imply such an endorsement.

The whole of this project can be found by looking at multiple documents. Some of the documents are original creations from the ITAR team and some of the documents were supplied by vendors as guidelines for developing a solutions architecture to meet their expectations.

ITAR VDC Documentation List

ITAR VDC Design Guide: This document provides the overall design of the management infrastructure of the ITAR VDC and the justifications for the design decisions.

ITAR VDC Implementation and Installation Guide: This document provides details on the configuration specifications for the installation and configuration of the management infrastructure. This document also details the physical setup of the entire ITAR VDC according to the elements in the ITAR VDC Design Guide and the guidelines provided by the VMware Authorized Training Center (VATC) Setup Guides.

ITAR VDC Operations Guide: This document provides details on the day-to-day operations of the ITAR VDC including how to setup and tear down the student VDC kits.

ITAR VDC Validation Guide: This document provides details on the steps required to perform validation testing on the architecture presented in the ITAR VDC Design Guide as implemented in the ITAR VDC Implementation Guide.

1. Project Overview

1.1 Project Description

IT Architect Resource (ITAR) is a division of ITAR that provides online and instructor-led training. The ITAR product line includes training across the spectrum of ITAR hardware products (servers, storage, and networking) and software products from leading vendors like VMware, Citrix, and Microsoft.

In 2008 as ITAR entered the VMware virtualization training market by joining other leading hardware vendors as a VMware Authorized Training Center (VATC) they found themselves in new territory. As ITAR entered into this new partnership with VMware they found themselves, like VMware and other VATCs, training their students on remote virtual datacenters (VDC) constructed, hosted, and managed by VMware. Unfortunately for ITAR the VMware managed training lab equipment was all designed and implemented on HP equipment. From a business perspective this didn't fit ITAR's training curriculum as delivering training to ITAR customers, looking to learn Dell hardware, on HP equipment did not make sense. ITAR quickly identified the infrastructure deficiencies and skills gap that left them struggling to find a way to deliver ITAR branded, ITAR hosted virtualization training.

As a contracted VMware training agency and an early partner with ITAR during their transition into VATC status, ITAR was able to offer a unique perspective on the existing and future VMware training market as well as the logistics required to help ITAR overcome the deficiencies and fill in the gaps to create a flexible, stable, reliable, and highly available VMware VDC training lab environment.

As the project and the partnership deepened and as the success of the ITAR-branded VMware lab environment flourished, ITAR found another need where our expertise in education lab management could facilitate the growth of their training product line. Specifically ITAR discovered a need to restructure their EqualLogic and Blades/DMC training to a VDC infrastructure with the same design qualities that were realized with the VMware training lab infrastructure we provided. With this discovery the project grew to include two major training product lines across VMware and ITAR product training.

ITAR was well equipped to strategically sell training services while ITAR was skilled in designing and managing training infrastructures that would provide customers with the opportunity to learn new technologies. As the ITAR/ITAR relationship moved forward it was important to for the architects to understand, not just the technical requirements, but the business requirements that the ITAR management team saw as critical for success. In order to ensure that ITAR was delivering on the ITAR message to customers, we asked the ITAR management team to provide us with a project mission statement.

"IT Architect Resource succeeds when customers' educational demands are exceeded by our sales team, our trainers, our courseware, and our facilities. In order to ensure that ITAR customers are retained as long term customers, we focus on the logistics of providing efficient and effective technology training that help them implement our products to better their own line of business. In order to evolve our own education product line we must adopt new technologies and infrastructure that provide multi-modal training experiences for today's fast-paced, mobile, and tech-savvy IT professional. The future of our business hinges on the construction of a reliable and scalable virtual datacenter that is accessible at anytime from anywhere." – John Doe, ITAR Infrastructure Manager

ITAR proposed the construction of a ITAR-branded virtual datacenter in our Johnstown, PA datacenter. At the agreement of both parties, the three year contract would stipulate that the VDC would be funded by IT Architect Resource while being designed, implemented, managed, and supported by the ITAR virtualization team. At the end of the three year contract ITAR can opt to renew the contract as it stands, relocate the infrastructure but retain ITAR for support and management duties, or assume the full accountability for the infrastructure absent the team from ITAR.

1.2 Requirements

In cooperation with the management and technical teams at ITAR, the following requirements have been identified and agreed upon for the ITAR/VMware training lab infrastructure:

1. Customer experience should remain above average as determined by post-class customer evaluations. Declining customer evaluations should result in infrastructure revisions that would improve customer experience.
2. Customer access to the VDC must use standard ports 3389 and/ or 443.
3. The VMware VDC must meet/exceed the VATC setup guidelines for the following courses:
    a. vSphere 4.1 Install, Configure, and Manage
    b. vSphere 4.0 Troubleshooting (2 kits)
    c. vSphere 4.0 Manage for Performance (2 kits)
    d. vSphere 4.0 What's New
4. Dell EqualLogic training must meet/exceed the ITAR specifications for the following courses:
    a. Dell EqualLogic Advanced
    b. Dell EqualLogic Business Continuity and Disaster Recovery
5. Dell Blades/DMC training must meet/exceed the ITAR specifications for the following courses:
    a. Dell Blades
    b. Dell Management Controller

6. Support must be provided beginning one hour before the start of class and ending hour after class on each class day for the respective time zone where class is being delivered.

7. Support requests must be responded to within 15 minutes.

8. Disruptions to VDC access must not exceed 2 hours, unless the root of the problem is failed student hardware for which ITAR knowingly has not provided the hardware required to achieve an N+1 redundancy. Under these circumstances the disruption time is determined by the business critical support contract for the failed device.

9. Disruptions to the VDC caused by complete storage array failure do not qualify for repair under the two-hour time constraint. A complete storage failure should be reported immediately to the instructor, ITAR management team, and ITAR infrastructure team. In this case a best effort will be made by the ITAR team to restore class to its normal operating environment.

10. VMware class compute workloads should not impact ITAR EqualLogic and/or ITAR Blades and DMC training. An overlap in networking is acceptable.

11. Student access to VDC kits should be limited to only the class for which they are enrolled and last only for the duration of the class.

12. Class setup and configuration is expected with as little as 2 business days' notice.

13. The VMware VDC, ITAR EqualLogic VDC, and Blades/DMC VDC should be modularized to support partial decommissioning upon request by ITAR.

14. The infrastructure must scale to accommodate the projected growth of the ITAR education products assembled for the ITAR specific training. VMware training was expected to remain stable but not require scaling beyond the initial infrastructure.

15. Due to the potential impact of resource contention on customer experience CPU and Memory resources should not be overcommitted.

16. The infrastructure design and management must be limited to technologies/features available to ITAR IT team. Any third-party products used to develop the infrastructure must be approved by the ITAR infrastructure team.

17. Design changes must be approved by the ITAR infrastructure team

18. Beyond the core infrastructure, failures in management infrastructure should be isolated to impact only one of the training product lines.

19. The infrastructure must support a simple and easy remote management as the principle engineers and support technicians are not local to the Johnstown, PA datacenter. This requirement was self-imposed and not suggested by the ITAR team.

Achieving success in this design was predicated on understanding how ITAR prioritized the design qualities of availability, manageability, performance, recoverability, and security and how well their priorities mapped to the requirements identified. These design qualities were defined in combination with the ITAR team as follows:

- Availability: the uptime of the system resulting in uninterrupted access.
- Manageability: the ease of provisioning, administering, and scaling the system to provide consistent operation and accommodate continued growth and change.
- Performance: the competence of the system to provide for step-by-step lab exercises as defined for each class without unreasonable delay.
- Recoverability: the restoration of the system in the event of an unplanned loss of a key component required for continued operation.

Security: the protection of system components against unauthorized access.

With both parties in agreement of the design quality definitions ITAR prioritized the design qualities in order of most important to least important as shown in Table 2.

Table 2 - ITAR Design Quality Ranking

	Rank	Design Quality
Most Important	1	Availability
	2	Performance
	3	Manageability
	4	Recoverability
Least Important	5	Security

Ranking Availability and Performance as 1 and 2 are in line with the ITAR requirement of maintaining above average customer experience (CE) ratings for the class deliveries. Both of these design qualities can be quantifiably traced back as having a direct impact on the CE.

Ranking manageability above recoverability was a surprise since recoverability can more directly relate to CE than manageability. However, looking at the possibility that this infrastructure could be relocated back to a ITAR managed facility at the end of the contract it is understandable that the ITAR infrastructure team would want to ensure reduced complexity of the overall solution coupled with easy to manage operational utilities and procedures.

A fifth ranked security was expected as this environment is used only for training, gets reset every week, and does contain any data that can be considered private corporate data that could jeopardize the competitive advantage of ITAR or ITAR.

Although the ITAR team ranked Security as the fifth and least important design quality there are aspects of the environment, to be noted throughout, where the ITAR team had to ensure that elements were adequately protected as a means of ensuring that the remaining design qualities were achievable.

1.3 Constraints

In cooperation with the management and technical teams at ITAR, the following constraints have been identified and agreed upon for the Dell/VMware training lab infrastructure:

1. Hardware is limited to hardware that can be provisioned by ITAR and can be accomplished within the budget for the project. The project included three separate budgets. One budget covered the requirements for the customer-facing VMware VDC kits, the second budget covered the requirements for the customer-facing Dell EqualLogic VDC kits, and the third budget covered the Dell Blades VDC kit.
2. Additional hardware purchases are limited beyond what is directly required for the direct customer-facing student VDC lab infrastructure.
3. Any required support for the VMware VDC beyond what can be provided by the existing infrastructure management team will be submitted to the ITAR Support Services.
4. Hardware for non-customer-facing management infrastructure has been provisioned by ITAR and is not included in the budget.
   a. Dell PowerEdge R710
      i. Dual Intel Xeon E5620, 64GB RAM
   b. Dell PowerEdge R610
      i. Dual Intel Xeon E5620, 32GB RAM
   c. Dell PowerEdge 2950 III
      i. Dual Intel Xeon E5405, 32GB RAM
   d. EMC CLARiiON CX3-20 (x4) and CX3-40 (x2) Fibre Channel Storage Arrays
      i. All drives in the arrays are 146GB 10k 2Gb FC drives
   e. Dell PowerConnect 6248 Gigabit Ethernet switches
   f. Dell PowerConnect 5448 Gigabit Ethernet switches
   g. Brocade 300 4Gb Fibre Channel Switches
   h. QLogic 2300 series Fibre Channel HBAs
   i. Intel Pro 1000 Gigabit Ethernet adapters

5. The VDC design must not include solutions or configurations for which the ITAR infrastructure team is not prepared to manage.
6. The vSphere troubleshooting class has strict requirements on the ESX /ESXi and PowerShell version for the configuration of the student servers and damage scripts to operate correctly. The version required is 4.0 with no update for vSphere and PowerCLI 4.0, however, the ITAR R610 with the H700 SCSI controller is not supported on this version of vSphere. It is supported on ESXi 4.0 Update 2.

1.4 Assumptions

In cooperation with the management and technical teams at ITAR the following assumptions have been identified and agreed upon for the ITAR/ VMware training lab infrastructure:

1. ITAR assumes all financial, legal, and logistical functions of the VMware Authorized Training Center agreement.
2. The VMware class requirements as outlined by the VMware created VATC setup guides are sufficient for achieving performance levels that result in adequate customer experience (CE) ratings.
3. Hardware provided by ITAR will scale to meet the VMware/Dell training demand. If demand exceeds the scalability of provided hardware and puts performance and CE in jeopardy ITAR understands that VDC labs will be provided only with an agreed upon adjustment to the performance requirements as stated in section 1.
4. All hardware (ITAR and non-ITAR) and software (VMware) issues can be resolved by the local datacenter staff or the ITAR Support Services.
5. ITAR customers will be able to accommodate the VDC access strategy.
6. Internet bandwidth in the datacenter is sufficient to handle remote connections to the VDC.
7. The power and cooling infrastructure at the physical datacenter is constructed with redundancy to ensure continued operations.

1.5 Risks

In cooperation with the management and technical teams at ITAR the following risks have been identified and agreed upon for the ITAR/ VMware training lab infrastructure:

1. Initial hardware specifications may not scale to educational demand.
2. Multiple hardware failures exceeding an N+1 redundancy design.
3. ITAR Support Services is unable to resolve a VMware issue.
4. No protection for complete site failure.
5. ITAR Blade class is delivered on two blade chassis. Loss of a Blade chassis incurs a loss of infrastructure for 50% of the class population.
6. The evolution of the class requirements outgrows the hardware provided resulting in a negative impact to the CE.
7. Loss of a ITAR EqualLogic iSCSI array that is part of the student infrastructure would be susceptible to the ITAR 4 hour business critical support contract.
8. The VMware vSphere troubleshooting student kits must be modified to use vSphere 4.0 Update 1. The PowerCLI will be update accordingly.
9. The EqualLogic VDC for Neptune and Jupiter have a dedicated IP storage network that is the same network as the Management and IP Storage network for the VMware VDC for Neptune and Jupiter. If EQL and VMware classes run simultaneously the two classes will share the same networks. In addition if the Neptune or Jupiter kit is used for a concurrent VMware and ITAR class it will push the EQL class to using a non-VMware supported nested ESXi solution. ITAR has acknowledged the risk and will try to avoid this scenario.
10. If ITAR decides to expand by adding an 8th kit the naming strategy will have to be revised or a new strategy begun on the new kit as it might be inappropriate to have students take a class on Uranus. ☺

1.6 Design Philosophy

It is often very easy to allow yourself to get carried away during the design process. Perhaps even more so when you work with technologies and features as cutting edge and "wow'ing" as some of those we find in the vSphere product. The goal of this design, however, is to solve a business problem for the IT Architect Resource division of ITAR. This is not an exercise or demonstration in implementing or using technology just for the sake of the technology. It is our due diligence to ensure that the design elements we work with to create this solution are all justifiable in the eyes of ITAR and our design team. Our efforts must focus on providing sound technical solutions that solve problems without undue complexity.

1.7 VDC Conceptual Design

The overall conceptual design of the ITAR virtual datacenter (VDC) addresses the two major classifications of training courses to be managed, VMware and Dell. The Solar01, Solar02, and Solar03 clusters are designed specifically as "management clusters" used to provide the required network applications, services, and Virtual Machines required for the different course titles that are delivered using the "production VDC kits" labeled Earth, Mars, Mercury, Saturn, Neptune, Jupiter, and Venus. The designation between a management cluster and production VDC kit (or student VDC kit) is whether the students are provided access to the underlying infrastructure. In the student VDC kit architecture, detailed in the ITAR Student VDC Design Guide, the students are able to access the hardware as required by the respective class requirements. The management cluster infrastructure is not accessed by students during any portion of the classes, however, students may access Virtual Machines hosted on a management cluster. Figure 8 shows the ITAR VDC conceptual design.

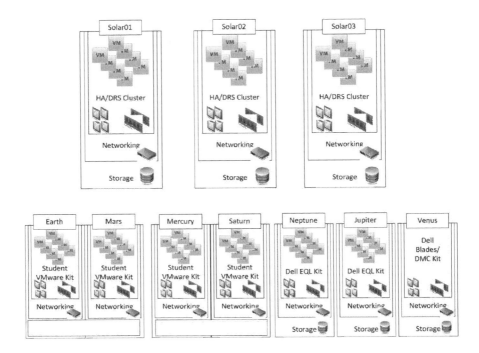

Figure 8 - The ITAR Virtual Datacenter (VDC) Conceptual Design.

The Solar01 cluster supports the VMware specific student virtual datacenter (VDC) kits of Earth, Mars, Mercury, and Saturn. The Solar02 cluster supports the ITAR EqualLogic/DMC/VMware kits of Neptune, Jupiter, and Venus. The Solar03 cluster is supports the VMware View virtual desktop infrastructure for accessing these same student VDC kits.

1.7.1 VDC Design Justification

A distinct separation between the equipment used for management of the lab infrastructure and the equipment used by the course attendees establishes boundaries for management that prevent students from accessing the support infrastructure and establishes separate execution zones and fault domains between the VMware and ITAR education product lines. A key driver behind the ITAR VDC design is the requirement to present a strong element of modularity to support the possibility that ITAR could decide at the end of the contract to return all or some of the infrastructure to a ITAR facility and may or may not assume the management and support duties.

Design qualities impacted: Availability, Manageability, and Security

Requirements Achieved: 10, 11, 13, 14, and 18

1.8 VDC Conceptual Access Strategy

Considering that this project revolved around a 100% remote global student demographic supported by ITAR it was important to strike a balance between ease of connectivity and conformity with the established training guidelines for each of the training products. While the external connectivity to the VDC is a centralized pair of firewalls, the connectivity decentralizes internally to provide access to the VMware VDC or the ITAR VDC as shown in Figure 9.

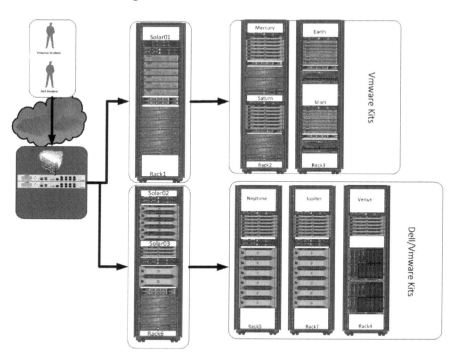

Figure 9 - ITAR VDC Conceptual Access Strategy

Separating the student access to the appropriate VDC (VMware or ITAR) is accomplished through a separation in access strategy techniques and/or external names or IP addresses provided for remote connectivity. Figure 10 shows a further logical breakdown of the access strategy into two different means of connectivity: Microsoft Terminal Services (port 3389) and VMware View (port 443).

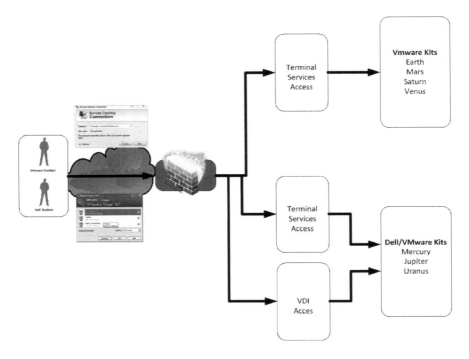

Figure 10 - VDC access with Terminal Services or virtual desktops through VMware View.

1.8.1 Access Strategy Design Justification

As identified in the VATC setup guides for the VMware training courses students access the VDC kits using the Microsoft Remote Desktop Client connected to a Windows Server running Terminal Services. The ITAR VDC kit specifications were less detailed with respects to technology but more specific with customer need. With ITAR providing many on-site training courses for organizations with a strict security policy it was mandated that access to the ITAR VDC be available over secure web-based ports and protocols. By introducing VMware View into the access strategy ITAR customers can satisfy the demands of their security policy and still complete their ITAR provided ITAR/VMware training.

Design qualities impacted: Availability, Manageability, and Security

Requirements achieved: 2, 3, and 4

2. VDC Cluster Design

2.1 Overview

The ITAR VDC Cluster Design provides details on the vSphere cluster configurations used to manage the infrastructure resources and student class resources for the ITAR training products.

2.2 Logical Cluster Design

At a high level overview the ITAR VDC is constructed within a single vCenter named vc.vdc-kits.com, a single datacenter named JST, and three management clusters named Solar01, Solar02, and Solar03. The three separate provide distinct execution zones for specific portions of the ITAR training courses, shown in Figure 11.

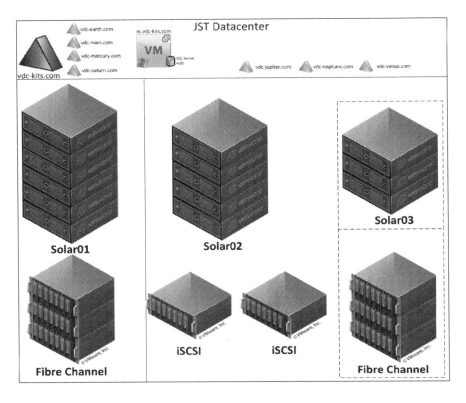

Figure 11 - ITAR VDC Logical Cluster Design

The Solar01 cluster hosts the infrastructure resources for the VDC-KITS forest root domain as well as the resources for the VDC-EARTH, VDC-MARS, VDC-MERCURY, and VDC-SATURN tree root domains. Solar01 hosts the Virtual Machines required for the VMware training products delivered on the kits respective to the four domains: Earth, Mars, Mercury, and Saturn. Solar02 hosts the Virtual Machines for the VDC-NEPTUNE, VDC-JUPITER, and VDC-VENUS domains.

The Active Directory (AD) domain design using a single forest with a forest root domain and multiple tree root domains presents connected but separate security and authentication boundaries for students to hold elevated and isolated privileges within a respective domain. Each AD domain maps to a specific kit architecture. Isolating the student accounts and VMs of a specific kit to a respective domain supports class requirements that require privileges that extend beyond just those granted to the default Domain Users group.

The ITAR VDC includes two EMC CX3-40 Fibre Channel storage arrays and two ITAR EqualLogic PS4000x iSCSI storage arrays. The Solar01 cluster utilizes one of the EMC CX3-40 arrays, the Solar02 cluster uses the second EMC CX3-40 array and the two PS4000x arrays, and the Solar03 cluster also connects to the second EMC CX3-40 exclusively. Though listed as a constraint, the storage hardware provisioned by ITAR, is not to be taken as if it were a direct limitation to the design options. Specifically in the case of storage, although the Fibre Channel storage arrays were not the latest make and model and could not run the latest Flare code we were able to provision a number of arrays and an ample number of hard drives to design a storage infrastructure that mapped well to the cluster design with a decentralized yet redundant storage infrastructure therefore eliminating the need for a single, centralized storage device.

With shared storage in place using both EMC Fibre Channel and EqualLogic iSCSI, all of the SolarXX clusters are enabled for High Availability (HA) and Distributed Resource Scheduler (DRS). The cluster configuration details for each of the Solar0X management clusters can be viewed in the ITAR VDC Implementation Guide.

2.4 Design Justification

Designing the ITAR VDC with three independent but interrelated clusters creates a set of natural boundaries for the isolation of workloads, segregation of fault domains, and modularity for (possible) disassembly and relocation.

Design Qualities Impacted: Manageability, Availability, Security

Requirements Achieved: 3, 7, 10, 11, 13, 14, 18

3. VDC Host Hardware Design

3.1 Overview

The natural thought of working directly with a PC manufacturer is that server hardware would be readily accessible and easy to come by. In the case of the ITAR VDC design we actually found that the server hardware introduced one of our largest constraints. The server hardware used to construct the customer-facing student kits was provisioned based on specifications obtained from the VATC setup guides or the ITAR course guides and had approved budget. The server hardware available for the non-customer-facing management infrastructure was provisioned from existing ITAR server stock. This equipment was excluded from any of project budgets.

3.2 Physical Hardware Configuration

Table 3 provides a summary of the hardware configurations that were available from the ITAR stock of servers for use in the design of the VDC management infrastructure that was not part of the customer-facing student kits and the cluster name that was assigned.

**Table 3 - Hardware provisioned by ITAR for use in
the design of the management infrastructure.**

Server Models in Cluster	CPU Models in Cluster	Memory Configuration per Host	vSphere Version	Cluster Name	# of Hosts in Cluster	Storage Access Technology
PowerEdge 2950 III	Intel Xeon E5405	32GB	4.1 U2	Solar01	6	Fibre Channel
PowerEdge R710	Intel Xeon E5620	64GB	4.1 U2	Solar02	5	Fibre Channel, iSCSI
PowerEdge R610	Intel Xeon E5620	48GB	4.1 U2	Solar03	3	Fibre Channel

Having learned early on that the Customer Experience as defined by ITAR would drive many of our design decisions we skewed the design to error on the side of caution by designing for situations where the VMs would all be in use for classes running simultaneously and labs coinciding. While it could be possible that every kit would be in use, it would be extremely unlikely that they would all be in use for the same times each day and that each class would be performing labs at the same time. Since resources in the VDC are only active while students are doing labs it would be more likely to see a mix of active and passive resource use at any given time. Considering the global nature of the ITAR course deliveries it is almost guaranteed that classes will be staggered across time zones with only partial overlap and even within that overlap the timings of the different courses and the delivery styles of the different instructors would introduce additional variables that could factor into an even more staggered active use time. The ITAR infrastructure team agreed that even though this "perfect storm" of class deliveries was unlikely it presented the safest method for designing to protect the integrity of the custom experience.

Note: The virtual machine specifications listed in the tables of this section are revisited in more detail in section 6 on Virtual Machine Design.

Each of the clusters would be enabled for HA with Admission Control enabled, and a percentage of resources left untouched to cover an HA failover event. The percentage of resources to be protected for failover is enough to cover the failure of a single host. A summary of the total and usable resources per cluster is shown in Table 4.

Table 4 - Resource summaries for the SolarXX clusters as totals and with HA considered.

Cluster	# Hosts	Ram/ Host	Total RAM	HA % Free	Usable RAM after HA	Sockets/ Host	Cores/ Socket	Proc Speed	Total CPU	Usable CPU after HA
Solar01	6	32	192	20	153.6	2	4	2	96	76.8
Solar02	5	64	320	20	256	2	4	2.4	96	76.8
Solar03	3	48	144	33	96.48	2	4	2.4	57.6	46.08

3.2.1 Solar01 Management Cluster

The Solar01 cluster is responsible for hosting (running) the Virtual Machines required for the Earth, Mars, Mercury, and Saturn student VDC kits. In addition it holds a handful of files required for the overall construction of the VDC.

With a choice to use any of the hardware options for any of the clusters, the PowerEdge 2950 III's were selected for Solar01 based on the virtual machine profiles of the virtual machines that were identified to run with that cluster. The virtual machines to be registered with Solar01 are a mixture of vCenter Servers, domain controllers, DHCP servers, and file servers.

Table 5 shows the virtual machine configuration profiles and resource calculations for the VMs to be hosted on Solar01. The average and peak CPU values for the VMs used in the VMware training classes were obtained by stepping the through performance monitoring of a VMware vSphere 4.1 Install, Configure, and Manage class. The performance metrics for the infrastructure servers were obtained from performance chart of existing servers with similar applications.

Table 5 - Solar01 Virtual Machine Resource Calculations Summary.

VMs	# VMs	RAM	Total RAM	# cpu	CPU count	vCPU GHz	Avg CPU Use %	Avg CPU Use GHz	Peak CPU Use %	Peak CPU Use GHz
Earth vCs	7	2	14	2	14	4	0.1	2.8	0.25	7
Mars vCs	7	2	14	2	14	4	0.1	2.8	0.25	7
Mercury vCs	8	2	16	2	16	4	0.1	3.2	0.25	8
Saturn vCs	8	2	16	2	16	4	0.1	3.2	0.25	8
DCs	8	1	8	1	8	2	0.01	0.16	0.01	0.16
DHCP	5	1	7	1	7	2	0.01	0.14	0.01	0.14
File Servers	2	2	4	2	4	4	0.25	2	0.15	1.2
UDAs	15	1	0.5	1	5	2	0.05	0.5	0.1	1
vCenter	1	8	8	2	2	4	0.1	0.4	0.3	1.2
Totals	61		88		86	30				34
Mean		2			10	3				

In the chart the configuration of the vCenter Server VMs was driven by the VATC setup guides first, and then determined if resource configuration alterations should be performed to drive up the ITAR customer experience. The light blue shaded rows of Table 5 identify VMs to which students will directly connect. For example, in a standard VMware vSphere 4.1 Install, Configure, and Manage students use Microsoft Remote Desktop Connection. From there they can access various lab elements like shared folders, management consoles, and any other utilities required for accessibility and management of the host. The remaining unshaded VMs in the chart represent the infrastructure VMs that supported the entire VDC for ITAR.

Among the hardware options that we were provided the ITAR PowerEdge 2950 III's were identified as the best fit for the cluster managing the VMs detailed in Table 5. The total memory configuration for the VMs of Solar01 is (rounded up to) 88 GB, while the total Peak CPU Usage from the VMs is (rounded up to) 34 GHz. This memory calculation value assumes that the Guest Physical Memory, or memory as seen by the guest, is held entirely in Host Physical Memory (actual physical RAM). This assumption provides a conservative value for memory use because it does not take into consideration any of the memory management techniques performed by the VMkernel (i.e. Transparent Page Sharing). Table 6 compares the CPU and Memory resource utilization summaries from Tables 4 and 5 showing that the cluster VMs have a total of 88GB of memory configured against the 154 GB of host physical memory available resulting in a difference of 66 GB. And along the same lines the sum of the Peak CPU Usage for the VMs is 34 GHz against the 77 GHz available for the cluster leaving a different of 43 GHz.

Table 6 - Solar01 resource usage vs. resource availability vs. remaining resources, with HA considered.

Memory Configured	**88**	
Total Memory Available	**154**	**66**
Peak CPU Usage	**34**	
Total CPU Available	**77**	**43**

Based on the data presented in the previous three tables it can be concluded that the dELL PowerEdge 2950 III's selected for the management cluster can handle the resource demands of the Earth, Mars, Mercury, and Saturn kits, even if all the kits were in use simultaneously and each VM use its approximate Peak CP Utilization value. But can it handle more?

Table 7 displays the CPU and RAM requirements for each additional VMware VDC kit to be managed by Solar01. For example the 8 student vCenter Server VMs would require 8GHz of CPU (based on data from Table 5) and 16 GB of memory. The numbers reflect that Solar01 could handle three more kits worth of VMs.

Table 7 - Solar01 can handle 3 more VMware VDC kits (the lesser of 3 and 5).

CPU	VM	RAM
8	vCenter x 8	16
0.02	DC	1
0.02	DHCP	1
0.2	UDA	0.5
8	SUM	19
43/8		66/19
5 kits	Estimated Additional Capacity	3 kits

Alternatively, the scalability of the Solar01 cluster beyond its existing VM pool could be determined by defining a unit of allocation equal to the mean RAM and mean vCPU GHZ which are 2 GB and 3 GHz respectively. If we divide these units of allocation into the remaining resources and then select the lower of the two values we can determine how many more VMs could run so long as they fit into that newly defined unit of allocation.

(Remaining Memory) / (Memory Unit of Allocation) = 66 GB / 2 GB = 33 VMs

(Remaining CPU) / (CPU Unit of Allocation x Peak Usage %) = 43 GHz / (3 GHz x .25) = 57 VMs.

In summary, the dELL PowerEdge 2950 III's were configured adequately to handle the infrastructure for four VMware Student kits and some of the infrastructure VMs. With 42.8% (1-(88/154)*100) and 55.8% (1-(34/77)*100) of the memory and CPU resources remaining, there is enough capacity to handle an additional three kits while still adhering to the admission control policy.

3.2.2 Solar02 Management Cluster

Based on the EqualLogic classroom specifications handed down by ITAR it seemed certain that the Solar02 cluster was going to consume a large amount of resources and as Table 8 shows, that assumption was correct. Just as in we did with Solar 01 we can look at Table 8 and Table 9 to review the VM and host calculations for Solar02.

Table 8 - Solar02 Virtual Machine Resource Calculations Summary.

VMs	#	RAM/ VM GB	Total RAM GB	No. of CPU	CPU Count	Ghz	Avg CPU Use %	Avg CPU Use GHz	Peak CPU Use %	Peak CPU Use GHz	Max CPU Use GHz
Neptune vCs	6	2	12	1	6	2.4	0.05	0.72	0.13	1.872	12
Jupiter vCs	6	2	12	1	6	2.4	0.05	0.72	0.13	1.872	12
DCs	8	1	8	1	8	2.4	0.01	0.192	0.02	0.384	16
DHCP	3	1	3	1	3	2.4	0.01	0.072	0.02	0.144	6
File Servers	1	2	2	2	2	4.8	0.1	0.48	0.15	0.72	4
UDAs	2	0.5	1	1	2	2.4	0.01	0.048	0.01	0.048	4
iSCSI tgts	6	0.5	3	1	6	2.4	0.01	0.144	0.01	0.144	12
SQL	24	2	48	1	24	2.4	0.1	5.76	0.2	11.52	48
Exchange	24	2	48	1	24	2.4	0.1	5.76	0.25	14.4	48
Nept ESXi	6	4	24	2	12	4.8	0.1	2.88	0.4	11.52	24
Jup ESXi	6	4	24	2	12	4.8	0.1	2.88	0.4	11.52	24
vc-Nept00	1	2	2	1	1	2.4	0.1	0.24	0.2	0.48	2
vc-Jup00	1	2	2	1	1	2.4	0.1	0.24	0.2	0.48	2
E-mail	2	2	4	1	2	2.4	0.05	0.24	0.1	0.48	4
Totals	96		193		109	41				56	218
Mean		2			8	3					

Table 9 - Resource usage vs. resource availability vs. remaining resources, with HA considered.

Memory Configured	193	
Total Memory Available	256	63
Total Peak CPU Usage	56	
CPU Available	77	21

Solar02 is home to both VMware VDC Kits and EqualLogic Kits so determining its scalability will depend on which type of class ITAR would like to include. The EqualLogic classes are much more intense from a resource perspective than the student VMware kits and as a result the Solar02 could not scale as far by adding more EqualLogic kits. Alternatively, as we saw in the previous section we can identify a unit of allocation for the cluster and back pedal into a number of VMs that can be added.

(Remaining Memory) / (Memory Unit of Allocation) = 63 GB / 2 GB = 31 VMs

(Remaining CPU) / (CPU Unit of Allocation x Peak Usage %) = 21 GHz / (3 GHz x .25) = 28 VMs.

In summary, the Dell PowerEdge R710s included hardware specifications that exceeded the initial roll out of all the Dell EqualLogic classes. With 24.6% (1-(193/256)*100) and 27.2% (1-(56/77)*100) of the memory and CPU resources remaining there is enough capacity to handle 28 VMs based on the units of allocation defined above while still adhering to the admission control policy.

3.2.3 Solar03 Management Cluster

The final cluster of the ITAR VDC management infrastructure, Solar03, is used as an aggregate of resources to support a VMware View Virtual Desktop Infrastructure that provides remote connectivity into the ITAR VDC. For Solar03, a trio of Dell PowerEdge R610s makes up the hardware configuration for supporting the VMware View infrastructure servers (Security Servers, Connection Servers) as well as the virtual desktops used for the Neptune, Jupiter, and Venus desktops. The Virtual Machine specifications for these components are detailed in Table 10 and the resource use summary is detailed in Table 11.

Table 10 - Solar03 Virtual Machine Resource Calculations Summary

VMs	#	RAM/ VM GB	Total RAM GB	No. of CPU	CPU Count	Ghz	Avg CPU Use %	Avg CPU Use GHz	Peak CPU Use %	Peak CPU Use GHz
Nept vDesktops	13	2	26	1	13	2.4	0.02	0.624	0.25	7.8
Jup vDesktops	13	2	26	1	13	2.4	0.02	0.624	0.25	7.8
Venus vDesktops	8	2	16	1	8	2.4	0.01	0.192	0.1	1.92
Security Servers	2	4	8	1	2	4.8	0.05	0.48	0.35	3.36
Connection Servers	2	4	8	1	2	4.8	0.05	0.48	0.35	3.36
Totals	38		84		38	17		2		24
Mean		3			8	3				

Table 11 - Resource usage vs. resource availability vs. remaining resources, with HA considered.

Memory Configured	84	
Memory Available	96	12
Total Peak CPU Usage	24	
CPU Available	39	15

Solar03, compared to Solar01 and Solar02, shows the highest relative memory resource utilization. With HA accounted for to ensure failover capacity equal to a single host, Solar03 has 12.5% (1-(96/24)*100) memory resources remaining and 38% (1-(24/39)*100) CPU resources remaining. Based on memory and CPU units of allocation defined as 2 GB and 600 MHz respectively, this cluster could support an additional six virtual desktops determined by dividing the remaining 12 GB memory by the 2 GB unit of allocation.

3.4 Design Justification

There were several key requirements that went into the overall hardware selection and design process. Having to select from a limited pool of different hardware architectures (2950, R710, and R610) was not a significant impact on the design as even with a similar pool of hardware the hardware design would have been split among multiple clusters to accommodate the requirement of isolating workloads and achieving modularity.

The planning and design meetings identified that the business projections for ITAR showed a consistent push for growth in the ITAR product training while the VMware training was expected to remain stable. ITAR does not anticipate that the VMware VDC kits will need to scale as rapidly, if at all, as the ITAR VDC kits for EqualLogic.

As it will be shown in section 6 on Virtual Machine design, the VMs that make up the EqualLogic training classes are larger VMs. For this reason the R710s were selected for Solar02 because they are the latest generation of ITAR enterprise rackmount server. In the event that the Solar02 cluster reached capacity it would be easier for ITAR to provision additional, similarly configured R710s than to try and provision legacy hardware (i.e. PowerEdge 2950). The systems also contained newer Intel Xeon processors based off the Westmere CPU architecture, which ensured longevity beyond the Intel Xeon 45nm Core 2 architecture of the PowerEdge 2950s. Similarly the R610's were selected for the Solar03 cluster, because like Solar02, the anticipation was that it would need to be scaled sooner than Solar01.

The demographic of customers and students that participate in ITAR delivered training classes not only span the globe but access the infrastructure through a variety of different network configurations. For this reason ITAR established a requirement for using port 443 as the standard for access to the ITAR VDC kits. Port 443 offers a standard, web-based, common port that is allowed by (or is acceptable to) most firewall administrators even in the most secure environments.

The glaring difference in this design process versus a more traditional design, stemmed from the fact that the hardware itself was not designed for all intents and purposes. Our responsibility in the hardware design was more of a scalability and capacity planning design to identify if the hardware we had to select from could sustain the workloads anticipated by ITAR. The understanding of how the required VMs and infrastructure VMs would scale on the given hardware resources was critical to providing

ITAR with data that could be analyzed and used to make decisions about the growth of their educational offerings.

Design qualities impacted: Performance, Availability

Requirements achieved: 2, 3, 10, 15, 16, and 18

4. VDC Network Design

4.1 Overview

Pick any one of the clusters isolated unto itself and the networking configuration is not so daunting and might even be considered simple. But looking down over the entire ITAR VDC to see all of the different silos of execution and bringing them together in a fluid IP network to meet the ITAR requirement took the design to the opposite side of simple. The network design was not focused on just the communication between clusters but had to bring together the multiple management clusters and then blend the VDC student kits into the mix to provide a stable, reliable, and scalable IP networking infrastructure that could support the dynamic growth of the ITAR training.

4.2 Logical Network Design

The logical assembly of the ITAR VDC networking,shown in Figure 12, identifies our reliance on a hybrid virtual networking design that used both vNetwork Standard Switches (vSS) and vNetwork Distributed Switches (vDS). Across all clusters the VMkernel-based IP communication was left to pass over a vNetwork Standard Switch architecture, while the VM traffic was handled by a single vDS.

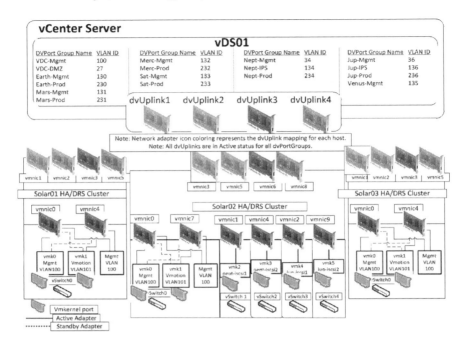

Figure 12 - Logical Networking Design of the ITAR VDC Clusters.

For each of the clusters the default vSwitch0 was reconfigured to include a second VMkernel port (vmk1) that is enabled for vMotion leaving the switch with 1 VM port group (Mgmt) and 2 VMkernel ports (vmk0, vmk1) for management and vMotion respectively. vSwitch0 is configured with 2 uplinks each provisioned from a different hardware bus (PCIe vs. on-board). The NIC teaming policy of each port/port group was modified as shown in Table 12.

Table 12 - Explicit Failover configuration for vSwitch0 ports and port groups.

Port/Port Group	vmnicX	vmnicY
vmk0	Active	Standby
vmk1	Standby	Active
Mgmt (VM Port Group)	Active	Active

The dynamic nature of the VMware and ITAR VDC kits and the possibility of continued growth provided the perfect business driver to include the vDS as part of the design. The centralized management architecture of the vDS allows the management cluster to quickly accommodate new VDC kits that are deployed with their own set of VLANs. A single vDS named vDS01 spans the three clusters. All of the hosts from each cluster are enrolled into vDS01 and participate with 4 uplinks. Solar01 and Solar03 are setup with four active uplinks; vmnic1, vmnic2, vmnic3, and vmnic5 are the respective dvUplink1, dvUplink2, dvUplink3, and dvUplink4.

The virtual networking of Solar02 is similar to that of Solar01 and Solar03 with the vSwitch0 configuration and the participation of four uplinks in vDS01. However, the hosts of the Solar02 cluster have four extra vSwitches (vSwitch1, vSwitch2, vSwitch3, and vSwitch4), each with a single VMkernel port (vmk2, vmk3, vmk4, and vmk5) which provide connectivity to two Dell EqualLogic PS4000X storage arrays. The detailed configuration of the VMkernel ports will be covered in Section 5 on the ITAR VDC Storage Design.

The entire ITAR VDC is made up of 24 logical IP networks used to support all of the management needs and the student VDC kit needs. All of the IP subnets use a 24-bit subnet mask. In addition each of the IP networks has an associated VLAN ID that matches with the third octet of the IP Network address. For example the IP network of 192.168.100.0/24 has a VLAN ID of 100, while the IP network of 192.168.132.0/24 has a VLAN ID of 132. The uplinks of the standard and distributed switches of each cluster were trunked appropriately to allow connectivity throughout the entire VDC. Figure 13 provides an overview of the IP networks and VLANs used for the management and student infrastructures of the ITAR VDC.

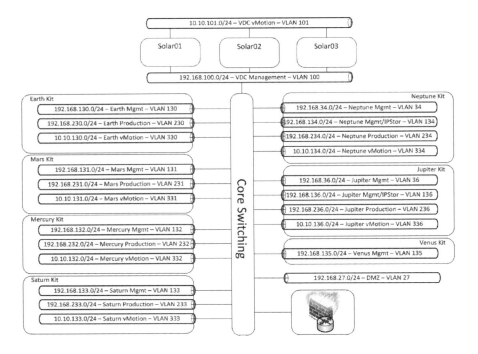

Figure 13 - The ITAR VDC is made up of 24 logical IP networks to support the management and student networks.

4.3 Physical Network Design

The 24 logical IP networks of the ITAR VDC are implemented and managed across a physical switching infrastructure that includes 15 gigabit Ethernet switches and a pair of SonicWALL NSA e5500 redundant firewalls. The internal switching architecture centers around a pair of Dell PowerConnect 6248 switches named CEswA and CEswB that are in a stacked configuration to be managed as a single switch. Spanning Tree priorities are configured to force CEswA as the primary and CEswB as the secondary.

Solar01 has a pair of Dell PowerConnect 6248 branch switches configured with a four port Link Aggregation between them. The primary switch, named S01-EswA is connected to the core switch CEswA and the secondary switch named S01-EswB is connected to the core switch CEswB. The

VLAN database of these switches includes all VLANs. The ITAR VDC Implementation and Installation Guide has details on the switch configurations.

Solar02 and Solar03 connect to a second pair of Dell PowerConnect 6248 branch switches with a four port Link Aggregation between them. The primary switch, named S02-3-EswA is connected to the core switch CEswA and the secondary switch named S02-3-EswB is connected to the secondary core switch, CEswB. The VLAN database of these switches includes all VLANs. The ITAR VDC Implementation and Installation Guide has the details on the switch configurations. Beyond those six switches used for the core switching and the branches for Solar01 and Solar02/3 the following physical switches are also deployed:

- 2 x Dell PowerConnect 6248 for Solar02 iSCSI.
- 7 x Dell PowerConnect 548 for each of the student kits.
- 1 x Dell PowerConnect 6248 hot spare
- 1 x Dell PowerConnect 5448 hot spare

There were not enough physical switches in the pool of physical from which we could operate so we narrowed it down to just core, branches, and IP storage switches to be redundant. In addition the number of PowerConnect 6248 was limited in comparison to the PowerConnect 5448. The hot spare switches with regularly scheduled switch configuration backups give an N+1 redundancy for any of the student kits that included only a single switch. Even though the support contract on the switches offered a four hour rapid response time we cannot afford for a student or two to be down for that duration of time. Each passing minute that a student cannot access a lab is one step closer to a negative customer experience.

Figure 14 gives a detailed look at the physical intra-switch connectivity.

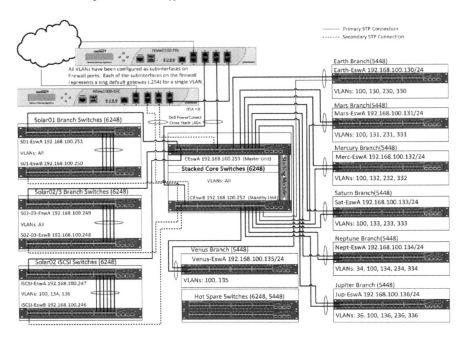

Figure 14 - The Physical Switching infrastructure of the ITAR VDC includes 24 IP networks across 15 physical switches.

NOTE: The physical network design diagrams only detail a single host of the cluster. However, care was taken to ensure that each host was cabled and configured identically. So representations of each individual host are redundant and unnecessary.

4.3.1 Solar01 Management Cluster

The ITAR PowerEdge 2950 III's in the Solar01 cluster have 2 on-board Broadcom Gigabit Ethernet adapters. An additional 4 NICs were added via an Intel Pro 1000 quad port adapter. All of the NIC assignments for the Solar01 hosts are shown in Table 13.

Table 13 - Solar01 host NIC identification and assignments.

vmnic	Location	Assignment	pSwitch Port Config
vmnic0	On-board Gb1 (left)	vSwitch0	Trunk
vmnic1	On-board Gb2 (right)	vDS01	Trunk
vmnic2	PCI-e3 Gb1 (left)	vDS01	Trunk
vmnic3	PCI-e3 Gb2	vDS01	Trunk
vmnic4	PCI-e3 Gb3	vSwitch0	Trunk
vmnic5	PCI-e Gb4 (right)	vDS01	Trunk

All ports on the physical switch to which ESXi host uplinks were connected were configured as trunk ports defined for multiple VLANs. The VLANs assigned to each trunk port were determined by the uplink mapping into the virtual switch. For example, the ports on the switch where vmnic0 and vmnic4 were connected were trunked for VLANs 100 and 101 as they were mapped to vSwitch0, which included VMkernel ports and VM port groups assigned those respective VLAN IDs. The remaining uplinks in the host were assigned as uplinks to vDS01 and therefore connected to switch ports trunked for all of the same VLAN IDs configured in the vDS. Figure 15 shows the mappings of virtual switch components to physical uplinks to physical switches.

The two branch switches for Solar01 are connected with a four-port link aggregation. Both switches are configured for all VLANs and each switch connects back to a single core Ethernet switch.

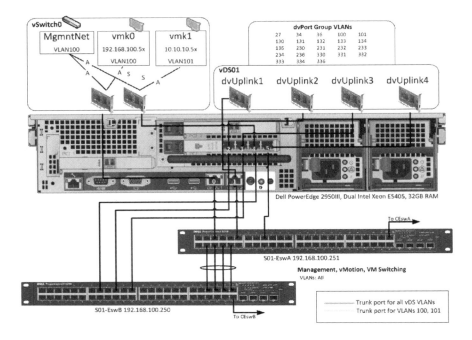

Figure 15 - Solar01 host physical network detail mapping virtual networking components to physical networking components.

4.3.2 Solar02 Management Cluster

The Dell R710's in the Solar02 cluster have 4 on-board Broadcom Gigabit Ethernet adapters. An additional six NICs were added via one quad port Intel Pro 1000 adapter and one dual port Intel Pro 1000 adapter. All of the NIC assignments for the Solar02 hosts are shown in Table 14.

Table 14 - Solar02 host NIC identification and assignments.

vmnic	Location	Assignment	pSwitch Port Config
vmnic0	On-board Gb1 (left)	vSwitch0	Trunk
vmnic1	On-board Gb2	vSwitch1	Access 134
vmnic2	On-board Gb3	vSwitch3	Access 136
vmnic3	On-board Gb4 (right)	vDS01	Trunk
vmnic4	PCI-e2 Gb1 (left)	vSwitch0	Trunk
vmnic5	PCI-e2 Gb2	vDS01	Trunk
vmnic6	PCI-e2 Gb3	vDS01	Trunk
vmnic7	PCI-e2 Gb4 (right)	vSwitch4	Access 136
vmnic8	PCI-e4 Gb1 (left)	vDS01	Trunk
vmnic9	PCI-e4 Gb2 (right)	vSwitch2	Access 134

The virtual and physical networking of Solar02 required additional consideration because of the need to connect these hosts to two EqualLogic PS4000x storage arrays. The vSwitch0 and vDS01 configuration of Solar02 was similar to Solar01 with the exception of the vmnics that were utilized as dvUplinks.

The extra four network adapters in the hosts of Solar02 were split to four different vNetwork Standard Switches (vSwitch1, vSwitch2, vSwitch3, and vSwitch4) with individual VMkernel ports created (vmk2, vmk3, vmk4, and vmk5). Two of the VMkernel ports were assigned IP addresses for the 192.168.134.0/24 network and the other two were assigned IP addresses on the 192.168.136.0/24 network. The uplinks were split amongst two physical switches and connected to physical switch ports configured as an access port for the corresponding VLAN (134 or 136). The four vSwitches and four VMkernel ports created for the iSCSI connectivity have been created from a command line so that Jumbo Frames (MTU 9000) is set. Jumbo Frames has also been enabled on the physical switch and the two EqualLogic PS4000x storage arrays. More detail on the technical configuration of the vSwitches, VMkernel ports, and physical switch ports can be found in the ITAR VDC Implementation and Installation Guide.

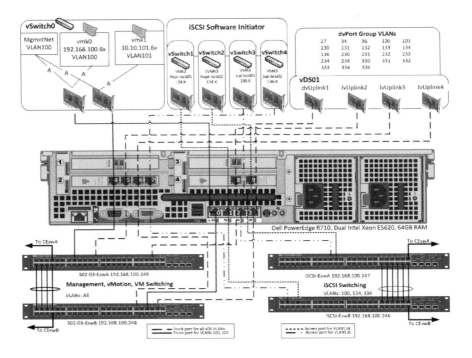

**Figure 16 - Solar02 host physical network detail mapping virtual
networking components to physical networking components**

The two branch switches for Solar02 are connected with a four-port link
aggregation. Both switches are configured for all VLANs and each switch
connects back to a single core Ethernet switch.

The two iSCSI switches for Solar02 are connected with a six port link
aggregation. Both switches are configured for VLANs 100, 134, and 136.
The management IP of the switch exists on VLAN 100. VLANs 134 and
136 are the IP Storage VLANs for the two respective arrays.

4.3.3 Solar03 Management Cluster

The Dell R610s of the Solar03 cluster have 4 on-board Broadcom Gigabit
Ethernet adapters. An additional two NICs were added via a single dual

port Intel Pro 1000 adapter. All of the NIC assignments for the Solar03 cluster are shown in Table 15.

vmnic	Location	Assignment	pSwitch Port Config
vmnic0	On-board Gb1 (left)	vSwitch0	Trunk
vmnic1	On-board Gb2	vDS01	Trunk
vmnic2	On-board Gb3	vDS01	Trunk
vmnic3	On-board Gb4 (right)	vDS01	Trunk
vmnic4	PCI-e1 Gb1 (left)	vSwitch0	Trunk
vmnic5	PCI-e1 Gb2 (right)	vDS01	Trunk

Table 15 - Solar03 host NIC identification and assignments

The hosts of Solar03, like the hosts of Solar01, have six NICs for participation as uplinks in virtual switches. Unlike Solar01, however, Solar03 has four on-board and two PCI-e. All ports on the physical switch to which ESXi host uplinks were configured as trunk ports defined for multiple VLANs. The VLANs assigned to each trunk port were determined by the uplink mapping into the virtual switch. For example, the ports on the switch where vmnic0 and vmnic4 were connected were trunked for VLANs 100 and 101 as they were mapped to vSwitch0, which included VMkernel ports and VM port groups assigned those respective VLAN IDs. The remaining uplinks in the host were assigned as uplinks to vDS01 and therefore connected to switch ports trunked for all of the same VLAN IDs configured in the vDS. Figure 17 shows the mappings of virtual switch components to physical uplinks to physical switches.

The two branch switches for Solar03 are connected with a four port link aggregation. Both switches are configured for all VLANs and each switch connects back to a single core Ethernet switch.

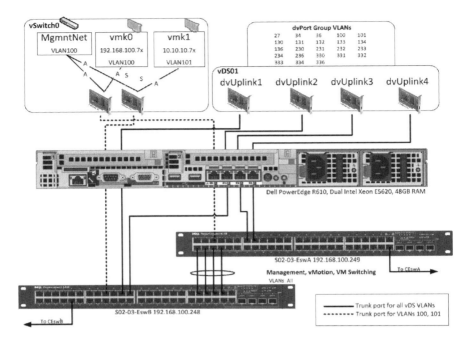

Figure 17 - Solar03 host physical network detail mapping virtual networking components to physical networking components

As previously noted, Solar03 was a cluster dedicated for the management of a VMware View VDI deployment used to provide VDC access over web based port 443. In the initial design, only the Neptune, Jupiter, and Venus kits were required to have access via View virtual desktops. Despite the fact that the dvUplinks on the Solar03 hosts were connected to trunk ports defined for all VLANs, only VLANs 34, 36, and 135 would be utilized by Solar03 VMs. The existence of the additional VLANs as managed by the vDS offered the flexibility to extend the VMware View deployment to the Earth, Mars, Mercury, and Saturn kits with very little administrative effort.

4.4 Design Justification

The logical and physical networking experienced a strong influence from several key functional and technical business requirements. Most significantly the VDC management networking design had to be resilient against a single point of failure. Using NIC teaming, redundant switches, redundant connections between switches, and redundant firewalls the network is protected against a single component failure.

With the exception of the two core switches, the switching architecture relies on link aggregation for inter-switch redundancy. Originally ITAR was not prepared to offer the necessary stacking modules for any of the switching architecture, however achieving a stacked configuration for at least the core switches was critical to the remote access availability of the entire VDC. By stacking the two core switches we can create redundancy to and from the pair of SonicWALL E5500 edge devices.

Separation of management and vMotion traffic from the VDC kit specific VM traffic using separate adapters helps isolate VM traffic. This also impacts the cluster design by allowing the HA isolation response to retain the default setting of leave powered on. Even though the HA heartbeat network (VMK port for management) is configured with an Active/ Standby NIC team, if an isolation event were to occur it does not signal that VMs have experienced any ill effects.

Having the hot standby switches ensures that in the event of a switch failure the physical networking infrastructure can quickly be returned to its redundant status. Even though the Dell hardware was tagged with a four response support policy we did not feel comfortable with a four window in which failure of another switch could possibly terminate access to a kit, a management array, or perhaps even the whole VDC.

The extra networking attention paid to Solar02 for its IP Storage access allowed he iSCSI communication traffic to exist on a dedicated and isolated network. Using a separate set of physical switches for ISCSI offers two significant benefits: 1) contention between iSCSI traffic and other host traffic (management, vMotion, VMs, etc.) is eliminated and 2) iSCSI traffic which is sent in clear text is protected.

The use of multiple VMkernel ports across separate vSwitches optimized the iSCSI storage access by allowing the iSCSI Software Initiator to have multiple Active I/O paths to the storage volumes. Additional info on the storage can be found in the ITAR VDC Implementation and Installation Guide.

Design Qualities Impacted: Availability, Manageability, Performance, and Security

Requirements Achieved: 2, 10, 11, 16, 18, and 19

5. VDC Storage Design

5.1 Overview

The decentralized resource management strategy introduced thus far through multiple HA/DRS clusters for infrastructure management and self-contained student VDC kits for designated class deliveries is a strategy rings true for the ITAR VDC storage design as well.

The Fibre Channel storage equipment provisioned by ITAR, while not the latest versions, was more than satisfactory for the demands of the VDC design, but still came with reservations about its longevity. ITAR made available to us a number of EMC CX3-40 and CX3-20 storage arrays that were decommissioned from their EMC CLARiiON education labs and repurposed for the VDC project. The age of the arrays eliminated their ability to provide for more recent features (i.e. VAAI) and did provide us with concern regarding their hardware stability but that did not exclude them from being capable of providing the storage infrastructure required. ITAR was also able to repurpose all of the Brocade 300 Fibre Channel switches from their EMC labs to the VDC project.

The iSCSI storage arrays provided for the project were purchased as part of the Dell EqualLogic training budget. Two Dell EqualLogic PS4000x storage arrays with 8TB of storage were provisioned for the management infrastructure along with another 12 storage arrays for the student VDC kits. Six of the arrays are dual controller PS6000x and the remaining six are single controller PS4000E arrays.

5.2 Logical Storage Design

The storage design of the ITAR VDC includes two CX3-40 Fibre Channel storage arrays used for the SolarXX management clusters, four CX3-20 Fibre Channel storage arrays used for the VMware VDC kits, two EqualLogic iSCSI storage arrays used by Solar02 exclusively, and twelve EqualLogic iSCSI arrays for the Dell EQL VDC kits. The storage design for the student VDC kits can be found in the ITAR VDC Student VDC Design Guide.

To eliminate a single point of failure in the storage access, the Fibre Channel design for each host in the Solar01 cluster includes two Fibre Channel HBAs each connected to a single Fibre Channel switch which is then connected to each of the storage processors on the Fibre Channel array giving each host four possible paths to the storage presented by the array as shown in Figure 18.

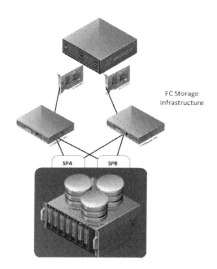

Figure 18 - The logical storage design for Solar01 includes 2 HBAs, 2 FC switches, and 2 SPs with 2 front-end ports each

The logical storage Fibre Channel design of the hosts in Solar02 was identical to that of Solar01. However Solar02 also required connectivity to a pair of iSCSI arrays. As shown in Figure 19, the hosts of Solar02 are configured with 4 network adapters connected to a pair of dedicated iSCSI switches that have redundant connections to the pair of controllers on each array.

NOTE: Please refer to the VDC Networking section of this document for details on the physical network design for Solar02.

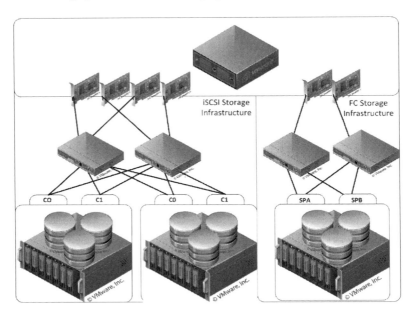

Figure 19 - The logical design of Solar02 includes 2 FC HBAs, 2 FC Switches, 2 SPs with 2 front-end ports, 4 NICS for iSCSI, 2 iSCSI Ethernet switches, and 2 controllers on each of the arrays

Like Solar01, the hosts of Solar03 had redundant connectivity only to a Fibre Channel storage array as shown in Figure 20.

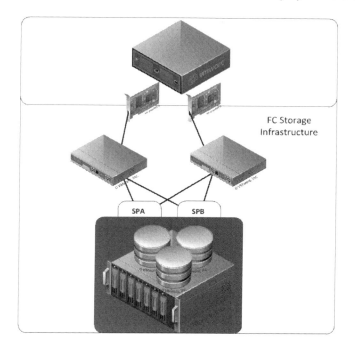

**Figure 20 - The logical storage design for Solar03 includes 2
HBAs, 2 FC switches, and 2 SPs with 2 front-end ports each**

5.3 Physical Storage Design

The ITAR VDC project presented a unique case where access to Fibre
Channel storage hardware was not a concern. The decision to go with EMC
CLARiiON storage was neither ours, nor ITAR's, as they had plenty of the
hardware from the recently terminated CLARiiON training products. The
decommissioned hardware available from ITAR for this project did not
constrain our ability to assemble the solution, but certainly did impact the
design as you will see. This was a rare case where storage was easier to
come by than servers! That being said we were not given free rein to just
take anything we pleased; we had to be sure to justify the provisioning of
Fibre Channel storage.

ITAR made sole decisions on the iSCSI storage devices. We were not consulted in any manner to discuss project requirements. The two EqualLogic arrays were purchased by ITAR as part of the budget for the EqualLogic training initiative. Lucky for us and our design effort the arrays came properly equipped with multiple controllers an overabundance over storage with 8TB over 16 500GB 7200RPM SATA drives.

As the logical storage design showed, we took every precaution to protect against a single point of failure in the storage design. Table 16 details the physical hardware that was provisioned from ITAR to support the Fibre Channel and iSCSI storage area networks.

Table 16 - ITAR provisioned hardware for support of the FC and iSCSI storage area networks.

Hardware	Make and model	Qty	Notes
FC Array	EMC CX3-40	2	4G
FC Array	EMC CX3-20	4	4G
FC DAE	EMC Ultrapoint DAE4	7	15 x 146GB 10K RPM
FC Switches	Brocade 300	9	24 port, 4G
FC HBAs	QLogic QLE2460	22	Single port 4G HBA
FC HBAs	QLogic QLE2462	3	Dual port 4G HBA
ISCSI Array	Dell EqualLogic PS4000x	2	16 x 500GB 7200RPM, Dual Controller 1Gbps
Ethernet Switches	Dell PowerConnect 6248	2	48 port, 1Gbps

As shown in Figure 21, the eight Brocade 300 FC switches were used to create four FC switched fabrics (A, B, C, and D), two for the management infrastructure and two for the student VDC kits.

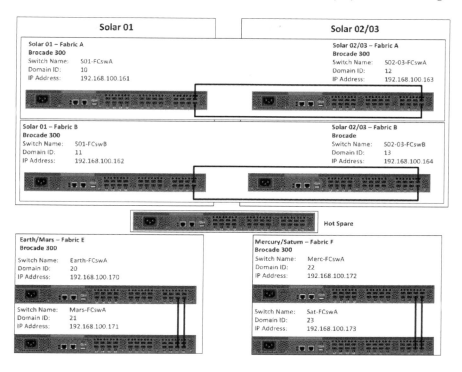

Figure 21 - ITAR VDC Fibre Channel switching design.

Although the Solar clusters operate independently of one another, the storage is not designed with that same level of independence. Given the age of the storage arrays, the critical nature of storage access, and the demand for availability, we wanted to take advantage of having access to storage components and use that advantage to provide a strong availability and recoverability solution. The single initiator / single target zoning of Fabric A and Fabric B creates an access strategy that permits the hosts in Solar01 and Solar02 to access both of the EMC CLARiiON CX3-40 arrays. Despite that connectivity LUNs for each cluster are presented only from a single array. The merging of the fabrics between the two clusters was done to allow for array level tasks that could protect data between the arrays. Section 5.4 on VMFS Design will offer more insight into how we utilized the Fibre Channel switched fabric to achieve better availability and recoverability. The 9th Brocade switch was maintained as a hot spare.

5.3.1 Solar01 Management Cluster

The Solar01 cluster uses Fibre Channel storage as its primary, and only, storage technology. Each host included two QLogic 2460 Fibre Channel HBAs. Each HBA was connected to one of the Brocade 300 Fibre Channel switches where its WWN was configured into a single initiator /single target zone with a WWN from the EMC CLARiiON CX3-40 array. Figure 22 shows the details of the physical FC connectivity of the Solar01 hosts.

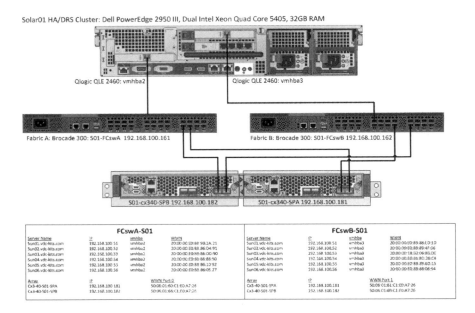

Figure 22 - Solar01 Fibre Channel connectivity

5.3.2 Solar02 Management Cluster

The Fibre Channel connectivity for the hosts of Solar02, shown in Figure 23, is identical to the configuration detailed for Solar01. Although the Solar01 cluster is constructed from older Dell PowerEdge 2950 hardware it is a 2U form factor like the newer PowerEdge R710 hardware used in Solar02. Thus both sets of hosts include enough expansion slots to outfit the server with two single port QLogic QLE 2460 FC HBAs. The WWNs of the

HBAs for the hosts in Solar02 were zoned to the WWNs of the array to offer redundant paths to the LUNs presented.

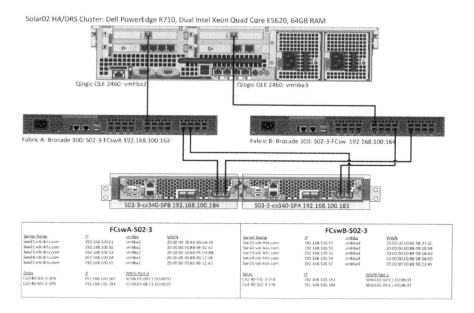

Figure 23 - Solar02 Fibre Channel connectivity

The hosts of Solar02 are the only hosts that are configured to access storage devices across more than just a Fiber Channel switched fabric. These hosts have extra network adapters used for connecting the VMkernel to an IP-based storage area network to accommodate the Dell EqualLogic training products. A set of dedicated Dell PowerConnect 6248 Gigabit Ethernet switches create the iSCSI network for connecting the hosts to two Dell EqualLogic PS4000x storage arrays; one for the Neptune kit and one for the Jupiter kit.

In the previous section on physical networking we introduced the multiple vSwitch / multiple VMkernel port design for the hosts in Solar02 to access the iSCSI targets. Each of the IP Storage specific vSwitch/VMkernel port configurations were bound to the VMware iSCSI Software initiator on the host. A single uplink was associated to each vSwitch/VMkernel configuration and then the uplinks were split between the two switches. Two of the VMkernel ports bound to the iSCSI software initiator were configured for and connected to the 192.168.134.0/24 IP network for connecting to the Neptune array, and the other two were configured for and connected to the 192.168.136.0/24 IP network for connecting to the Jupiter array.

The switches were not stacked switches, due to a ITAR imposed constraint that prevented obtaining the necessary stacking modules for the PowerConnect 6248 switches, with the exception of the core switches. The iSCSI switches were interconnected with a four port link aggregation (LAG). Dell EqualLogic recommends that link aggregations contain as many ports as there are active iSCSI ports in the arrays. In this case each of the two arrays has two active iSCSI ports, and therefore four ports in the LAG.

The third Ethernet connection on each of the controllers for the arrays is a port dedicated for managing the array.

Figure 24 shows the iSCSI storage area network design for the hosts of Solar02 and the associated PowerConnect switches and EqualLogic Storage arrays.

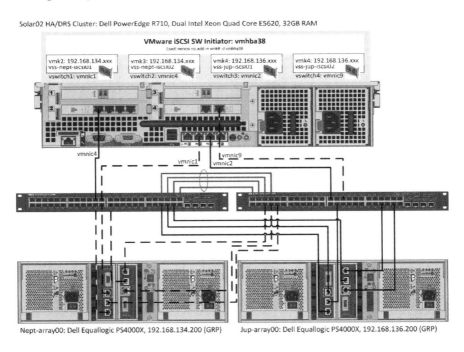

Figure 24 - Solar02 iSCSI connectivity

5.3.3 Solar03 Management Cluster

The Dell PowerEdge R710 hosts of the Solar03 cluster are configured for storage access almost identically to the manner in which the Solar01 hosts are configured. The difference, as shown in Figure 25, is that due to the 1U enclosure there were not enough expansion slots to accommodate two single port Fibre Channel HBAs and thus a single QLogic QLE 2462 dual port FC card is used. This poses a documented and increased risk for the hosts of Solar03 because if the card fails both FC paths will fail along with it.

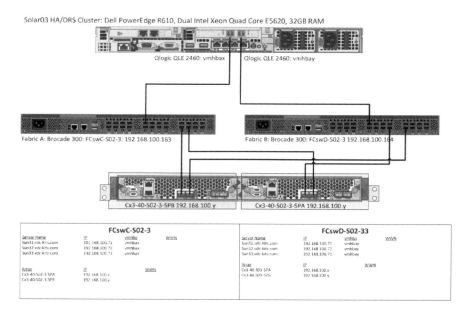

Figure 25 - Solar03 Fibre Channel connectivity

5.4 VMFS Design

With the storage access design in place we can turn our attention to the presentation of LUNs/volumes to the hosts of the SolarXX clusters. It was noted earlier that the age and previous use of the arrays for classroom training was a bit of a concern as they were now being repurposed for a more production like environment.

The primary EMC CX3-40 supporting Solar01, named S01-CX340, included 2 storage processors with 2 front end ports each and 4 DAEs with a full 15 disks. Each of the disks are 146GB 10K RPM 4G drives. The array was setup so that DAE0 and DAE2 shared back-end bus 0 (BE0) while DAE1 and DAE3 shared back-end bus 1 (BE1). The second array, named S02-3-CX340, also included 2 storage processors with 2 front end ports but only 3 DAEs, each full with 15 disks of similar specification. On S02-3-CX340 DAE0 and DAE2 shared BE0, while DAE1 sat solo on BE1.

For both availability and performance reasons RAID groups, or collections of disks in a RAID configuration, are built using RAID 1/0 (or RAID10). The mirrored stripe configuration of RAID 1/0 is ideal for achieving both performance and availability, but is not ideal for maximizing available space. Each of the RAID 1/0 RAID groups is constructed using disks from DAEs of different back-end architectures creating additional resilience beyond just disk failure. Given that access to additional storage capacity was not significantly constrained RAID 1/0 was all round ideal for the ITAR VDC LUN design.

Not all of the RAID groups, however, where RAID 1/0. LUNs to be used for backups were carved from RAID groups that used a RAID 5 configuration. RAID 5 offered protection against disk failure and increased storage capacity for backups.

The workloads of the VMs would not be considered intense workloads and are intermittent at best given they dynamic nature of a given class day where a portion of the day is in lecture (minimal I/O) and a portion of the day is in labs (increased, but not significant I/O). With these types of sporadic and minimal workloads the carving of LUNs was less impacted by disk contention and more impacted by being consistent, to facilitate VM provisioning. As shown in Figure 26, the LUN designed settled at creating 500GB or 700GB LUNs (on RAID 1/0) for the storage of VMs and 1 TB LUNs (on RAID 5) for backups. The 1TB LUN (LUN17) used for backups is replicated to an equally sized LUN on the second CX3-40 array.

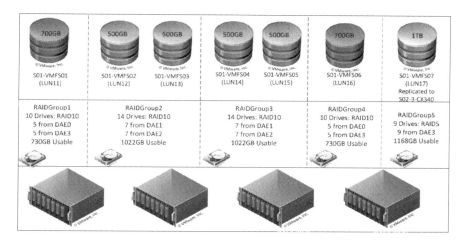

**Figure 26 - RAID groups, LUNs, and VMFS for
storage available to the hosts of Solar01**

RAID groups with multiple LUNs will still compete for the same of underlying disks. The storage size of the LUNs could be any combination that sums to the available space. For example, RAIDGroup2 could have been carved up as a 700GB LUN and a 300GB LUN instead of two 500GB LUNs. Either way the LUN design would result in three different size LUNs; 700GB, 500GB, and 1TB or 700GB, 300GB, and 1TB. The same number of LUNs (7) would have been available under either design.

A host's access to a Fibre Channel LUN within the array is governed by the association of a host and LUN within a storage group. A single storage group, named SG01, is created on S01-CX340. The storage group includes all of the hosts from Solar01 and LUNS 11, 12, 13, 14, 15, 16, and 17).

Solar02 hosts are configured for connectivity to both Fibre Channel and iSCSI storage area networks. Each of these hosts has access to the S02-3-CX340 Fibre Channel array and both the Nept-array00 and Jup-array00 iSCSI storage devices.

Like the Fibre Channel storage arrays, the iSCSI storage arrays had enough capacity to support using a RAID 1/0 configuration. The EqualLogic devices, however, use a different approach to LUN configuration. Unlike the EMC arrays, where specific RAID groups are constructed for the carving of LUNs, the EqualLogic iSCSI arrays use all available disks for LUNs that are created. Nonetheless we are consistent in the use of RAID 1/0 across both storage topologies.

Two of the disks in each iSCSI array were designated as spare disk leaving 14 disks to participate in the enclosure level RAID configuration. With a 50% loss in capacity due to RAID 1/0 each iSCSI array was left providing 3.5 TB of usable space (14 disks x 500GB/disk x .5 RAID1/0 penalty). The available 3.5 TB of space from each array is carved up as two 700GB LUNs and a single 1TB LUN. The 1TB LUNs are used for backups and like the 1TB LUN on S01-CX340 these LUNs are replicated to protect against array failure.

Each of the Solar03 hosts has access to only the storage devices carved on the S02-3-CX340 Fibre Channel array. S02-3-CX340 includes a single storage group, named SG01, that includes all of the hosts from Solar02 and Solar03 and LUNs 21, 22, and 23. Figure 27 details the storage devices designed for the hosts in Solar02 and Solar03.

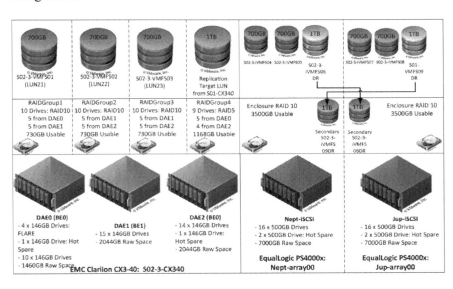

Figure 27 - Fibre Channel storage design for Solar02 and Solar03 and iSCSI storage design solely for Solar02

Note: The 1TB LUN on S01-CX340 is replicated to S02-3-CX340, however a reciprocal replication configuration is not configured. The backups performed through the Solar02 cluster are stored in the iSCSI storage area network and replicated between the two EqualLogic arrays.

5.5 Design Justification

The ITAR VDC storage design is impacted by all of the design qualities. Using RAID 1/0 RAID groups across multiple DAEs and back-end bus architectures improves the availability and performance of the overall system. Using RAID 1/0 eased the fears associated with the age and wear and tear on the arrays having been decommissioned from a classroom architecture.

Although all of the hosts in all three clusters were zoned properly for access to both Fibre Channel storage arrays the LUN presentation strategy prevented Solar01 from access to LUNs on S02-3-CX40 and vice versa for Solar02 and Solar03. However, with the zoning in place, if a storage array failure were to occur for either array the ITAR VDC support team could quickly place registered hosts into existing Storage Groups and begin the recovery process. This strategy allows LUNs of each array to be protected from access by unauthorized hosts until a failure event occurs and access becomes needed. With the zoning in place however, there is a risk that incorrect hosts are presented to LUNs prior to a failure event. Alternatively the zoning could have been eliminated and added to the recovery steps, however, in the event of complete SAN failure classes will be impacted and time is of the essence to get the environment returned to a functional state so that classes can proceed. Students are in class for a limited amount of time, and any time denied to the environment will be reflected upon negatively in the customer experience.

By replicating the LUNs holding backups of the infrastructure we enhance the recoverability of environment and protect against loss of backup data in the event of a complete array failure.

This design adopts the adaptive LUN design scheme in which a fewer number of larger LUNs is preferable to a larger number of smaller LUNs.

The adaptive LUN design improves manageability by reducing the number of LUN options when provisioning new virtual machines. If I/O requirements would have deemed it necessary we would have opted for a more hybrid approached that would include the predictive LUN design scheme in which LUNs are built with more specificity to the Virtual Machine workloads.

Design Qualities Impacted: Availability, Manageability, Performance, Recoverability, and Security

Requirements Achieved: 10

6. Virtual Machine Design

6.1 Overview

The ITAR VDC is a deviation from traditional enterprise design because of its infrastructure within an infrastructure solution. Systems that are traditionally classified as management are used in the ITAR VDC as service offerings to the user base, or in this case the students attending class. For example, VMware vCenter Server would not normally be considered a VM offered up as a production VM for end user access but rather a management infrastructure component for the IT staff. However, in the ITAR VDC one of the core VMs provisioned for students will be used as a vCenter for the student kit in which they build their class infrastructure. The same can be said for the SQL Servers and Exchange Servers that, in the case of the ITAR VDC, are offered as utilities for enabling the classroom learning. Each of the SolarXX clusters provides a specific functional solution as a part to the whole of the ITAR VDC solution. Each has a set of VMs that are unique to that cluster, but in a handful of cases they host VMs that play similar function between among the clusters.

6.2 Solar01 Management Cluster VMs

The Solar01 cluster is home to all of the VMs that make up the Earth, Mars, Mercury, and Saturn student VDC kits. This includes all of the infrastructure services required to operate each of those kits including domain controllers, DNS servers, DHCP servers, deployment appliances, and all of the additional course specific VMs as outlined in the VMware Authorized Training Center (VATC) setup guides for the official VMware training classes. In some cases the VMs built for class exceed the VATC recommendations in order help ITAR meet their goal of ensuring customer experience. More information on the setup recommendations and management of the classroom infrastructures can be found in the ITAR VDC Operations Guide and the ITAR VDC Student Design Guide.

Although the hosts of the Solar01 cluster are collectively responsible for over 60 VMs and templates the bulk of the VMs, 30 to be exact, are transient VMs that exist only if and when a class is in progress for a given week. Table 17 details the configuration of the VMs hosted on Solar01.

Table 17 - VMs hosted on Solar01

VM	#	RAM GB	Total RAM GB	HD Size GB	HD Size Total GB	# cpu	CPU count	vCPU/ VM GHz
Earth vCs	7	2	14	30	210	2	14	4
Mars vCs	7	2	14	30	210	2	14	4
Mercury vCs	8	2	16	30	240	2	16	4
Saturn vCs	8	2	16	30	240	2	16	4
Dcs	8	1	8	30	240	1	8	2
Dhcp	5	1	7	30	150	1	7	2
File servers	2	2	4	130	260	2	4	4
UDAs/iSCSI	15	1	0.5	15	225	1	5	2
Vcenter	1	8	8	145	145	2	2	4
Totals	61		88		1920		86	30
Mean		2		52				
Mode		2		30		2		

If the Earth, Mars, Mercury, and Saturn kits are all in use during a given week then the VMs in Table 17 would all be deployed and running. But if a kit is empty for a given week then those VMs would be excluded from the VM count for that week. In addition, just because all four kits are in use does not guarantee that resource utilization will be simultaneous. With classes running in different time zones the resource utilization of the four sets of vCenters would be staggered. So the VM metrics used to determine host scalability were "worst case" scenarios in which all VMs are running and consuming resources.

What sets Solar01 apart from the other 2 clusters is that it is also the home the domain controllers of the forest root vdc-kits.com, the DHCP server for the management network, and the vCenter Server from where all of the ITAR VDC is managed. The vCenter Server is configured with 2 vCPUs, 8GB RAM, 1 vNIC, and three VMDKs of 40GB, 25GB, and 80GB to hold the Windows Server 2008 R2 operating system, SQL Server 2008, and VMware applications respectively. Figure 28 shows the vCenter design.

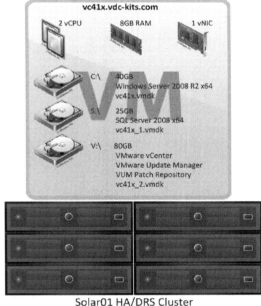

Solar01 HA/DRS Cluster

* VUM installation requires 32-bit DSN created from C:\Windows\Syswow64\odbcad32.exe

Figure 28 - VMware vCenter Server 4.1 configuration

Since the Fibre Channel storage is presenting 700GB LUNs to be formatted as VMFS datastores, and each of those LUNs is built off of similar disk structures (type of disks, speed of disks, and RAID type) it should not be expected that any one datastore would be a better fit for a given virtual machine, however to provide the best spread of I/O across the physical disk subsystem within the array the vCenter VMs for Earth, Mars, Mercury, and Saturn are deployed so that each set of VMs are split among the four 500GB VMFS datastores built from the RAID 1/0 RAID groups. For example if the Saturn kit has 8 vCenter server VMs deployed those 8 VMs would be split into pairs with each pair being stored on a different LUN among LUNs 12, 13, 14, and 15. Figure 29 details the VM placement for the Solar01 VMs.

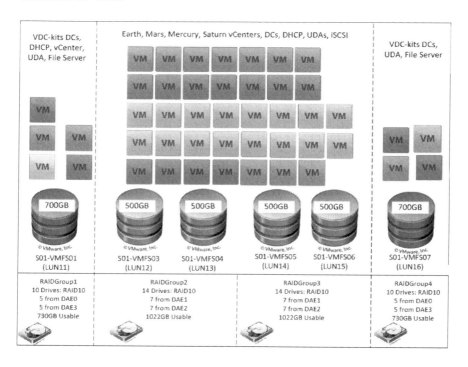

Figure 29 - VM placement on Fibre Channel storage for Solar01

6.3 Solar02 and Solar03 Management Cluster VMs

The Virtual Machine design on Solar02, like Solar01, was driven primarily by the course design specifications; however the total number of VMs to be managed by Solar02 if all kits were full in a given week is close to 100 VMs. As previously noted, though, there is a staggered nature of resource usage due to the class location, class start time, and instructor pace.

The Solar02 kit is home to the transient and low impact VMs that are used by the Dell EqualLogic students in the ITAR four-day class on Dell EqualLogic. These VM include application VMs like SQL Server, Exchange Server, and vCenter Server. The Neptune and Jupiter kits can pull double duty and function as both the delivery infrastructure for Dell EqualLogic classes and VMware classes alike.

Note: Pending no availability of other kits, it is possible to use a single Neptune or Jupiter kit to concurrently run a VMware class and an EqualLogic class. However, doing so requires a contingency plan for using a virtualized infrastructure for the VMware integration labs. More information about this contingency plan can be found in the ITAR VDC Student Design Guide.

Table 18 - displays the details of the VMs hosted on Solar02.

Table 18 - VMs hosted on Solar02

VMs	#	RAM/VM GB	Total RAM GB	HD Size GB	Total HD Size GB	# CPU	CPU Count	vCPU/VM Ghz
Neptune vCs	6	2	12	30	180	2	12	4.8
Jupiter vCs	6	2	12	30	180	2	12	4.8
DCs	8	1	8	30	240	1	8	2.4
DHCP	3	1	3	30	90	1	3	2.4
File Servers	1	2	2	130	130	2	2	4.8
UDAs	2	0.5	1	15	30	1	2	2.4
iSCSI tgts	6	0.5	3	15	90	1	6	2.4
SQL	24	2	48	30	720	1	24	2.4
Exchange	24	2	48	30	720	1	24	2.4
Nept ESXi	6	4	24	15	90	2	12	4.8
Jup ESXi	6	4	24	15	90	2	12	4.8
vc-Nept00	1	2	2	30	30	2	2	4.8
vc-Jup00	1	2	2	30	30	2	2	4.8
email	2	2	4	30	60	1	2	2.4
Totals	96		193		2680		123	50
Mean		2		33				
Mode		2		30		2		4.80

The VMFS datastores formatted from iSCSI storage are home to all of the SQL Server, Exchange Server, and vCenter Server systems used in the ITAR EqualLogic training class. Labs specific to those VM have been written with instructions that should be followed properly to ensure success of the step-by-step labs.

Solar03, home to the VMware View virtual desktops, only has access to the Fibre Channel network and therefor will use the LUNs carved and presented from the CX3-40. The design here is consistent with the prior in that the LUNs carved from the array are RAID 1/0 using disks from different BAEs and different back-end bus architectures. Figure 30 provides a high level overview of the design of the EqualLogic VDC kit virtual machines.

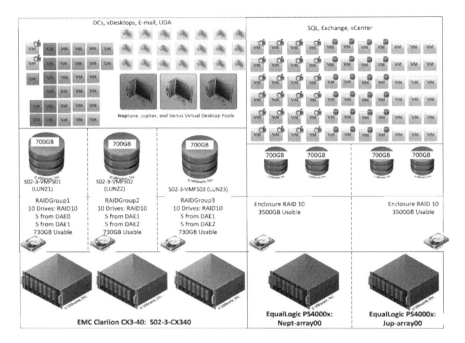

Figure 30 - VM placement for VMs hosted on Solar02 and Solar03

6.4 Solar 03 VDI Design

The VMware View deployment included in the ITAR VDC design was critical to satisfying the access requirements of the VDC. The solution was kept simple to solve the business problem revolving around secure access over a standard, common Web port (i.e. 443).

6.4.1 Logical VDI Design

Using VMware View to provide students with access to the ITAR VDC meant that even though design was to be kept simple it had to be highly available. For this reason two VMware View Security Servers participate in a Microsoft NLB cluster and then each one maps to a VMware View Connection Server. Under this design the student access requests balance between the Security Servers and get passed along to the Connection

Servers. If a Security Server failed, any existing connections would terminate but students would then be able to reconnect through the remaining server.

The VMware View Connection Servers share a common configuration of three Linked Clone Dedicated Pools. Figure 31 provides an overview of the VMware View logical design, it does not however reflect the firewall's inspection of traffic between the Security Server and the Connection Server.

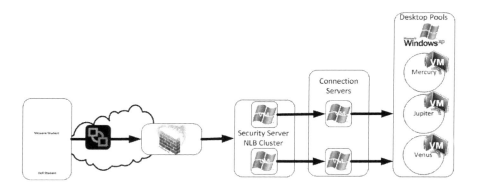

Figure 31 - VMware View logical design for the ITAR VDC

By placing the Security Servers in front of the Connection Servers we can offer a consistent access method over port 443 but still protect the domain data from direct external access. Without the Security Server the Connection Servers, which belong to the Active Directory domain, would be direct targets for Internet attacks.

Figure 32 provides a sample traffic flow as communication originating outside of the enterprise is passed through the Security Server, on to the Connection Broker for desktop assignment, and then finally communicate with the target virtual desktop.

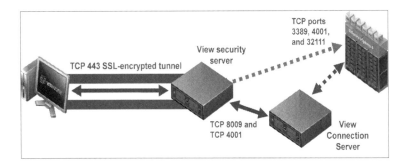

Figure 32 - External customer connections are protected using an SSL-encrypted tunnel to the Security Server

6.4.2 Physical VDI Design

The ITAR VDC View implementation is built entirely in Virtual Machines. The NLB cluster of Security Servers runs Windows Server 2003 Service Pack 2 on 1 vCPU, 4GB of RAM, and a 25GB virtual hard disk. The shared cluster name that is resolves externally and then gets forwarded through the firewall is vportal.vdc-kits.com. This name resolves to the IP of 8.225.211.230 and then gets forwarded through the firewall to the DMZ VLAN where the Security Servers each have a unique IP address 192.168.27.231 and .232 but also share an internal IP address of 192.168.27.230/24. The firewall then permits the Security Servers to communicate with the Connection Servers located on the internal network at 192.168.100.231/24 and 192.168.100.232/24.

The desktop pools are accessed on the 192.168.34.0/24, 192.168.36.0/24, and 192.168.135.0/24 networks. Figure 33 provides design details on the VMware View architecture for student access.

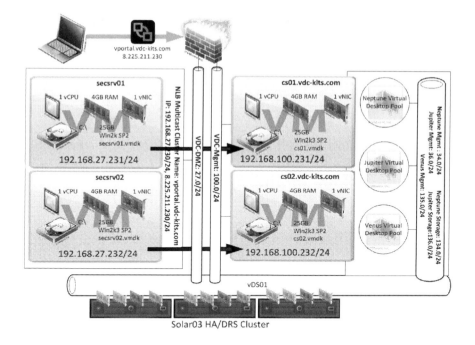

**Figure 33 - Technical design details on accessing the
ITAR VDC using VMware View virtual desktops**

6.4.3 Virtual Desktop Design

The virtual desktops for the Neptune and Jupiter kits were designed not just as part of the access strategy but are utilized in the EqualLogic labs. The virtual desktops for each of these two kits are configured with three network adapters. One network adapter is connected to the management network, 192.168.34.0/24 for Neptune and 192.168.36.0/24 for Jupiter, and then two additional network adapters connected to the IP storage network, 192.168.134.0/24 for Neptune and 192.168.136.0/24 for Jupiter. The network adapter on the management network is used exclusively for the VMware View connection traffic while the second and third NIC become part of the Microsoft iSCSI initiator and Dell EqualLogic HIT kit for accessing the respective iSCSI storage arrays.

Although not part of VMware View, the additional VMs running Microsoft Exchange and Microsoft SQL Server are configured this same way. Students use their virtual desktop to establish a remote desktop connection to the other two VMs in order to work through the iSCSI configuration and complete the labs. Figure 34 shows the virtual desktop and additional VM configurations used in the Dell EqualLogic training classes. By using the virtual desktops as part of the lab environment as opposed to just an access VM we were able to eliminate an additional 24 Virtual Machines that would have been required.

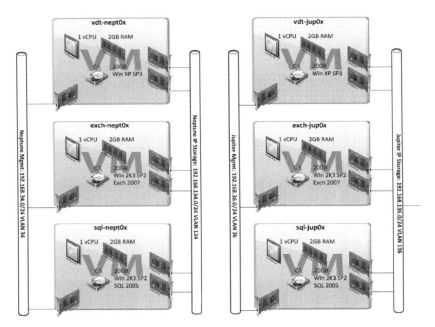

Figure 34 - ITAR EqualLogic class VMs (virtual desktop provisioned by VMware View, Windows Server, Exchange Server 2007, and SQL Server 2005

6.5 VM Design Justification

Most of the VMs in the SolarXX clusters are created according to configuration specs detailed by the training vendors, so we cannot offer much insight into the design decisions for those VMs. There are, however, adjustments that have been made to some of the configurations in order to better accommodate ITAR's consistent thriving for good customer experience. For example, the VMware Authorized Training Center (VATC) setup guide for vSphere 4.1 Install, Configure, and Manage provides configuration details for the student vCenter servers as needing only a single CPU. This despite the VMware defined minimum requirements of two 64-bit CPUs or one 64-bit dual core processor. So our adjustment to 2 vCPUs for the student vCenters was justified on two fronts; 1) it helped improve the customer experience in effort to achieve business driver and 2) it followed more closely to the real-world practices as suggested by VMware's internally created vSphere documentation.

The design of vCenter in a virtual machine offers several advantages but perhaps none more profound than in the area of availability. As a virtual machine, vCenter can be protected using the VMware High Availability feature. It is commonly thought that vCenter must be available for HA to function but this rumor is easily disproved by watching an HA event take place and noticing that none of the occurrences of VMs being revived by HA are reflected in the recent tasks of vCenter. Or if you prefer evidence that is a little more convincing then place vCenter on a host and cause the host to fail. When vCenter comes back on line on a remaining host it will be all the proof you need.

The design of the virtual desktops as noted in the last section was driven by the requirements of the Dell EqualLogic lab and our desire to eliminate redundant VM purposes. It is not feasible to deploy additional VMs when existing VMs can be configured to handle he same workloads.

The design of the infrastructure VMs like domain controllers, DHCP servers, and file servers was focused on creating VMs with consistency. By having consistent VM configurations it is easier to plan for and identify the need for change.

Design Qualities Impacted: Availability, Manageability, Performance, and Security

Requirements Achieved: 1, 2, 3, 4, 5, 8, 10, 13, and 15

7. Disaster Recovery and Business Continuity Design

7.1 Overview

Even though the key stakeholders ranked the Recoverability design quality second to last, in front of only security, it is still an important quality for ensuring a continued operation of the VDC. Designing the disaster recovery and business continuity (DRBC) for the ITAR VDC can only be successful upon a detailed and thorough inspection of all the elements making up the design, including hosts, networking devices, storage devices, and management services.

7.2 Host Protection

Of all the infrastructure elements, the ESXi hosts are probably the easiest to address when it comes to the DRBC planning because of their static nature. In the ITAR VDC specifically, the hosts are enrolled to a vNetwork Distributed Switch to accommodate the dynamic and growing networking, but the other remaining configuration settings of the host are very static in nature. Settings such as NTP, DNS, standard switches, VMK ports are not elements that require consistent review and reconfiguration. Our approach to capture this static configuration hinges on two different features: 1) host profiles and 2) vicfg-cfgbackup.

Once the hosts of the management cluster were set with their initial configuration host profiles are captured using the vSphere client. An additional ESXi host configuration backup performed using the vicfg-cfgbackup command from the vSphere Management Assistant (vMA), provides a second backup.

Keeping in mind that losing a host does not mean losing VMs, in the event that either the host profile or the vicfg-cfgbackup initiated backup is unavailable for recovery, a reinstallation of ESXi and a full post-installation configuration can still be done little to no impact on the VMs of the environment.

Estimated time to recover: < 45 minutes

7.3 Network Protection

The core switching architecture, the Solar01 branch networking, the Solar02 and Solar03 branch networking, and the production iSCSI networking were all designed with redundant Dell PowerConnect 6248 Gigabit Ethernet switches.

The student VMware VDC kits only include a single Dell PowerConnect 5448 Gigabit Ethernet switch.

Even though all the switches were covered under a 4-hour support agreement by ITAR, the four window for replacement was not acceptable as that could half of a day of training lost. So to reduce this time down to the agreed upon and acceptable down time interval an extra switch of each type is kept as a hot standby.

After the initial setup of the physical switches (and then again upon any change) the switch configurations are backed up to a folder in the replicated DFS folder structure. Should any of the production switches fail anywhere in the ITAR VDC the failed switch will be swapped out with the hot standby of similar type and the most recent backup configuration will be restored.

Estimated time to recover: < 60 minutes.

7.4 Storage Protection

Covering storage failure is critical because failed storage means no Virtual Machines and no Virtual Machines means no lab. No lab means unhappy students.

As we have shown thus far storage availability is achieved with multiple Fibre Channel switches, appropriate RAID types, and proper array cabling. The VMFS LUN design outlined in section 5.4 identifies a 1TB LUN from

S01-CX340 that is replicated to S02-3-CX340 as means of protecting the backup data. That same section also details a reciprocal replication strategy for 1TB LUNs on both of the iSCSI storage arrays accessed by the hosts of the Solar02 cluster.

Virtual Machines are protected via the VMware Data Recovery appliance as well as a simple export to OVF. In the event of storage failure (S01-CX340 or S02-3-CX340) there is not an automated process of any sort (HA, SRM) in place to facilitate the recovery of lost VMs and services.

The contingency plan for loss of an entire array is to present storage from a surviving array, then recover the VMs necessary to return classes to an operational status. The administrative effort involved in this process is difficult to pinpoint because the VDC kit usage varies by week. In the worst-case scenario we would have to restore all of the student VMs and management infrastructure VMs from the failed storage array.

By having a domain controller from each domain on both Solar01 and Solar02 we eliminate the urgent need to recover AD/DNS services. Priority would begin with recovering vCenter (pending it was part of the failure) and then recovering the student VMs that were in use for the class. If the failure occurred on the first morning of the first day of class the recovery would be a simple deploy from template with application of a custom specification file initiated from a PowerCLI command. But if the failure occurs on the afternoon of the last day, the recovery process would incur much more administrative effort as even after the restoration of the student systems it would take time to return it to the same state.

Estimated time to recover: 1 to 4 hours

7.5 vCenter Protection

VMware vCenter is not a single point of failure in the infrastructure and is not the first domino that can trigger a chain reaction of bad events however it is important for the day-to-day management and critical in the destroy/rebuild process that occurs each week as classes complete and new classes begin.

The rapidly changing nature of the ITAR VDC means that the vCenter database is constantly being updated. Objects are created, then deleted, and replaced once again. Eliminating orphaned objects and/or out-of-sync issues requires a DRBC strategy that keeps vCenter Server protected at regular intervals.

The vCenter Server service and its back-end database are hosted on the same system which also includes VMware Update Manager and its database.

The vCenter Server is protected using the following techniques:

1.   Application consistent backup using the VMware Data Recovery appliance.
2.   Clone of the VM.
3.   SQL Server backup strategy consisting of:
     a.   Full backups every Saturday morning. (Class configurations are destroyed Friday night and new classes are built on Saturday evening and Sunday.
     b.   Differential backups on each evening Sunday through Thursday
     c.   Transaction log backups every four hours. (Although an installation note refers to a VMware knowledge base regarding shifting the database to Simple Recovery model doing so would eliminate the transaction log backup capability as Simple Recovery operates under truncate log on checkpoint procedure.)

Estimate time to recover: < 2 hours

7.6 Infrastructure Services Protection

Domain controllers, DNS servers, DHCP servers, file servers, and other network applications and services running inside of a Virtual Machine are protected using the VMware Data Recovery appliance. Pairs of Domain controllers (DNS servers) for each of the domains are split among the

Solar01 and Solar02 clusters and are backed up by different vDR appliances to different storage arrays.

All of the SQL and Exchange VMs for the Dell EqualLogic classes are backed with the vDR and have also been exported to an OVF and archived on an external storage device. Since each of those VMs exist in its own silo environment as a domain controller of its own domain there are no implications on AD replication.

The appliances specific to each of the classes have also been exported to an OVF and archived on an external storage device.

Estimated time to recover: < 1 hour

7.7 Design Justification

All of the DRBC procedures in the VDC were motivated by achieving a level of recoverability that allowed us to meet or exceed the service level agreement agreed upon at the onset of this project.

Design Qualities Impacted: Recoverability

Requirements Achieved: 8, 13

CHAPTER 5

SERVER VIRTUALIZATION: INSTALLATION, VALIDATION, AND OPERATIONAL EXAMPLES

"Excellence is an art won by training and habituation. We do not act rightly because we have virtue or excellence, but we rather have those because we have acted rightly. We are what we repeatedly do. Excellence, then, is not an act but a habit."
— *Aristotle*

This chapter provides a set of reference material, in the form of installation guides, validation guides, and operational process guides that should be included in all Architectures for an infrastructure. There are some core examples provided in this chapter. These are not all of the possible guides that would be included in a solution. These example documents are complete, in their context here, but may have areas that need to be expanded on for a particular integration.

The result of this chapter is to enable the reader with a template of how to create procedural guides for installation processes, validation processes, and operational processes. Using the examples provided, it should be easy for you, the reader, to take these formats, and work through creating your own documentation. Feel free to borrow the formatting of these guides from this chapter. There are many exercises in Appendix D – Building a Design Lab, where it asks you to create your own documentation. Use this formatting to start building your own set of documentation, as it can provide you a format that works. It will require effort to do so the first time, but once you create a document set that works, it can be reused over and over. When you find new items that need to be included, you can update your documentation to reflect this new information.

The contents of this chapter provide the following Installation Guides, Validation Plans, and Operational Process Guides as a baseline for creating your own documentation:

- ESXi Installation Guide
- vCenter Installation Guide
- VMware Cluster Configuration Guide
- vSphere & VMware Cluster Validation Plan
- Windows 2012 R2 Virtual Machine Template Build Process
- Deploy Virtual Machine from Template Process

The choice on how you combine or separate material in your design submission is up to you and is not a scoring area, however it is important to have a consistent flow within and across the documents.

Keeping track of the multiple documents required to successfully integrate a solution may become difficult to manage if left unchecked. Creating a high level document that summarizes the overall procedure, which then calls out each of the actual processes, could make managing and sequencing the events required to successfully integrate a simpler task.

ESXi Installation Guide

This installation guide is designed to capture all information needed to install an ESXi server, adjust base configuration at time of installation, and prepare ESXi server to be managed by a vCenter Server.

Additional configurations, such as vSwitches, datastores, or other advanced parameters are not define herein, as these parameters are defined and configured differently depending on the VMware Cluster that the ESXi host will be a member of.

Information Required For Installing ESXi

This section is in place to gather all the information required to perform the installation of the ESXi Hypervisor. The lead Architect, or a member of his team, should lead a customer through the process of gathering the information in this section, so that the teams responsible for installation and maintenance of the solution understand all the choices and values entered into this table.

Table 19 - Information Required for Installation

Parameter	Notes	ENTER VALUE HERE
Hostname	The Fully Qualified Hostname of the ESXi host about to be deployed i.e. esx01.itaresource.com	
TCP / IP Information	The IP Address associated with the Hostname of this ESXi server i.e. 192.168.10.11	
Subnet Mask	The subnet mask associated with the Hostname / IP address of the ESXi server i.e. 255.255.255.0	
Gateway Address	The Default Gateway Address (router address) associated with the Hostname/IP address of the ESXi server, where all routed traffic will pass i.e. 192.168.10.1	
DNS Server Addresses	The DNS servers that will provide name resolution for the ESXi Servers. There must be one (1), should be two (2) i.e. 192.168.10.3 192.168.11.3	
Additional DNS Suffixes	By default, and ESXi server will use its domain name, which is entered in the hostname as FQDN, to perform host based lookups. If Additional DNS namespaces are to be queried, list them here. i.e. lab.itaresource.com sales.itaresource.com	
Root Administrator Password	The password for the root Administrator of the ESXi VMkernel. This is equivalent to the Administrator password on a Windows system. i.e. Not$ho4ingYouMyPass4ord	

Parameter	Notes	ENTER VALUE HERE
Visio Diagram of VMNIC to vSwitch/vDS	Must have a Visio drawing of the physical NIC, its correlated VMNIC #, and PCI Address. The Visio will have planned redundant network connectivity for vSwitches/DVS i.e. Onboard LAN1 VMNIC0 PCI Address: 05:01:01	Visio Available, complete with planned NIC to VMNIC mappings
Physical switch ports that each VMNIC is connected to	What upstream switch and corresponding port does the ESXi server's physical NICs connect to? Required to make appropriate connections to vSwitches, and configuration of VLAN traffic. Can be included in the Visio. i.e. VirtualConnect Cisco Switch <name-of-switch>-port1/2/3	
VMNIC for VMkernel	Which VMNIC will handle the initial VMkernel Management traffic after the installation of ESXi. i.e. vmnic0	
VLAN Tag for VMkernel	If a VLAN tag is required for VMkernel Management, this tag must be entered or no communication will occur. This tag is a number between 1 – 4096. This field will be left as NONE if the port is not trunking VLANs to it.	
Syslog Servers	vSphere 5 Has a Syslog Server that can run on vCenter Server. Up to two syslog hosts can be entered i.e. vc01.itaresource.com syslog.itaresource.com	
ESXi Dump configuration	vSphere 5 has an ESXi Dump Collector can collect coredumps over the network. Hostname: vc01.itaresource.com IP Address: 10.10.10.20 VMkernel Interface: vmk0 IP Port: 6500	
NTP Servers	To synchronize time. Typically a Unix based service, though Windows Domain Controllers can act as an NTP server. i.e. ntp.itaresource.com ntp1.itaresource.com ntp2.itaresource.com	
IPMI / iLO / DRAC Settings	If using Distributed Power Management, this information must be acquired. Administrator name: Password: BMC IP Address: BMC MAC Address:	

Parameter	Notes	ENTER VALUE HERE
Preferred Multipath Settings	This is dependent of the Storage Array in use. Different arrays have different settings for different versions of vSphere. Verify your settings with the storage vendor. i.e. *3Par 7400* VMW_SATP_ALUA VMW_PSP_RR *EMC VNX 5500* VMW_SATP_ALUA_CX VMW_PSP_RR	
Lockdown Mode	Lockdown Mode prevents remote Administrators from logging into an ESXi host. When enabled, Administrators can only manage the server at the local console or vCenter Server. The default is disabled	

The following figure is a logical diagram of an ESXi server hardware, how the onboard NICs are allocated and named, and a summary of how these VMNICs are assigned to vSwitches/Distributed vSwitches.

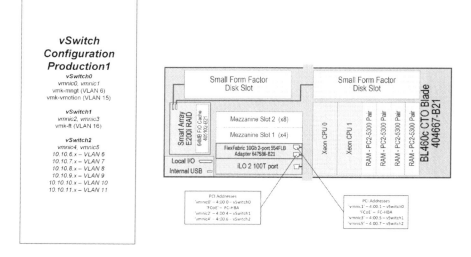

Figure 35 - Logical ESXi Server

The following figure is another logical diagram of how vSwitches are configured, assigned to physical NICs / VMNICs, and allocation of bandwidth to the HP c7000 FlexFabric interconnects configured in the chassis.

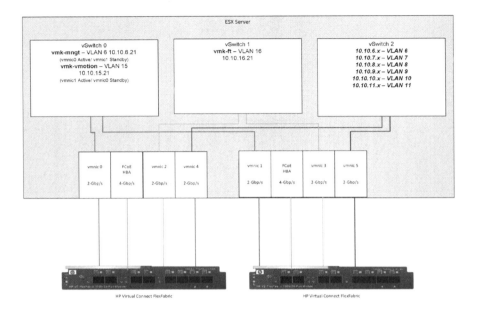

Figure 36 - Logical ESXi Server vSwitch Mapping

ESXi Installation & Configuration

This is the process for installing ESXi Server from an ISO file over IPMI / iLO/ DRAC or from a CD-ROM at the console of the ESXi Server. An assumptions that the reader is familiar with connectivity of IPMI / iLO / DRAC is made, that this is a new installation of ESXi on a new server, as well as a base familiarity with the ESXi software.

Please sign off each task as it is completed.

Table 20 - ESXi Installation & Configuration

Completed	Tasks / Notes
	Validation of DNS Name Resolution Prior to performing installation tasks These should be done from an administrative workstation.
	Ping the shortname of the ESXi Server being deployed. You are not expecting a response. You are validating Name Resolution works correctly. i.e. ping esx01
	Ping the FQDN of the ESXi Server being deployed. You are not expecting a response. You are validating Name Resolution works correctly. i.e. ping esx01.itaresource.com
	Perform an nslookup of the IP address of the ESXi Server. You will get the FQDN response back. i.e. nslookup 192.168.10.16
	Verify BIOS Settings are configured per design guide
	Connect to the console of the ESXi host Verify settings, such as hyperthread & power settings, are configured as specified in the design guide. Do not disconnect from the console
	Being Installation of ESXi
	Present the installation media (be it ISO or actual CD-ROM media) to ESXi host Boot from media A boot menu will appear after the boot media is read and initiated The standard installer will begin the installation process A loader screen will show the VMkernel loading from the boot media
	Completing the ESXi Installation
	Once able to interact with the installation, there are a few prompts to answer At the Welcome Screen, hit Enter to continue. At the EULA screen, hit F11 to continue. At the Select Disk to Install or Upgrade, select the appropriate destination drive At the Select Keyboard Layout, select your appropriate keyboard layout At the Root Password Screen, enter the 'root' Administrator's password twice. At the Confirm Installation Screen, hit F11 to accept and initiate installation Installation takes 10-15 minutes. You are prompted to reboot. Remove ESXi ISO / CD-ROM, and reboot. Stay connected to the console.

Completed	Tasks / Notes
	Post Installation Configuration – Management Network

Once the reboot has completed you will see prompts to use F2 to customize the system, or F12 to Shut Down / Restart the system. Hit F2 to begin customizing the system

Navigate the menu to Configure Management Network, and select Select Network Adapters.
Verify desired VMNIC is being used, adjust if necessary. Hit Enter to accept

Select VLAN (optional)
Leave blank if not using VLANs, enter VLAN ID if using VLAN tags.
Hit Enter to accept.

Select IP Information
Choose Set Static IP Address and Network Configuration
Enter IP Address, Subnet Mask, and Default Gateway.
Hit Enter to accept.

Select DNS Configuration
Enter the primary and secondary DNS servers
to Administrator for name resolution.
Enter the hostname (Fully Qualified). i.e. esx01.itaresource.com
Hit Enter to accept

Select Custom DNS Suffixes
Enter any custom DNS Suffixes required.
Hit Enter to accept.

Hit Escape to back out of this menu.
You are prompted to apply changes, and restart management network.
Hit Y to accept.
You are now back at the main configuration page.

Post Installation Configuration – Testing Management Network

After the configuration of the management network, validate the configuration can communicate with the network as expected.

Navigate the menu to Test Management Network.
Hit Enter to accept the default test (ping DNS Servers, Gateway, resolve the configured hostname of the ESXi host).
All should come back OK, hit Enter to continue.
If any issues, resolve before continuing.

You are now back at the main configuration page.

Completed	Tasks / Notes
	Enable ESXi Shell
	This is to allow local login as root, to perform additional configurations at the command line interface
	Navigate the menu to Troubleshooting Options. ESXi Shell is disabled by default. Hit Enter to Enable ESXi shell.
	Enter ESXi Shell via keyboard command ALT+F1 Login as root, with the password you configured. You should see a prompt.
	Configure the ESXi Dump Collector Settings
	Review current configuration via command: esxcli system coredump network get
	Specify the VMkernel interface to use (vmk0 is typical) (IP address used in command example below should be IP of your vCenter) esxcli system coredump network set --interface-name vmk0 --server-ipv4 10.10.10.10 --server-port 6500
	Enable network coredump configuration esxcli system coredump network set --enable-true
	Confirm the configuration esxcli system coredump network get
	Stay logged in to the console
	Configure SATP and PSP settings
	At the console, type the command appropriate for your array. An example is provided here for syntax. esxcli storage nmp satp set -s VMW_SATP_DEFAULT_CX--p VMW_PSP_RR
	Type exit to log out of the console
	Disable the ESXi Shell
	This is to lock down local login, locking down the console of the ESXi host.
	Return to the ESXi DCUI via keyboard command ALT+F2 You should still be in the Troubleshooting Options Screen. Hit Enter to Disable ESXi Shell
	Log out of the ESXi host.

ESXi Final Configurations

These additional steps are to finish the core configuration of an ESXi host's core settings.

Table 21 - ESXi Final Configuration

Completed	Tasks / Notes
	The following tasks are performed at an administrative workstation using the vSphere Client, or the vSphere Web Client, connected to the vCenter Server.
	Add ESXi Server to vCenter Server Inventory.
	Navigate to the Hosts & Clusters View. Select the Datacenter the ESXi host is to be added to. Right Click Datacenter object, select Add Host. Do NOT add ESXi host to cluster at this time.
	Enter the FQDN of the ESXi host. i.e. esx01.itaresource.com Enter the account, root, and password you configured. Hit Enter. You are prompted to accept the self-signed certificate. Accept to continue. A summary of the host is displayed. Click Next to continue. You are prompted to assign a license key. Select one, click Next to continue Disable or Enable Lockdown mode, click Next to continue. There should be no Virtual Machines to place in folders, click Next to continue. Click Finish.
	Configure NTP Settings of ESXi Server
	In the vSphere Web Client, select the newly added ESXi host on the left. Navigate to the Manage Tab, and select the Settings Tab. Navigate to System → Time Configuration, and click Edit. Select the radio button to Enable NTP Enter the NTP Servers to be used. Select this service to Start & Stop with Host Click Start to Start the Service. Click OK to finish this configuration
	Configure Syslog Server settings of ESXi Server
	In the vSphere Web Client, select the newly added ESXi host on the left. Navigate to the Manage Tab, and select the Settings Tab. Navigate to System → Advanced System Settings. Find the setting: syslog.global.loghost. select this line, and click Edit. Enter the FQDN of the syslog server(s) to send data to. Click OK to finish this configuration

Completed	Tasks / Notes
	Configure Security Profile to allow Syslog traffic
	In the vSphere Web Client, select the newly added ESXi host on the left. Navigate to the Manage Tab, and select the Settings Tab. Navigate to System → Security Profile. Under the Firewall heading, click Edit. Find the Syslog service, and enable it through the firewall. Click OK to finish this configuration
	You are finished the base ESXi Configuration
	Additional configuration of vSwitches and Datastore presentation is defined in the VMware Cluster guidelines, and should be completed and validated before adding this ESXi host to an active VMware Cluster.

vCenter for Windows Installation Guide

This installation guide is designed to capture all information needed to install a vCenter server, adjust base configuration at time of installation, and prepare vCenter server to be capable of managing ESXi servers.

Additional configurations, such as Distributed Virtual Switches, VMware Clusters, Datastore Clusters, VM & Template Folders, or other advanced parameters are not defined herein.

Information Required For Installation

This section is in place to gather all the information required to perform the installation of the vCenter Server. The lead Architect, or a member of his team, should lead a customer through the process of gathering the information in this section, so that the teams responsible for installation and maintenance of the solution understand all the choices and values entered into this table.

Table 22 - Information Required for Installing vCenter

Parameter	Notes	ENTER VALUE HERE
Hostname	The Fully Qualified Hostname of the vCenter Server about to be deployed i.e. esx01.itaresource.com	
TCP / IP Information	The IP Address associated with the Hostname of this vCenter Server i.e. 192.168.10.11	
vCenter Server Instance ID	The instance ID that will be set for this instance of vCenter Server. The value can be between 0-63	
vCenter Server Linked Mode	Will this vCenter participate in a linked mode vCenter group? If yes, enter FQDN of the existing vCenter Server. If this is the first vCenter Server, ignore this requirement This is not configured during setup	
Memory & CPU	How Many hosts will you be managing? Sizing of 8-GB RAM and 2 x vCPU is minimal, and provides support for < 100 hosts.	
SSL Certificate	Is there an in-house Certificate Authority that publishes SSL certificates, and manages the lifecycle of Certificates? If so, additional planning and processes are required for Signed SSL Certificate	No
SSO Administrator	VMware SSO requires an administrator of SSO environment. This is separate from any type of domain admin. Default is administrator@vsphere.local	administrator@ vsphere.local
SSO Administrator Password	The Password for the SSO Server Administrator 8 characters, 1 number, 1 special character	
SSO Site	Name of the SSO site you are installing. Aligning this name with the AD Sites & Services name for this site is acceptable.	
SQL Server	The SQL server that the databases will be housed on	
SQL Database for vCenter	Include the vCenter name/instance ID into the DB name if possible i.e. vcenter18 is the database name for vCenter18	
SQL Database for Update Manager	Include the vCenter Name/instance ID into the DB name if possible i.e. vcenter18um is the database name for vCenter Update Manager	

Parameter	Notes	ENTER VALUE HERE
ODBC Connection for vCenter	Include the name of the vCenter Database if possible i.e. vcenter18 is the name of the 64-bit ODBC connection to the vCenter DB	
ODBC Administrator/ Password for vCenter	Administrator and password of named SQL account that has DBO access to the DB for vCenter	
ODBC Connection for Update Manager	Include the name of the vCenter Database if possible i.e. vcenter18um is the name of the 32-bit ODBC connection to the vCenter DB	
ODBC Administrator/ Password for Update Manager	Administrator and password of named SQL account that has DBO access to the DB for vCenter Update Manager	
vCenter Service Account	If required to have an Active Directory Service Account to start the vCenter Server Windows services (can be run as system account)	vmware.vcenter
AD Group for Administrative Permissions in vCenter	The Active Directory Group Given Admin permissions in vSphere	vSphere-Admins
SNMP Info	Will vCenter send SNMP alerts, and if so, what are the community strings and SNMP trap destinations	
SMTP Info	The mail server and its account that vCenter Server will send alerts as	
vSphere Licensing	Validated vSphere licensing is available for assignment after the installation process.	
Media	SQL Client is required to connect to the DB vCenter Sysprep is required to populate the vCenter Server directory to deploy from template and integrate sysprep for legacy Windows OS's. TFTP Server to enable AutoDeploy	
vCenter Functions	Will the Syslog Server be installed?	Yes
	Will the ESXi Dump Collector be installed?	Yes
	Will the Update Manager be installed?	Yes
	Will the AutoDeploy be installed?	No
	Will the Authentication Proxy be installed?	No

vCenter Installation & Configuration

This is the process for installing vCenter Server from a network share. An assumptions that the reader is familiar with vCenter Server terminology, that all components are being installed on the vCenter Server, that the operating system supporting the vCenter Server has been deployed per existing documentation, is a member of an Active Directory Domain, self-signed certificates are being used, and that the installer has access to the console (RDP is acceptable).

These tasks are broken up into sections, and corresponding tables, to make the tasks more manageable.

Please sign off each task as it is completed.

Table 23 - Preparations for vCenter Server & Components

Completed	Task / Notes
	Validation of DNS Name Resolution Prior to performing installation tasks These should be done from an administrative workstation.
	Ping the shortname of the ESXi Server being deployed. You are not expecting a response. You are validating Name Resolution works correctly. i.e. ping vcenter01
	Ping the FQDN of the ESXi Server being deployed. You are not expecting a response. You are validating Name Resolution works correctly. i.e. ping vcenter01.itaresource.com
	Perform an nslookup of the IP address of the ESXi Server. You will get the FQDN response back. i.e. nslookup 192.168.10.16
	Logon to the vCenter Server with Administrative Account
	Verify that you have logged in to the domain that vCenter is planned for.
	Add vCenter Active Directory Service Account to the Local Administrators group.
	Verify appropriate Memory & CPU has been allocated.
	Verify network share has the software available to perform the installation

Completed	Task / Notes
	Install Adobe Flash This is not typically done on servers. This is being done on the vCenter Server, to enable connectivity to the vSphere Web Client from the vCenter Server itself, during initial setup, but more so for any potential troubleshooting in the future. If Adobe Flash has an auto-update feature, do not enable it.
	SQL Client Verify that the appropriate Microsoft SQL Client software has been installed. If not install the latest Microsoft SQL Client software, to enable creation of the ODBC connections required
	Create ODBC Connection for vCenter Server Database Control Panel → Administrative Tools → ODBC Data Sources (64-Bit) System DSN Click Add Choose the Correct SQL Client Driver In Name, type the name of the ODBC Connection In Server, type in the name of the SQL Server hosting the DB Use SQL Server Authentication Change the Default Database to … Next, Finish, Test connection.
	Create ODBC Connection for vCenter Update Manager Database Control Panel → Administrative Tools → ODBC Data Sources (32-Bit) System DSN Click Add Choose the Correct SQL Client Driver In Name, type the name of the ODBC Connection In Server, type in the name of the SQL Server hosting the DB Use SQL Server Authentication Change the Default Database to … Next, Finish, Test connection.
	Launch the vCenter Autorun Splash Screen From the network share, navigate to the folder for vCenter Server installation. Launch the Autorun.exe in the root of that folder.
	Do not log out. Ongoing processes start from this point….

Table 24 - Installing vCenter Single Sign On

Completed	Task / Notes
	From the vCenter Autorun splash screen, select VMware Single Sign On on the left, and on the right, click Install.
	Welcome Screen. .Net will have finished configuring. Click Next.
	End Administrator License Agreements. Accept. Click Next
	vCenter Single Sign On Prerequisites Shows hostname, FQDN, and IP. Checks are placed next to 'joined to domain' and DNS checks. Click next.
	VMware SSO Server Information Choose "vCenter Single Sign-On for your first vCenter". Click Next.
	vCenter Single Sign On Information Default SSO Administrator: administrator@vsphere.local Default SSO Administrator password: < enter twice > Click Next.
	vCenter Single Sign-On Configure Site Type in the name of the Site Click Next
	vCenter SSO Port Settings Click Next.
	Destination Folder Click Next
	Ready to Install Click Install
	Finish the installation.

Table 25 - Installing vSphere Web Client

Completed	Task / Notes
	From the vCenter Autorun splash screen, select vSphere Web Client on the left, and on the right, click Install.
	Welcome Screen Click Next.
	End Administrator License Agreements. Accept. Click Next
	Destination Folder Click Next

Completed	Task / Notes
	Configure Ports Click Next
	vCenter Single Sign On Information
	Enter administrator@vsphere.local Enter password Verify the Lookup Service URL (make sure it is all lower case)
	Click Next
	Click Yes to accept SSL SHA1 Fingerprint
	Click Install Certificate to accept Certificate
	Ready to Install Click Install
	Click Finish to finish the installation. Wait 5 minutes for the service to start before continuing to the next step.

Table 26 - Active Directory / LDAP Authentication

Completed	Task / Notes
	From your desktop, open the vSphere Web Client
	Install the Client Integration Plugin (bottom left of the page) Accept all the defaults.
	Log In to vSphere Web Client Using administrator@vsphere.local
	Enter AD / LDAP Authentication
	On the left, go to Administration Go to configuration Go to Identity Sources
	Highlight your AD / LDAP. 4th icon in, is set default Directory. Click it
	Close Web Client and continue installation.

Table 27 - Installing vCenter Inventory Service

Completed	Task / Notes
	From the vCenter Autorun splash screen, select vCenter Inventory Service on the left, and on the right, click Install.
	Choose the language
	Welcome Screen Click Next

Completed	Task / Notes
	End Administrator License Agreement Accept Click Next.
	Destination Folder Click Next
	Local System Information FQDN of vCenter Server Click Next
	Configure Ports Click Next
	Java Virtual Machine Memory Size Choose. Click Next
	vCenter Singe Sign On Information Enter administrator@vsphere.local Provide Password. Verify the Lookup Service URL to be FQDN Click Next
	Certificate Installation for Secure Connection Install Certificate
	Ready To Install Click Install
	Click Finish to finish the installation.

Table 28 - Installing vCenter Server

Completed	Task / Notes
	From the vCenter Autorun splash screen, select vCenter Server on the left, and on the right, click Install.
	Choose the language
	Welcome Screen. .Net will have finished configuring. Click Next.
	End Administrator License Agreements. Accept. Click Next
	License Key Leave the license key empty for now. Click Next.
	Database Information Choose 'Use an existing supported database' Choose your vCenter DSN that you configured. Click Next.

Completed	Task / Notes
	Database Options Enter the appropriate password for the DB/Administrator If you have an error here, you do not have DBO permissions. Click Next
	vCenter Server Service Enter, if the service account (in domain\Administrator format) Make sure the Fully Qualified Domain Name is correct. Click Next.
	Linked-Mode Options In the vCenter Server Linked mode Option, leave the default, Standalone vCenter. Click Next
	Configure Ports Click Next.
	JVM Memory Size Choose the size of the JVM Memory based on sizing. Click Next
	vCenter Single Sign On Information Enter: administrator@vsphere.local Enter his password Verify the Service Lookup URL to be FQDN (all lower case) Click Next
	Accept Certificates
	vCenter Single Sign On Information Change the name to vSphere-Admins@itaresource.com Click next.
	vCenter Inventory Service Information Click Next
	Destination Folders Click Next
	Ready to Install Click Install
	Click Finish to finish the installation.

Table 29 - Installing VMware vSphere Client

Completed	Task / Notes
	From the vCenter Autorun splash screen, select VMware vSphere Client on the left, and on the right, click Install.
	Installation of client is all default choices.
	Click Finish to complete the installation.

Table 30 - Installing vSphere Update Manager

Completed	Task / Notes
	From the vCenter Autorun splash screen, select vSphere Update Manager on the left, and on the right, click Install.
	Choose the language
	Welcome Screen Click Next.
	End Administrator License Agreements. Accept. Click Next
	Support Information Leave the checkbox to 'Download Updates ....' Click Next
	vCenter Server Information Enter the FQDN of the vCenter Server (do not use IP) Enter the Domain\vmware.vcenter credentials and its password Click Next.
	Database Information Use an existing supported database, and choose your 32-bit ODBC connection configured earlier Click next
	Enter the password for the SQL account, and click next
	In the vSphere Update Manager Port Settings Choose the FQDN, not the IP in the pull down box. Click next to continue
	Destination Folders You will get an error if there is less than 120- GB Free. You can ignore this for now. Click Next to continue
	Click Install to install
	Click Finish to finish the installation

Table 31 - Installing vSphere ESXi Dump Collector

Completed	Task / Notes
	From the vCenter Autorun splash screen, select vSphere ESXi Dump Collector on the left, and on the right, click Install.
	Welcome Screen Click Next.
	End Administrator License Agreements. Accept. Click Next

Completed	Task / Notes
	Destination Folder Click Next
	Setup Type VMware vCenter Server installation Click Next
	vCenter Server Information Enter the FQDN of the vCenter Server (do not use IP) Enter the Domain\vmware.vcenter credentials and its password Click Next.
	SSL Warning Click Accept
	ESXi Dump Collector Port Settings Click Next
	ESXi Dump Collector Port Identification Make sure FQDN is shown Click Next
	Ready to Install Click Install

Table 32 - Installing vSphere Syslog Collector

Completed	Task / Notes
	From the vCenter Autorun splash screen, select vSphere Syslog Collector on the left, and on the right, click Install.
	Welcome Screen Click Next.
	End Administrator License Agreements. Accept. Click Next
	Destination Folder Click Next
	Setup Type VMware vCenter Server installation Click Next
	vCenter Server Information Enter the FQDN of the vCenter Server (do not use IP) Enter the Domain\vmware.vcenter credentials and its password Click Next.
	SSL Warning Click Accept
	Syslog Collector Port Settings Click Next

Completed	Task / Notes
	Syslog Collector Port Identification Make sure FQDN is shown. Click Next.
	Ready to Install Click Install
	Click Finish to finish the installation
	Additional configuration of the ESXi servers is required. This is covered outside this guide.

Table 33 - Post install vCenter Configurations

Completed	Task / Notes
	Log in to the vCenter Server with the same Administrative credentials.
	Add Sysprep folders
	From the network share, navigate to the folder where you legacy Windows sysprep files can be found.
	Copy the appropriate files to the vCenter Server C:\ C:\ProgramData\VMware\VMware VirtualCenter\sysprep The directory structures there are empty, and expect the content of the appropriate version of sysprep.
	Newer Windows OS's do not require this, as they have sysprep integrated into their OS.
	Launch the vSphere Client
	Log into the vCenter Server using FQDN. Accept the Certificate by clicking 'Install this certificate...' and clicking Ignore.
	In the vSphere Client, go to Home → Administration → vCenter Server Settings Items not being configured here are not mentioned.
	Statistics Default statistics are acceptable for normal runtime. NOTE: vCenter DB Sizing tool here if needed
	Runtime Settings Change the Unique ID Enter the IP Address in Managed IP Addresses (some vApps require this setting) Make sure the name is the FQDN of the vCenter server
	Mail Enter the FQDN of the SMTP server The sender account is how vCenter Server sends email notifications when alarms/alerts are triggered. Make sure no authentication is required for this send.

Completed	Task / Notes
	SNMP Enter up to 4 SNMP trap/destination/community strings
	Database Retention Policy Click the box to Retain both Tasks & Events for 180 days
	Go To Home Administration Licensing Enter all of your vSphere 5 License Keys Assign the keys for vCenter to the vCenter Server
	Go to Home → Management → Customization Specifications Manager This is answer files for Windows & Linux. Configure answer files for the Operating Systems being deployed, to take advantage of automation when deploying from template.
	Install the vCenter Update Manager Plug-In Go to the Plug-Ins Pull Down Menu, and select Manage Plug-Ins
	Click Download & Install vSphere Update Manager Use all the default choices to complete the installation. Close the Plugins Manager
	Place a check in the box, and Ignore the Warning if not using SSL in-house
	Go to Home → Solutions & Applications → Update Manager
	Go to the Configuration Tab
	Adjust the Download Schedule Set this task run at 7:40 AM on Monday, weekly. Enter the email to send that the task was completed to.
	Adjust the Notification Check Schedule Set this task run at 7:30 AM on Monday, weekly. Enter the email to send that the task was completed to.
	Virtual Machine Settings Turn off Take Snapshot
	ESXi Host/Cluster Settings By Default, I change to the following: VM Power State: Do Not Change Power State Retry is enabled, 5 minute delay, 3 retries Enable 'Temporarily disable any removable....' Enable the Temporary Disable of "DPM" Enable the Temporary Disable of "HA Admission Control" Enable the Temporary Disable of "Fault Tolerance" DO NOT Enable the Temporary Disable of "Enable Parallel...." Enable the Temporary Disable of "Migrate Powered Off &...."
	Restart the vCenter Server (reboot the OS)

Completed	Task / Notes
	You have finished the base configuration of vCenter Server.
	All other actions/functions will vary.
	Configuration of different Hosts & Clusters, VM Folders, Datastores, vSwitches, Distributed vSwitches, Host Profiles, and all other configurations are outside the scope of this document.

VMware Cluster Configuration Guide

The configuration of VMware Clusters in any environment may be different between cluster objects. Each Cluster being created should have its own configuration guide. There is an assumption that the administrator implementing this has a familiarity with VMware vSphere.

Table 34 - Configuration of VMware Cluster <NAME-OF-CLUSTER>

Completed	Task / Notes
	Log in to vSphere Web Client.
	Navigate to Home → Inventories → Hosts & Clusters Expand out the vCenter object
	If no datacenter object exists yet
	Right click on the vCenter Object, and select New Datacenter. Name the datacenter according to the naming standard i.e. Boston for a Boston located datacenter Click OK to create the new datacenter object.
	Create a New Cluster
	Expand the datacenter object Right click the datacenter object, and select New Cluster. Name the cluster, according to the naming standard.
	Enable DRS (by putting a check in the box). Default settings for DRS should be fully automated & migration threshold should be set to its middle setting.
	Enable EVC (use the pull down menu to select the appropriate mode). In this Cluster, Intel "Sandy Bridge" Generation is being set
	Click OK to configure the cluster

Completed	Task / Notes
	Add a minimum of three (3) ESXi hosts at this time.
	Right click the cluster and select Add Host
	Enter the FQDN of the host to add, and click next.
	i.e. esx01.itaresource.com
	Enter the Administrator name (root) & password you had
	set previously on the ESXi host, and click Next.
	You are prompted to accept the SHA1 fingerprint of the server, click Yes.
	A summary of the host appears, and should
	not contain any VMs. Click Next.
	Assign the appropriate license key to the ESXi host, click Next.
	Enable / Disable Lockdown Mode, based on this clusters setting.
	(Lockdown mode is not being used in this cluster). Click Next.
	Select "Put all of this host's Virtual Machines in the
	Cluster's resource pool. Resource Pools currently
	present on the host will be deleted." Click Next.
	A summary screen appears. Click Finish to add the host.
	Repeat for the additional ESXi hosts being added at this time.
	Review Cluster Settings, and enable High Availability
	Select the newly created cluster on the left.
	Select the Manage tab on the right pane, and the Settings sub-tab.
	Select vSphere DRS.
	Verify Fully Automated for DRS automation
	Verify Power Management is Off.
	Select vSphere HA
	Edit vSphere HA
	Turn vSphere HA On
	Expand Admission Control. Configure for 1 Host of Failover Capacity.
	Expand Datastore Heartbeating. Select Use Datastores only from
	the specified list. Select the first two (2) sequentially named LUNs
	(do not select the LUN dedicated to Template VMs/ISO files).
	Click OK.
	Select Configuration → General.
	Edit Default VM Compatibility.
	Set appropriately for the Cluster.
	Click OK.
	Application of Host DRS Group, DRS VM Groups,
	DRS Rules, may be applied at this time.
	Application of Host Profiles may be applied at this time.

vSphere Cluster Validation Plan

The procedures contained in this Validation plan can be used to verify the operational functionality of essential components in the vSphere implementation. This plan is written with the assumption that an administrator who is testing and validating these milestones is familiar with VMware vSphere, has basic understanding of Ethernet connectivity, has a basic understanding of SAN connectivity, and has been allocated the permissions to open a support case with VMware.

Table 35 - Host(s) Checks

Completed & Successful	Task / Notes
	Verify NTP Verify NTP is configured to start and stop with host. Verify NTP is syncing time
	Verify DNS Verify DNS is able to resolve hostnames of Cluster Members Verify DNS is able to resolve Windows Domain Controllers
	Verify Redundant Power Pull power supply 1, and host remains running Pull power supply 2, and host remains running Pull power from PDU 1, and hosts remains running Pull power from PDU 2, and hosts remains running
	Test vSwitch Failover Pull vmnic0, and verify communications to Host / VM Pull vmnic1, and verify communications to Host / VM Pull vmnic2, and verify communications to Host / VM Pull vmnic3, and verify communications to Host / VM Pull vmnic4, and verify communications to Host / VM Pull vmnic5, and verify communications to Host / VM
	Test Fiber Channel Failover Pull vmhbaX, and verify connectivity to the SAN has failed over Pull vmhbaY, and verify connectivity to the SAN has failed over Remove FC-SwichX, and verify connectivity to the SAN has failed over Remove FC-SwichY, and verify connectivity to the SAN has failed over Remove SAN Controller X, and verify connectivity to the SAN has failed over Remove SAN Controller Y, and verify connectivity to the SAN has failed over

Table 36 - Cluster Check

Completed & Successful	Task / Notes
	vMotion Validation Host 1 to Host 2 Host 2 to Host 3 Host 3 to Host 4 Host 4 to Host 5 Host 5 to Host 6 Host 6 to Host 1
	DRS Full Automation Validation Deploy new VM spreads out workload Synthetic workloads cause DRS migrations to occur
	High Availability Validation Verify VMs restart after failure of Host 1 Verify VMs restart after failure of Host 2 Verify VMs restart after failure of Host 3 Verify VMs restart after failure of Host 4 Verify VMs restart after failure of Host 5 Verify VMs restart after failure of Host 6

Windows 2012 R2 VM Template Build Process

Information Required For Creating Template

This section is in place to gather all the information required to perform the deployment of a Virtual Machine, which will become a vCenter Template. The administrator, or a member of his team, should have gathered this information, to be review all affected components prior to the deployment of the Virtual Machine.

Table 37 - Information Required for Windows 2012 R2 VM Template Build

Parameter	Notes	ENTER VALUE HERE
VM Hardware Version	vSphere 5.5 should be Hardware Version 10. Limited use for Hardware Versions prior.	10
VM Name	The name for the template VM should reflect the OS and installation. i.e. win2k8r2sp1	w2012r2sp1
Datastore Used	There should be a LUN named Template. This varies between clients.	Templates
VM Port Group	The network label that the template Virtual Machine should use for creation.	
TCP/IP Address	This should be DHCP, though in rare instances, this could be Static.	
Size of C:\	This should be 25-GB. It is easy to grow, and impossible to shrink this disk.	25-GB
Windows Installation Media	There should be a LUN named Templates, with a folder named ISOs, containing all the media for installation of OS.	templates:\iso\ win.2012.r2.sp1.iso
VM Folder	There should be a VM folder named Templates, where all template Virtual Machines are kept.	Templates
VMware Cluster	Which VMware Cluster should the templates run on.	
Windows 2012 R2 License Key	Is there a KMS server, or are you required to enter a license key? A KMS server SHOULD be in place with appropriate licensing already enabled.	
Server Core or GUI	Will Windows have a GUI or be the Core version	GUI

Windows 2012 R2 Template VM Build Process

The procedures contained herein is written with the assumption that an administrator who is familiar with VMware vSphere, and has basic understanding of Windows 2012 R2.

Table 38 - Windows 2012 R2 Template Build Process

Completed	Task / Notes
	Create a new Virtual Machine in the Templates Virtual Machine folder, and run this on the appropriate cluster.
	Perform a custom configuration. VMware Hardware Version 10 Name the VM Only a single CPU and single Core are given to the template VM Only 2-GB of RAM is given to the template VM The network card must be explicitly selected as a VMXnet3 adapter Select the ParaVirtual SCSI Controller A 25-GB hard disk drive should be configured as SCSI 0:0 Click Finish.
	Edit The Virtual Machine Settings
	Present the FLP file to the Floppy Drive from the appropriate datastore, and choose to have it Connected At Power On When you browse for the image, it is located in: VMimages, Floppies, pvscsi-win2008.flp (Yes, use the one labeled win2008)
	Present the ISO file to the CD-ROM from the appropriate datastore, and choose to have it Connected At Power On
	In the Options tab, VMware Tools section, verify the power controls are set for graceful shutdown and reset.
	In the Options tab, Memory/CPU Hotplug section, enable both Memory & CPU Hot Plug While it is enabled, whether you choose to do this with the Guest OS is up to you. This is enabled now, by default. Not all OS's support this.
	In the Options tab, Advance/Boot Options, Force BIOS Setup
	Click OK to save the settings
	Open the VM Console, and power on the Virtual Machine.
	Change BIOS Settings
	In the Boot Screen, change the boot order to be in this sequence: CD-ROM, HDD, Network, Removable Media (Floppy)
	Go to the Advanced, I/O Device Configuration of the BIOS. Change 3 options to disabled. Both Serial Ports, and the Parallel Port We will disable the Floppy Drive Later.
	Save BIOS and exit BIOS utility

Completed	Task / Notes
	Edit The Virtual Machine Settings
	As the Virtual Machine boots from ISO media, edit the settings. In the Options tab, Advance/Boot Options, Force BIOS Setup Put a check in this box. Click OK.
	Windows 2012 Installation will begin.
	Enter the product key
	Choose Server Core or GUI Choose GUI in this instance.
	License Agreement
	Choose Custom Installation
	At the driver screen, select to load an additional driver, and choose the ParaVirtual driver on the Floppy Drive of the Virtual Machine.
	Click Continue to initiate the Installation
	During the first reboot, you will be back at the BIOS Screen
	Power Off The Virtual Machine.
	Edit the Virtual Machine settings
	Edit the Floppy Drive to be a Client Device. Remove the Floppy Drive.
	In the Options tab, Advance/Boot Options, Force BIOS Setup Put a check in this box. Click OK.
	Power on the Virtual Machine Remove Floppy Drive from the BIOS On the Main Screen, set the Floppy Drive A:\ to none On the Advanced, I/O Device Configuration of the BIOS, set the Floppy Drive to none/disabled Save the BIOS and reboot the Virtual Machine
	Continue through the installation of Windows 2012
	You will be prompted to create a password for the Administrator account. The password will be changed after the first boots
	DO NOT JOIN ACTIVE DIRECTORY DOMAIN! Keep the machine in a work group.
	Installation has finished, and you are at the desktop.
	Edit Setting of the Virtual Machine. Change the CD-ROM to Client Device (to clear any connected CD-ROM).
	Install VMware Tools
	Reboot the Virtual Machine

Completed	Task / Notes
	Change Settings in Server Manager → Local Server
	Activate Windows This should show Windows is activated
	Configure Remote Desktop Settings (enable)
	Set Time Zone
	Disable Firewall
	Change Computer Name Make it w2012r2sp1
	Reboot the Virtual Machine
	Change the Password Policy of the Virtual Machine Windows Key → Administrative Tools → Local Security Policy Located under Security Settings, Account Policies, Password Policy Enforce Password History = 0 Maximum Password Age = 0 Minimum Password Age = 0 Minimum Password Length = 0 Password Must Meet Complexity Requirements = Disabled Store Passwords Using Reversible Encryption = Disabled Close the Local Security Policy when done.
	Change the password of the Administrator account Set the password to be blank (not the word, but there should be no password on the Administrator account)
	Delete Task Scheduler Items Server Manager → Local Server → Tasks → Computer Management Under System Tools → Task Scheduler → Task Scheduler Library → Microsoft → Windows → Delete the following folders by deleting all contents, then Delete folders when empty. (some folders cannot be deleted) Application Experience Autochk Customer Experience Improvement Program → Server Customer Experience Improvement Program Defrag Memory Diagnostic MUI Power Efficiency Diagnostics Windows Error Reporting
	Install SNMP Control Panel, Programs & Features, Windows Features Choose ALL of the SNMP subsections

Completed	Task / Notes
	Create A Power Plan Control Panel, Power Options, Create A Power Plan Based on High Performance, should be Always On, Never turn display off, never put computer to sleep
	Verify and/or Change the registry settings for the following: Change the Disk Timeout Value HKLM\System\CurrentControlSet\Services\Disk\ TimeOutValue (REG_DWORD) 0x0000000be (180)
	Perform Windows Updates
	Server Manager → Local Server Make sure to have all Optional Updates performed as well. Make sure to continue to rescan until all updates have been applied, and a Check For Updates does NOT return any additional updates.
	Reboot the Virtual Machine
	Release the PCI NIC, VMXNET3
	Open an elevated command prompt Run ipconfig /release
	Open device manager Find VMXNET3, right click, uninstall DO NOT remove the drivers!!! If asked, do not reboot....
	Shut Down the Virtual Machine
	Convert the Virtual Machine to a Template Virtual Machine Right Click the Virtual Machine, Template, Convert To Template

Deploy a VM from Template Process

This section is in place to gather all the information required to perform the deployment of a Virtual Machine from a vCenter Template. The administrator, or a member of his team, should have gathered this information, to be review all affected components prior to the deployment of the Virtual Machine.

Table 39 - Information Required to Deploy VM from Template

Parameter	Notes	ENTER VALUE HERE
OS / VM Template	Which OS are you deploying? What is the name of the Virtual Machine template that this is being built from?	Windows 2012 R2

Parameter	Notes	ENTER VALUE HERE
Computer Hostname	What is the hostname of the operating systems being deployed? This will also be the name of the Virtual Machine for consistency.	
TCP/IP Information	Get a static IP Address for the Virtual Machine, as well as subnet mask, Gateway, and DNS servers.	
DNS Entries	Create DNS Host (A) entry for planned hostname and IP address, along with reverse lookup (PTR) record.	
vCenter Server	Which vCenter will manage this Virtual Machine?	
VMware Cluster	Which VMware Cluster will run this Virtual Machine?	
Resource Pool	Will there be a Resource Pool that this Virtual Machine is nested under, or will the cluster object be the resource pool?	
Datastore	Which VMware Datastore will hold the files for this Virtual Machine	
Resize of C:\ required?	Template VM has a small C:\ (25-GB). Conservatively, how large does this drive need to be (you can always grow it at a later time).	
Additional Data Drives	Will there be a requirement for additional data drives? If so, what size requirement? Keep the drive small. It is easy to grow, and impossible to shrink.	
Port Group	Which VMware Port Group will this Virtual Machine have network connectivity on?	
VM Folder	Which Virtual Machine Folder will this Virtual Machine be placed in, on the vCenter Server's Virtual Machines & Templates Folder	
vCPU and RAM Required	Template VM has a small allocation (1 x vCPU and 2-GB RAM). Conservatively, how much RAM and how many vCPUs are required? You can always add more at a later time.	
Active Directory	Which Active Directory will this computer be joining?	
Active Directory Organizational Unit	Which OU will this server be placed into after deployment	
Appropriate OS Deployment Guide	This document only covers the deployment of the operating system. Each OS has its own guide, with its own configurations and details that must be followed after the completion of this document, which deals with Virtual Machine deployment.	Windows 2012 R2

The procedures contained herein is written with the assumption that an administrator who is familiar with VMware vSphere, and has basic understanding of Windows 2012 R2. It also expects that Customization Specifications (answer files) have been created to join the domain this machine is being deployed to.

Table 40 - Deploy VM Template Process

Completed	Task / Notes
	Ping the shortname of the Virtual Machine being deployed. You are not expecting a response. You are validating Name Resolution works correctly. i.e. ping newvm
	Ping the FQDN of the Virtual Machine being deployed. You are not expecting a response. You are validating Name Resolution works correctly. i.e. ping newvm.itaresource.com
	Perform an nslookup of the IP address of the Virtual Machine. You will get the FQDN response back. i.e. nslookup 192.168.10.4
	Verify computer account has been added to the correct Active Directory Organizational Unit. This allows for appropriate policy based management upon deployment of the operating systems / Virtual Machine.
	Open a connection to the vCenter Server where the Virtual Machine is being deployed to.
	Select & Deploy the Template VM for the OS/VM you are deploying. Home, Inventory, Virtual Machines and Templates. Find the folder named Template VMs. Right Click on the Virtual Machine template, and choose Deploy Virtual Machine from this Template.
	Name the Virtual Machine based on its FQDN. If the FQDN of the Virtual Machine is newvm.itaresource.com, then the name for the Virtual Machine should be newvm. MAKE SURE THIS IS ENTERED IN ALL LOWERCASE CHARACTERS!
	Select the appropriate Virtual Machine folder to host this Virtual Machine.
	Select the appropriate VMware Cluster and Resource Pool (if required) to host this Virtual Machine.
	Select the appropriate VMware Datastore to host the Virtual Machine.
	Choose the Virtual Machine Disk Format. Choose same as source. Virtual Machine Template is built with Thick Eager Zeroed Virtual Disk. Thin Provisioning is performed on the SAN, not in the VMware Software.

Completed	Task / Notes
	Customize the Operating System

Select Customize Using an Existing Customization Specification radio button.
Choose the appropriate Answer File for the OS being deployed.
Enable the option to, Use the Customization Wizard to
Temporarily adjust the Specifications Before Deployment. |
| | Walk Through the Customization Specification, and change IP.
Click next at the Administrator/Company name.
Click Next at the NextBIOS name.
Click Next at the Windows License.
Click Next at the Administrator Password.
Click Next at the Time Zone.
Click Next at the Run Once.

Change Network to Custom Settings, and click Next.
Click on the Radio Button next to NIC 1
Configure a static TCP/IP Address
Configure an appropriate subnet mask
Configure an appropriate gateway.
Configure two (2) DNS Servers.
Click OK.
Click Next.

Verify the Active Directory Domain To join is correct, and click Next.
Click Next at Generate a new Security ID (SID).
Click Finish to finish walking through the answer file. |
| | Click Finish to finish the build of the Virtual Machine.
DO NOT enable Power On Virtual Machine after creation.
DO NOT enable Edit Virtual Hardware. |
| | Edit the Virtual Machine Network Settings Settings

Verify the Network Adapter is on the appropriate VMware Port Group.
Modify if needed.
Click OK to accept settings. |
| | Power on Virtual Machine. |
| | Wait 20 minutes.
This allows for domain join, and other functions to complete. |
| | Log in to the Virtual Machine

Verify that the computer joined the domain.
Verify connectivity to gateway.
Verify connectivity to external website. |
| | Adjust Virtual Machine's Resources

Edit the settings of the Virtual Machine.
Edit the vCPUs
Edit the RAM allocated
Edit the size of Hard Drive 0 (the C:\)
Add additional Hard Drive, if required.
Click OK to accept changes. |

Completed	Task / Notes
	Verify Changes
	Switch focus back to Virtual Machine Console Open Server Manager, navigate to Storage Management Rescan disks if needed, to see newly allocated space. Expand C:\ size. Write signature, online, and format additional data drive. Quit Server Manager.
	Open task manager Verify vCPU count, and RAM allocated. Quit task manager.
	Switch to the appropriate OS configuration Guide to complete the configuration of the system prior to letting the business group know that this is completed.

CHAPTER 6

DESKTOP VIRTUALIZATION ARCHITECTURE DESIGN EXAMPLE

"Producing a detailed design for a datacenter solution is a balancing act between meeting the customers requirements, working within the constraints such as technology or budget and minimizing risk. The next challenge is making the solution as simple as possible to implement while reducing operational complexity and cost. The design should be documented to a point where it can be picked up by an engineer to implement without involvement from the architect. To achieve this the architecture must have clearly documented all design decisions with requirements, justifications, alternatives and implications. Supporting documentation such as Implementation Guide, Operational Verification & Operational Procedures are critical to ensure the success of not only the implementation phase but the ongoing management & support of the solution.
— *Josh Odgers, VCDX-090*

This chapter builds upon the previous chapter to cover the desktop virtualization aspect of the Case Study.

In this chapter, a VMware Horizon View design is presented. You will notice that many of the core items specific to vSphere are not called out in this design. This was done to save space in the book, and allow this chapter to focus on the specifics that are unique to a VMware Horizon View implementation.

If working on a design to submit for the customer or even a VCDX defense, remember that the underlying vSphere design must be included and covered as part of your submission. When submitting your Desktop Virtualization Design, be sure to include all components. This chapter makes references to the previous chapter's architecture (Chapter 4), and is not included herein to keep the focus on the components that are specific to the Virtual Desktop Infrastructure Design.

Chapters 4 and 6 provide slightly different writing styles for the corresponding design documents. They were written by different authors, using a different style for presentation of information and different hardware used in the solution. This is done intentionally to highlight different ways architects may approach documentation development and expression of the design material. All designs are tied to the case study from Chapter 3, representing the needs of different business units at a company.

As stated in the last chapter, the choice of how you combine or separate material in your design submission is up to you.

Project Overview

Project Description

IT Architect Resource (ITAR) provides online and instructor-led training. The ITAR product line includes training across the spectrum of hardware products (servers, storage, networking) and software products from leasing vendors such as Citrix, Microsoft, and VMware.

In 2014, as ITAR prepares to enter the VMware Virtualization training market as a VMware Authorized Training Center (VATC), they find themselves in familiar territory, just like other VATCs and VMware Hands on Labs, training their students on remote Virtual Datacenter, constructed and hosted in a centralized datacenter.

Building upon the success of the vSphere Infrastructure that ITAR has recently completed, where all servers supporting the classes and remote offices have been virtualized and centralized, the next step in their strategy is to virtualize all the student desktops, and create an experience for the users that feels as good (or better than) a traditional desktop.

This project focuses on the build of a Virtual Desktop Infrastructure (VDI) that was proposed alongside the virtualization of servers and infrastructure that allows ITAR to deliver training to its students. It reduces the ongoing maintenance of desktops required to support the classes that are held by

ITAR, and creates a streamlined process to deploy desktops operating systems for students, in a dynamic, and on demand, fashion.

Building a VDI solution in the Johnstown, PA datacenter, where the servers that support the ITAR infrastructure and classes reside, will allow for centralized management, and local access to the resources where the classes are held.

ITAR believes that to achieve success in this project, it has prioritized Availability, Manageability, Performance, Recoverability, and Security.

Availability

The uptime of the systems, resulting in uninterrupted access by students, should be key to the design. ITAR's centrally located IT service now has a high level of availability, due to a virtualized infrastructure, which now make it possible to ensure and deliver the SLAs for applications to the business units.

ITAR requires the same level of availability for its desktop services to ensure that end users have the access to their desktops, and to enable the creation of a desktop services SLA. This availability will need to prove better than the existing decentralized model of distributed desktops.

Manageability

As ITAR is investing in standardization of technology and processes across the region there is a high expectation for the design to provide a simplified management layer which will reduce operational complexity and enhance the overall efficiency in monitoring, re-porting and managing the environment.

Performance

ITAR has decided that no negative performance impact should be noticeable by end users as a result of virtualizing the desktop workloads. In order to achieve this, existing desktops and applications have been benchmarked using Liquidware Labs Stratusphere UX, and the same workloads will also be measured post-migration using the same tools.

Centralizing the desktops will also enable ITAR to centralize and virtualize servers that have been left at remote locations due to client-server network traffic requirements.

Recoverability

Service continuity upon outage is of utmost importance, especially with regulatory compliance requiring ITAR to prove the business continuity capabilities. In doing so, ITAR has invested in a disaster recovery site to run its production server workload in the event of a disaster

Desktop Services will build upon this continuity by designing a Virtual Desktop Infrastructure that spans both production and DR sites. The Virtual Desktop Infrastructure will be a single namespace that spans both datacenters, and using global load balancing policies to direct traffic to the appropriate datacenter both during normal production, and in the event of a disaster.

Alongside making the Virtual Desktop Infrastructure continuously available, being able to recover the end users' data personalization, and applications is required to align with the Recovery Time Objectives and Recovery Point Objectives in the event of a disaster.

Security

Due to the nature of ITAR's business there is requirement for moderate, centralized access control, which needs to be included in the proposed solution. Authentication, authorization, and access control must utilize existing Active Directory Users and Groups configuration.

Keeping the ITAR corporate data in the datacenter has become a requirement, as concerns over theft or loss of ITAR's intellectual property have begun to arise. Access to the Virtual Desktop from outside the corporate network must be as secure as ITAR's current remote access VPN solution.

Access to administrative functions also needs to be a role based, rather than user based, and all access to the environment must be kept on record to comply regulatory requirements.

This prioritization is listed in the following table.

Table 41 - Design Quality Rankings

	Rank	Design Quality
Most Important	1	Availability
	2	Manageability
	3	Security
	4	Performance
Least Important	5	Recoverability

Requirements

Requirements are the key demands on the design. Sources include both business and technical representatives.

Table 42 - ITAR's Requirements

ID	Requirement	Source	Date Approved
R01	Design must take into account VMware Best Practices for VMware vSphere 5	**ITAR CIO**	
R02	The design must use the vSphere Architecture & Design ITAR has for its server infrastructure as the basis for hardware, storage, network, and operational process.	**ITAR CIO**	
R03	IPMI Management must run in its own network	**Network Architect**	
R04	vSphere Management and backend functions must run in their own networks	**Network Architect**	
R05	Infrastructure and Virtual Desktops must be able to recover from a physical hardware failure of single server, network devices, or storage device.	**Infrastructure Manager**	
R06	Storage selected for use must have adequate capacity and performance.	**Infrastructure Manager**	
R07	The Architecture and Design Guide must be written to support 4,000 users, and scale to 8,000	**ITAR CIO**	
R08	Prevent use of external media (USB Hard Drives / Thumb Drives) by users	**Security Manager**	
R09	Design must allow for consistent processes to onboard additional classes (Desktop Pools)	**ITAR CIO**	
R10	Allow for simple reallocation of resources, at as high a level as possible	**Infrastructure Manager**	
R11	Antivirus / malware protection must be part of the solution.	**Security Manager**	
R12	Over commitment of resources should be kept to a minimum, to provide a 'good' desktop experience for students.	**ITAR CIO**	
R13	Access to Virtualized Desktops must be secure, and use well know TCP ports for connectivity.	**Security Manager**	
R14	Reduce ongoing management tasks for desktops administrators	**ITAR CIO**	
R15	Each class must run its desktops in a separate network	**Network Architect**	

Constraints

Constraints limit the logical design decisions and physical specifications. They are decisions made independent of this engagement, and may or may not align with the stated objectives.

Table 43 - ITAR's Constraints

ID	Constraint	Source	Date Approved
C01	Design will take into account server hardware in use by ITAR, the HP c7000 Class chassis and c-class blades	Infrastructure Manager	
C02	FlexFabric Virtual Connect interconnects are the preferred manner to connect the c7000	Infrastructure Manager	
C03	Upstream Cisco core switches are not stacked	Network Architect	
C04	HP FlexFabric Converged Network Adapters will be used in the ESXi hosts	Infrastructure Manager	
C05	HP 3Par is the preferred Storage Vendor	Infrastructure Manager	
C06	Brocade 5100 Fabric switches are in use, and have adequate ports for this project	Infrastructure Manager	
C09	SQL 2012 is the current MS database server standard	Infrastructure Manager	
C10	Windows Server 2012 R2 is the current Wintel server operating system standard	Infrastructure Manager	
C11	Windows 7 SP1 is the current Wintel desktop operating system standard.	Infrastructure Manager	
C12	Antivirus in use today is Trend Micro Deep Security	Security Manager	
C13	HP OneView will be managing the HP chassis, servers, and storage in the next calendar year.	Infrastructure Manager	
C14	The Load Balancer in use is F5's Big IP, and supports both internal and external load balancing.	Network Architect	
C15	Boot from SAN should be avoided.	Infrastructure Manager	

Assumptions

Assumptions are introduced to reduce design complexity, and represent design decisions that will be factored into the environment to meet the business requirements.

Table 44 - ITAR's Assumptions

ID	Assumption	Source	Date Approved
A01	ITAR has the necessary resources to successfully configure the existing and new HP server hardware according to the design	Consultant	
A02	Performance is considered acceptable if the end user does not notice a difference between the original platform and the new design: The desktop must look and feel just like a physical desktop when in use.	ITAR CIO	
A03	To improve availability of the vSphere cluster, another chassis will be purchased in due course	Consultant	
A04	New application resource requirements are undefined, therefore ITAR will routinely monitor capacity as more users are migrate, and a new process defined to bring on new applications.	Consultant	
A05	ITAR will monitor the consumed bandwidth on the network links between the HP chassis and Core switches to ensure capacity is always available.	Consultant	
A06	ITAR will monitor the consumed bandwidth of each network type to enforce bandwidth limits in alignment with SLAs	Consultant	
A07	All physical cabling will provide redundancy against cable or switch failure.		
A08	All power in the datacenter is redundant per rack, and the loss of a single rack PDU will not affect the operations of hardware in the rack	Consultant	
A09	Additional VLANs and subnets may be required to support and segregate Virtual Desktops, server workloads, and Access Devices	Consultant	
A10	HP c7000 Chassis in use will have all power and fan modules populated	Consultant	
A11	DHCP, DNS, NTP services are highly available at ITAR, and are always available.	Consultant	
A12	Creation of desktop pools, and their required application sets, is the responsibility of ITAR's teams. Desktop Pools referred to in this document are for reference purposes.	Consultant	
A13	Adequate Internet bandwidth exists to support students accessing the Virtual Desktop Infrastructure, and that latency is less than 200ms.	Consultant	

Risks

Design risks represent items where the design may not meet business requirements and were identified as such during the design phase. Risks can be caused by design constraints.

Table 45 - ITAR's Identified Risks

ID	Design Risks	Accepted by	Date Approved
K01	The purchase of one HP chassis enclosure will be a Single Point of failure. Building a Block with two chassis allows for mitigation of chassis failure.	ITAR CIO	
	A blade server will only use the LAN on Motherboard for network and FC connectivity. Loss of the LOM would result in a host failure. This risk has been deemed low. Mitigation would require additional PCI / Mezzanine cards, as well as additional c7000 Interconnect modules.	ITAR CIO	
K02	Consolidation ratio for existing desktop is based on a Liquidware Labs Stratusphere UX reports executed between February 2014 and April 2014. Compute resource utilization outside of this period is unmeasured.	ITAR CIO	
K03	The Stratusphere UX report contains 62 specific users in February 2014, which has determined the hardware recommendation.	ITAR CIO	
K04	All risks in the vSphere Architecture & Design Guide apply here for the deployment of the vSphere for Virtual Desktop Infrastructure	ITAR CIO	
K05	Use of a single SAN shelf (for drives) allows for a shelf failure to bring down a block. Additional Drive shelves were added, for redundancy, to survive the loss of a drive shelf, and not lose any data / volumes.	ITAR CIO	
K06	Use of a single SAN Storage array will have the potential to impact existing workloads if a SAN array fails. This is a low risk.	ITAR CIO	
K07	Site failure is not currently part of this VDI deployment. Adding additional desktops in another site to address DR is possible, and requires additional resources not currently available at ITAR.	ITAR CIO	

Conceptual Design

The VDI solution is built upon the foundation of VMware vSphere. ITAR has a production VMware vSphere Infrastructure today, that provides server virtualization, and which will provide the footprint for the management servers required to support a VDI vSphere Infrastructure.

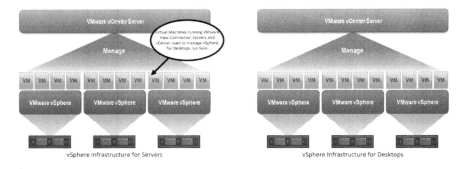

Figure 37 - vSphere Infrastructures

The wording in Figure 37 states that the servers required to provide functionality of the VMware Horizon View Infrastructure should run on the vSphere Infrastructure that exists today for virtualization of server operating systems.

VMware Horizon View provides us with a dynamic and automated deployment of desktop operating systems.

Liquidware Labs ProfileUnity allow for us to control the location of user data (the user persona), and delivery of applications to specific groups. This data is stored on existing Windows file servers in the production environment.

Using technology, software, and hardware that ITAR is familiar with, and uses today, simplifies the transition to Virtualized Desktops. As part of the approach to implementation, new technologies and features in software were reviewed, and included if they added value to the operations of this environment or solved business requirements.

VMware Horizon View Pod

The VDI solution starts with the definition of a VMware Horizon View Pod. A Pod can support up to 10,000 desktops, is built with 5 VMware Horizon View Blocks, and has a set of external dependencies to fully enable the solution.

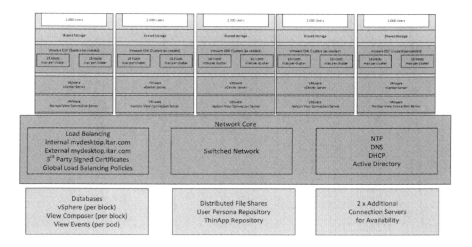

Figure 38 - VMware Horizon View Pod

The external Components are described in the next section.

VMware Horizon View Block

Looking at the VMware Horizon View Block, it is simply a vSphere Infrastructure (vCenter and ESXi Clusters) that provides the resources for running the desktops that are a result of the VDI solution, as well as the additional of VMware Horizon View Connection Servers.

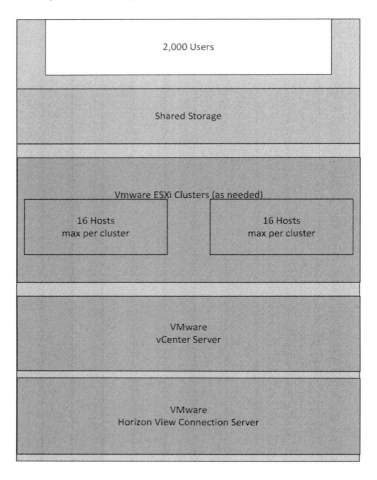

Figure 39 - VMware Horizon View Block

ESXi Clusters can actually have 32 nodes per cluster. Sixteen (16) nodes was selected as the design's initial maximum, to allow for additional growth of clusters that did not violate Cluster Maximums of a VMware Horizon View solution.

Design Justification

Using Blocks designed to support 2,000 users keeps the VMware Horizon View solution in line with maximum supported values. An example would be that each vCenter Server can support up to 10,000 virtual machines, though VMware's design best practices and validated solutions keep this number at 2,000 users (desktops).

Shared Storage is allocated per Block, to address the IOPs required to support a VDI solution. If 2,000 users were all accessing their desktops, the potential to have 100,000 or more IOPs required of the Storage Array (2,000 Users x 50 IOPs/User = 100,000 IOPs).

Shared Storage could be presented to more than one Block, though this is being avoided for ITAR, to have Blocks that are well defined, and simplify the provisioning of additional VMware Horizon View Blocks that are part of a VMware Horizon View Pod.

Conceptual Access Strategy

Connection Servers are VMware Horizon View servers that provide the mechanism for user login, authentication against Active Directory, and provide a desktop to an end user, internal to the corporate network, or from the Internet.

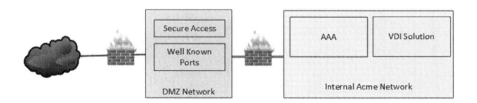

Figure 40 - Authorization, Access, & Accounting

There are two types of Connection Servers. The first server installed is referred to as a Standard Server installation. Every other Connection Server installed into the single View Solution is called a replica server. A load balanced Virtual Namespace is provided, via ITAR's Load Balancers, allows for the single namespace, mydesktop.itaresource.com, to abstract the specific Connection Server handling administrative or end user requests.

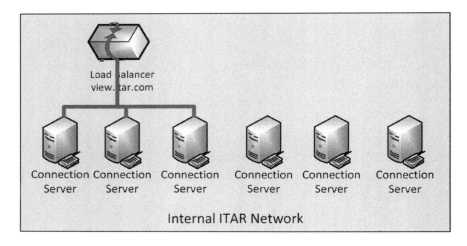

Figure 41 - Internal Access

Security Servers are server that resides in the DMZ, and communicates through the corporate firewalls to the VMware Horizon View Connection Brokers. Users can access their Virtual Desktop by authenticating through the VMware Horizon View Security Server. Only authorized and then authenticated users may access their Virtual Desktop through the Security Server. This server should not be a member of the Active Directory.

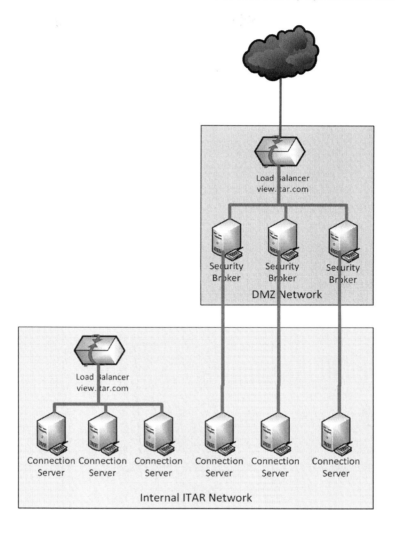

Figure 42 - External Access

Client Access to Desktop, Internal

Access inside the corporate network will be allowed via wired and wireless networks. The goal is to support any device wishing to connect to the Virtual Desktop Infrastructure, while inside the corporate network.

The Access network allows only the TCP/IP ports, called out in the Appendix, required for access to the Virtual Desktop Infrastructure, which in turn, provides access the corporate network. This minimal set of ports allows for connectivity to all required features (a Virtual Desktop). Once in the Virtual Desktop, 'normal' access to ITAR's corporate resources is permitted.

Primarily, Thin/Zero clients will replace traditional desktops, and laptops of users who are in the corporate facilities. Zero Clients will be the new standard for ITAR moving forward, as they minimize the management of the end user Access Devices

Client Access to Desktops, External

User located outside the corporate network (including home office and remote users) will utilize the Virtual Desktop Infrastructure, unless otherwise stated. Remote users will require Internet connectivity, and a computer from which to run the VMware Horizon View Client, to connect to the ITAR Virtual Desktop Infrastructure.

Users outside the corporate network still connect to the same namespace, mydesktop.itaresource.com, as they would on the internal corporate network. Although externally, they will first connect to a security server in the DMZ to provide authentication and authorization prior to being presented a Virtual Desktop.

VMware Horizon View Client is available for Windows, OS X, iOS, Android, and Linux.

Tunneling UDP packets in a TCP based VPN should be avoided at all times.

Access Strategy Design Justification

Access to administrative functions also needs to be role-based, rather than user-based. A minimal set of permissions, enough permissions to perform job functions, will be allocated to each role type. All access to the environment must be kept on record to achieve regulatory compliance.

Cluster Design

Overview

ITAR will utilize all integration and design decisions from vSphere Architecture & Design document. Deviations from the existing design will be articulated herein.

Each VMware Cluster in this design will be HA and DRS enabled. No VMware Cluster will contain more than sixteen (16) hosts in the initial implementation. This will provide the ability to add hosts to a cluster if additional resources are required.

VMware Horizon View Servers which are required as part of this implementation will be deployed as Virtual Machines on the existing vSphere Infrastructure that currently supports all server workloads, and be integrated into ITAR's server infrastructure. This will provide the server workloads hosting the VMware Horizon View Connection Brokers with all the benefits of backup, availability, and security provided by to all workloads running in the vSphere Infrastructure.

Cluster Design

ITAR will define a VMware Cluster to be configured as a sixteen (16) node cluster as its base configuration, allowing for horizontal scaling of ESXi servers. It will configure these clusters with two (2) nodes for High Availability. This will define the base 14 + 2 Cluster – A cluster of 16 nodes where the VMware High Availability tolerance is configured to allow for two (2) nodes to fail, configured via policy in HA settings.

How many desktops can reside on each is a limitation of the resources available on the ESXi server. Memory is typically the limiting factor. VMware has validated and has published works that show an average of 10 Virtual Desktops can run on a single CPU Core.

The number of ESXi servers, and the number of VMware Clusters, required would depend on the workload requirements of the Desktop Pools, which deliver the resources to run Virtual Desktops in this solution. Virtual Machine density, the number of Virtual Machines per host or per core, is expected to be higher in a Virtual Desktop Solution. For example, in a Virtual Desktop Infrastructure, an ESXi server with 256-GB of RAM would be expected to run 100-150 Virtual Desktops, while in a vSphere Infrastructure for servers, this configuration may only run 20-30 Virtual Servers.

Table 46 - ESXi Cluster Resources

ESXi Host Resources	
# of CPU Sockets	2
# of Logical Processors / (Cores per) Socket	10
GHz per Logical Processor	2.3
GHz per Socket	23
GHz per ESXi Host	46
Max Average CPU Utilization	80%
Available GHz per ESXi Host	36.8
GHz Per 14+2 Cluster	588
RAM per ESXi Host (GB)	256
Max RAM Utilization	80%
Available RAM per host (GB)	200
RAM per 14+2 Cluster	3,200-GB

Cluster Settings

Called out in vSphere Architecture & Design.

Variances

- Sizing VMware Clusters with VMware Horizon View Composer limits you to thirty-two (32) nodes per cluster. This design has been written to utilize sixteen (16) nodes per cluster, allowing scaling of each cluster up to thirty-two (32) nodes.
- High Availability (HA) polices would be configured to allow for two (2) nodes to fail, providing a 14+2 Cluster, or six servers worth of resources. Admission Control policy will be enabled, and a custom slot size of 100-MHz and 1-GB or RAM will be created. vShield Endpoint Virtual Machines will be excluded from HA. The first two LUNs dedicated to each cluster will be used for Datastore Heartbeat. No other HA settings shall be configured.
- Distributed Resource Scheduler (DRS) policies will be set to full automation. vShield Endpoint Virtual Machines will be excluded from DRS automation. No other DRS settings shall be configured.
- The number of clusters required will vary in any block, though is expected to be no greater than two (2) clusters for any given VMware View Block.

Host Compatibility (CPU)

- Because all ESXi blades will have the same CPUs, Enhanced vMotion Compatibility will not be implemented on any cluster in the vSphere Infrastructure providing resources for VMware Horizon View.
- In the event that additional ESXi hosts are required, and compatible CPUs are no longer available, a new cluster of VMware ESXi hosts will be created using the new CPUs available at that time.

Resource Pools

- Two resource pools will be created per VMware Cluster.
- No reservations or limits will be applied during the implementation, unless explicitly called out here.
- Infrastructure Pool will consist of Virtual Machines providing vShield Endpoint functions, Virtual Machine Templates, and Virtual Machines being used as the Master Virtual Machine for Linked Clones. This pool will have a reservation set to support the vShield Endpoint Virtual Machines, and Master Virtual Machines.
- Virtual Desktop Pool will consist of all other Virtual Machines that are deployed.
- A resource pool will be created on the cluster supporting the IT Team's Desktop Pool. This resource pool will be allocated High shares for both CPU and Memory.

Design Justification

Due to the automation and policies driving Virtual Desktop Deployment, implementation of hardware and the VMware Clusters is being kept consistent across the environment, to allow for simplified allocation of resources, or changes in the existing allocation to VMware Clusters.

Thirty-two (32) node clusters are now supported. Starting the 'maximum' at 16 nodes allows for 100% growth per cluster.

VMware View Documentation limitations, coupled with existing vSphere Architecture & Design documents at ITAR have been analyzed to create as few new management points (things to do from an ongoing administrative perspective) as possible. While this may have a slightly higher acquisition cost, the ability to manage this environment requires fewer administrators, and allows for identical processes to be used in the server and VDI vSphere Infrastructures.

Host Hardware Design

Overview

Today, a VMware Horizon View Building Block is two (2) Hewlett-Packard c7000 chassis. These chassis have the capability to support 32 ESXi servers, creating 2 VMware Clusters of sixteen (16) nodes each. The current network configuration provides two (2) 20-GbE LACP links communication to the production VLANs providing access to the ESXi hosts, as well as all Virtual Machines. Two 8-Gb Fibre Channel connections, per FlexFabric module are also available to provide the connectivity to the Fibre Channel array, which is a 3Par 7450 2 Node array. Details on the connectivity of the c7000 chassis is in the Network and Storage sections of this document.

It has been explicitly stated that ITAR may wish to extend the VMware Horizon View Building block to incorporate up to three (3) c7000 chassis. This would allow for up to two (2) VMware Clusters of up to twenty-four (24) hosts each to provide the resources for a single VMware Horizon View Block supporting up to 2,000 users.

In respect to external SAN storage, if additional capacity is required, or if additional IOPs are required, these can be added to the SAN, and provide the scalability required for a VMware Horizon View Block.

Connectivity of Storage and Networking is available in the corresponding sections in this guide.

Physical Hardware Configuration

HP c7000 Chassis

Each HP c7000 chassis will be configured as follows.

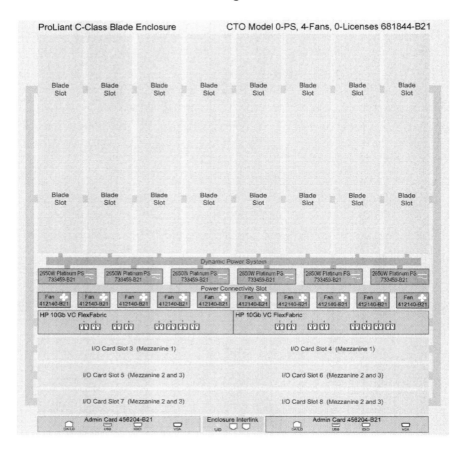

Figure 43 - c7000 Configuration

An accompanying Bill of Materials (BOM) will detail out the components required, as well as for the rest of the hardware detailed in this section.

The only configurable items here are the Virtual Connect FlexFabric modules (detailed in the next section), and the Onboard Administrators.

Onboard Administrators will be configured according to the integration guide, and will be integrated for Active Directory Authentication. Permissions to manage the chassis will be given to the VDI Admins Active Directory Group.

HP Virtual Connect FlexFabric

Virtual Connect provides the means to manage WWNs and MAC Addresses of the blades that are in the chassis. This feature will be enabled on all c7000 chassis, and allow for the integration of HP OneView software to manage the provisioning of the chassis, as this software is deployed.

Each FlexFabric module has 24 ports. Of these, sixteen are internal for blade connectivity, and eight are external, with external ports being numbered 1-8. Ports are allocated as such:

- Ports 1 and 2 are dedicated for FC connectivity, directly to the 3Par.
- Ports 5 and 6 are dedicated for 10-GbE connectivity, and will connect to upstream Cisco switches in an LACP configuration.
- Ports 7 and 8 are dedicated for cross-interconnect traffic between the two FlexFabric modules installed in a chassis, and happen internal to the chassis.
- Ports 3 and 4 are unused, and can be allocated to either FC or Ethernet use, if required.

FlexFabric modules are managed through Onboard Administrators, and allocated their IP addresses from the Onboard Administrators.

Virtual Connect accepts multiple VLANs from the Ethernet switches it is connected to. Shared Uplink Sets (SUS) will be configured to pass all VLANs required to the chassis.

For presentation of VLANs to blades, a Profile will be created. This profile dictates the configuration of the FlexLOMs (on the Blades), how they are allocated, and what they can connect to. Each blade has 2 FlexLOMs, which can then be sub-allocated as 4 Logical Devices, either 4 Ethernet NICs or 3 Ethernet and 1 FC adapter.

The Profile will define the FlexLOMs, and its 10-GbE per FlexLOM, and present as follows:

- FlexLOM 1 (10-GbE)
  - NIC 0 – 2-GbE
  - Fiber Channel – 4-GbE
  - NIC1 – 3-GbE
  - NIC2 – 1-GbE
- FlexLOM 1 (10-GbE)
  - NIC 3 – 2-GbE
  - Fiber Channel – 4-GbE
  - NIC4 – 3-GbE
  - NIC5 – 1-GbE

This will provide the connectivity required by each ESXi server to provide adequate resources to network and SAN. Details of these connections are in the Network and SAN sections respectively.

HP BL460 G9 Blades

HP BL460 G9 blades were chosen for populating the c7000 with ESXi hosts. Each blade will be configured as follows.

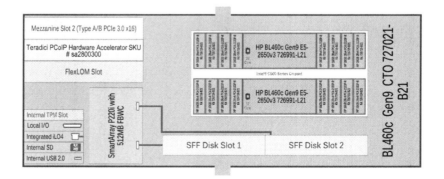

Figure 44 - HP BL460 G9 Blade Servers

Each blade was configured with 256-GB of RAM, and 20 cores, to serve up to 100 Virtual Desktops.

Blades will have WWNs and MAC addresses allocated by Virtual Connect, to make blades simpler to manage in the environment, especially if swapping blades or their hardware components.

vSphere Infrastructure for Servers

This is referenced as an existing vSphere Infrastructure that exists at ITAR today, and provides the Virtualized Infrastructure that runs most of ITAR's servers. The vSphere Architecture & Design Guide for ITAR details this hardware configuration, and is not included here.

vSphere Infrastructure for VDI

All Management servers will run in the vSphere Infrastructure for Servers environment (details of Virtual Machine design are available in the section, Virtual Machine Design, Management Servers).

Design Justification

The VMware Horizon View Block was built to address 2,000 Users actively using Virtual Desktops. Two HP c7000 Chassis are used to address a chassis failure impacting the solution, and allowing for two (2) VMware Clusters to be built across chassis.

Blades were selected, and configured with 20 cores and 256-GB of RAM to run up to 100 desktop VMs.

This requires a minimum of 20 blades, and a maximum of 32 blades to be acquired as part of this solution.

Configuration of blade profiles through Virtual Connect allows for simple add / remove / repurposing of blades, and potentially physical movement of blades to other chassis to provide resources in other VMware Horizon View Blocks.

Network Design

Overview

There is a dependency on a resilient network infrastructure to eliminate single points of failure in datacenter communications.

Planning and configuration of NTP, DNS, DDNS, DHCP, DHCP scopes, IP Helpers, and new corresponding VLANs and Subnets are required when designing a VDI solution.

Network latencies in the LAN should be less than 5ms. Packet loss in the network will provide a poor user experience, and if discovered, must be resolved to deliver a successful VDI solution. A Quality of Service (QoS) should be configured to prioritize PCoIP above all other traffic, except Voice over IP (VoIP).

Latency also has an effect on the users' desktop experience. Low latency is 5ms. Latencies of > 200 ms have an adverse effect on the perceived performance of a Virtual Desktop, from the end user consumption perspective. Up to 150 ms is acceptable for most applications.

Some core network services that are required for a VDI solution are discussed here.

DNS and Naming Conventions

DNS must be configured to provide name resolution between vCenter, ESXi servers, Active Directory, Virtual Machines, Storage Networks,

Management Tools, and any other devices requiring network connectivity. Both forward and reverse lookup zones are required.

Wherever possible, Fully Qualified Domain Names will be used to reference all systems and components.

Virtual Machine will be named based on the pool they are provisioned for, as detailed in the section Virtual Machine Naming Conventions. All desktops will be in the itar.priv domain.

DHCP and Naming Conventions

DHCP must be configured for all Virtual Desktops running in a VMware Horizon View Virtual Desktop Infrastructure, as well as for internal Access Devices. Access Devices may be thin clients, zero clients, laptops, desktops, or any mobile device capable of connecting to a Virtual Desktop.

Additional DHCP scopes will be required to support the VDI solution.

Separate scopes for Access Devices are recommended. This subnet will have limited access to the ITAR network. Lease time for these scopes will be set to 8 hours.

Separate scopes for each Virtual Desktop Pool will be configured, as mentioned in the previous section. Lease time for these scopes will be set to 2 hours, to allow for potential recompose operations, additional desktop requirements, and other maintenance functions to be performed, and allow for the DHCP scope to scavenge records and ensure that an adequate number of leases remain available during maintenance processes.

DHCP scopes will be named according to the subnet / VLAN that they serve.

IP Helper Addresses will be configured at the routers, to pass DHCP requests to the appropriate DHCP Servers.

Time Synchronization

vSphere ESXi Servers

All ESXi hosts will have their Time Configuration configured to use ntp. itar.priv as their authoritative time source.

VMware Horizon View Servers

All VMware Horizon View Servers on the internal network will run as Virtual Machines on the vSphere Infrastructure for servers in place at ITAR. VMware Horizon View Servers will be running Windows Server 2012 R2, and are joined the Active Directory Domain, which provides authoritative time for all systems in the Active Directory Domain. Active Directory is using the internal ntp.itar.priv timeserver as its authoritative time source. As a result, no additional configurations are required for VMware Horizon View servers in the corporate network.

All VMware Horizon View Security Servers need in the DMZ segment of the network will run as Virtual Machines on the vSphere Infrastructure for servers in place at ITAR. VMware Horizon View Security Servers will be running Windows Server 2012 R2, and will not join the Active Directory Domain. VMware Horizon View Security Servers will be configured to use the ntp.itar.priv timeserver as their authoritative time source.

Virtual Desktops

All Virtual Desktops, which run Windows 7, are expected to join the Active Directory Domain, which provides authoritative time for all systems in the Active Directory Domain. Active Directory is using the internal ntp.itar. priv timeserver as its authoritative time source As a result, no additional time configurations are required for the Virtual Desktop.

Logical Network Design

Separation of management traffic, vMotion traffic, and Virtual Machine traffic is preferred by ITAR, and can be accomplished through VLANs dedicated to specific functions.

VMkernel traffic, dedicated to the Management of ESXi, will exist on its own VLAN.

VMkernel traffic dedicated to vMotion functions of ESXi, will exist on its own VLAN.

Virtual Machine networks will align Desktop Pools to particular VLANs, and each Desktop Pool will have its own subnet, providing isolation between pools and broadcast domains.

Physical Network Design

ITAR has two (2) network core switches, which are not 'stacked'.

Each FlexFabric module (2 per chassis) will have a 20-GbE LACP (2 x 10-GbE connections) connecting to one of the network core Switches.

The Virtual Connect Domain will be configured in an Active / Passive configuration. This simplifies the presentation of VLANs at the Virtual Connect layer, and still provides 100% of the bandwidth required to support the solution, in the event of a network component failure.

Onboard Administrators in each of the c7000 Chassis will connect to the existing 1-Gbp/s Cisco switches, used in the iLO / IPMI network. Each c7000 has 2 x Onboard Administrators, and connecting each to a different 1-Gbp/s Management Switch provides redundancy at the iLO / IPMI layer, not available with traditional rack mount servers (which have only a single iLO / IPMI connection.

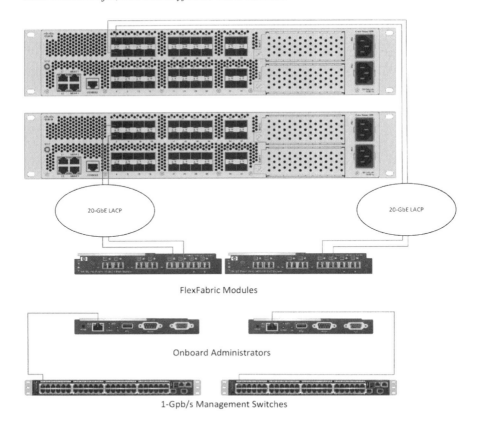

Figure 45 - c7000 Network Connections

Specific connectivity of each c7000 to switch ports is in the implementation guide, accompanying this Architecture and Design Guide.

Distributed Virtual Switches will be used for all connectivity of ESXi hosts and Virtual Machines. The exception is a single Standard Virtual Switch will be implemented on each ESXi host to support vShield Endpoint functionality.

iLO IPMI Networks

ITAR standard practices require isolation of the Out Of Band management solutions to a dedicated VLAN / Subnet. HP c7000 Chassis, their blades, and their Interconnect Modules, will run in a dedicated network to meet the isolation requirements.

Connectivity of a single c7000 Chassis require 2 x 1-Gbp/s NICs (one per Onboard Administrator) to provide redundancy and manage all devices in the chassis.

One VMware Horizon View Pod, in this hardware configuration, can potentially utilize 200 TCP/IP addresses, and is therefore allocated a net new subnet/VLAN.

VMkernel Networks

A distributed Virtual Switch will be used for the VMkernel networks required for management and vMotion. Configurations are detailed further in this section, though a summary is made here.

Table 47 - VMkernel Port Configuration

Port / Port Group	vmnicX	vmnicY
vmk0 (Management)	Active	Standby
vmk1 (vMotion)	Standby	Active
VMs on VMkernel	Active	Active
vdivc01-02	Active	Active
vdivc01-03	Active	Active
04 -49	Active	Active
vdivc01-50	Active	Active

Noting explicit failover for both VMkernels allows for dedicated bandwidth during normal operations, and redundancy, though shared bandwidth, in the event of a component failure.

A Virtual Machine Port Group, not expected to be used by any Virtual Machine, would allow for a VM to exist on the same VLAN/Subnet as the VMkernels, if a requirement for such communication arises.

Virtual Machine Networks

ITAR has determined that Desktop Pools will not exceed 100 desktops per pool. Requirements today deem 20-40 desktops per class are required. This allows for substantial growth per class, without impacting the design or operations of each class / Desktop Pool. Each Desktop Pool created will require one additional subnet / VLAN. All subnets/VLANs that are implemented to support this will have a subnet mask of 255.255.255.0, for standardization of all subnet masks, subnet sizes, and address space allocation.

Virtual Machine networks will align Desktop Pools to particular VLANs.

This will allow for each Desktop Pool to be sized for number of desktops, provide 200% of the required IP addresses per Desktop Pool. This will guarantee operations when recompose operations are required, and staging of a whole desktop pool is required during normal operations when the entire desktop pool is in use. This will also provide simplified network access policies to other network resources, as each pool resides in one subnet/VLAN, allowing for flexibility of network based Access Control Lists to control access in the network.

VLANs and Subnets

Initial subnets/VLANs are planned as follows:

Table 48 - VLANs, Subnets, & VM Port Groups

VLAN ID	Network Address Range	Desktop Pool or VMkernel Function	Virtual Machine Port Group
125	192.168.125.0 – 192.168.125.255	Servers in Prod vSphere Supporting this VDI Solution	N / A vSphere for Servers External Dependency
1100	10.10.0.0 – 10.10.0.255	iLO (IMPI) Management	N / A
1101	10.10.1.0 – 10.10.1.255	VMkernel Management	vmk-mngt
1102	10.10.2.0 – 10.10.2.255	VMkernel vMotion	vmk-vmotion
1103 – 1109	10.10.3.0 – 10.10.9.255	RESERVED FOR FUTURE Management Features	N / A
1110	10.10.10.0 – 10.10.10.255	Trend Micro Virtual Appliances	10.10.10.x-Trend
1111	10.10.11.0 – 10.10.11.255	IT Team Desktops	10.10.11.x-IT-Team
1112	10.10.12.0 – 10.10.12.255	Desktop Pool A	10.10.12.x-Pool-A
1113	10.10.13.0 – 10.10.13.255	Desktop Pool B	10.10.13.x-Pool-B
1114	10.10.14.0 – 10.10.14.255	Desktop Pool C	10.10.14.x-Pool-C
1115	10.10.15.0 – 10.10.15.255	Desktop Pool D	10.10.15.x-Pool-D
1116 – 1199	10.10.16.0 – 10.10.99.255	RESERVED FOR ADDITIONAL Desktop Pools	N / A

Distributed vSwitch Configuration

A consistent configuration of vSwitches across all ESXi hosts is made easier with Distributed Virtual Switches (vDS). All ESXi hosts will belong to the vDS, which will be configured per vCenter Server's datacenter object.

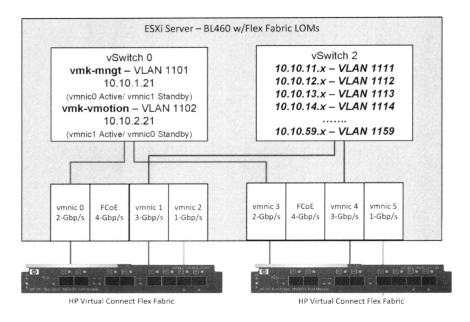

Figure 46 - Distributed vSwitch Configurations

Network IO Control (NIOC) will be enabled on both Distributed Virtual Switches in the solution, as NIOC can control the different types of traffic being sent over physical NICs. While separation of the VMkernel(s) and Virtual Machine traffic is done using the multiple NIC capabilities of the Virtual Connect FlexFabric, this allows for additional traffic types to be added to both Distributed Virtual Switches, and prioritization of traffic types if required.

NIC Teaming for the Management Distributed Virtual Switch will be configured to have the VMkernel for Management prefer vmnic0, and the VMkernel for vMotion prefer vmnic3, at the Port Group level. Allowing for the other NIC in each port Group to be a Standby Adapter provides redundancy.

Load Balancing will be configured for Physical NIC load, which recommended by both HP and VMware when using NIOC and Distributed Virtual Switches.

Storage Design

Overview

A Storage Area Network (SAN) is required for realization of VMware operations such as High Availability (HA) and Distributed Resource Scheduler (DRS). Selection of the type of SAN, drive types available in the SAN, and alignment of their functionality to the VMware Horizon View VDI solution vary for each implementation.

The focus of selection should be around Disk I/O, or IOPs capability, that a Storage Controller can provide, as Virtual Desktop Infrastructures have a different pattern of disk access than typical server workloads. Most VDI solutions that were problematic can be tied back to insufficient sizing of a Storage Controller's ability to provide enough IOPs. Peak IOPs can be ten times the normal number required, such as during a boot storm, login storm, or an antivirus storm. Operational considerations are being given to reduce these potential impacts. Read / Write ratios of 80/20% can occur during boot, and 20/80% during normal operational use.

Storage capacity requirements are important, though these are considered second, after IOPs. Consideration of both capacity and IOPs are given throughout the design.

3Par 7450 SAN was selected for this project due to multiple features.

- 900,000 IOPs per 3Par 7450 maximum
- 10,000 IOPs per Solid State Drive (SSD)
- Shelf Level Redundancy (3 shelves required)
- Direct Attach to FlexFabric (c7000 Interconnect) mitigates SAN switch requirement with up to 128 Hosts per 3Par port
- Inline Deduplication (10:1 is marketed, 4:1 is expected) per CGP

Logical Storage Design

All LUNs will be presented to all ESXi servers managed by a vCenter Server, even though 2 clusters will be created. This breaks the best practices rule of only presenting storage to all the nodes inside of a cluster. This is being done to meet a customer's request to allow for easy migration of desktop pools resources inside of a VMware View Block.

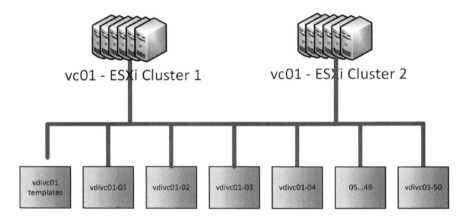

Figure 47 - Storage Presentation per Cluster

This graphic represents an example of the naming convention of LUNs per vCenter, and for the VMware Clusters managed by vCenter Servers in a VMware Horizon View Block.

Physical Storage Design

No Raw Device Mappings will be used in the Virtual Desktop Infrastructure.

All VMware Clusters managed by a single vCenter Server shall share a templates LUN.

Each vCenter Server shall maintain a single template LUN.

This LUN will hold all Template & Master (parent) Virtual Machines.

All LUNs / Datastores will be configured with Round Robin Multipathing, per 3Par Best Practices.

All Datastores will have Storage IO Control (SIOC) enabled, to enable automatic control of ESXi host device-queue depths. Recommended Latency should be configured to 10-15 ms for SSD, per the 3Par Best Practices.

A single Common Provisioning Group (CPG) will be used for the 3Par 7450. This simplifies administration, and enables Inline Deduplication across the entire array.

All LUNs presented from the 3Par will be Thin Dedup Provisioned, taking advantage of Inline Deduplication, and Thin Provisioned LUNs, with reclamation of unused space.

All LUNs will managed in a single Volume Set, as all LUNs are presented to all ESXi hosts capable of using this array.

All ESXi hosts will be added to a single Host Set, as all ESXi hosts capable of using this array will see all LUNs.

The Host Set (containing the ESXi hosts) will be presented the Volume Set (containing all the LUNs) via the Export function of the InServ 3Par software.

Connectivity of the 3Par Controllers to the four HP FlexFabric (two per chassis) is shown in the figure below.

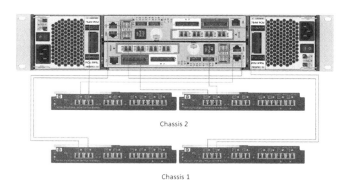

Chassis 2

Chassis 1

Figure 48 - 3Par to c7000 Connections

Adequate connectivity exists if another chassis is to be added to this storage array, allowing for 50% additional chassis (16-blades) to connect to the 3Par Storage Controllers.

VAAI and VASA

vSphere 5, along with 3Par InServ 3.1.1 and later, provides enhanced support for the T10 standards without the need to install a plug-in, enabling vSphere to directly utilize more advanced features of the storage array. Because T10 support is native at both the ESXi hosts and storage array, ESXi hosts communicate directly to 3PAR Array and do not require a plug-in for VAAI. This enables Hardware Assisted Locking, Fast Copy, and Block Zeroing.

vSphere 5 introduced vSphere Storage APIs for Storage Awareness (VASA), which can detect the Storage Arrays' LUNs capabilities, such as Replication state, RAID level, thick/thin provisioning, and back end disk type (SSD, FC, or nearline). All of this information is no available to administrators in the vSphere Interface. This will require HP 3PAR Management Software Plug-In for VMware vCenter to be installed.

Reducing Storage Requirements with View Composer

Because View Composer creates desktop images that share virtual disks with a base image, it is possible to reduce the storage capacity required by the Virtual Desktop by 50 to 90 percent.

View Composer uses a base image, or parent virtual machine, and to 1,000 Linked-Clone Virtual Desktops per pool. Each Linked-Clone acts like an independent desktop, with a unique host name and IP address, yet the Linked-Clone requires significantly less storage since all desktops leverage the same base image.

This will further reduce the storage capacity required in the SAN, and complements the 3Par Inline de-duplication feature.

Hypervisor Boot

All ESXi servers will use an SD card to boot the ESXi Hypervisor.

All logging will be sent to the ITAR Syslog server, as well as the vCenter Syslog server.

All ESXi servers will be configured to use vCenter as the VMkernel Dump.

Although Auto Deploy was considered, it is not to be used at this time in the Virtual Desktop Infrastructure, due to the perceived risk by ITAR staff.

Storage Presentation to Virtual Machines

No Virtual Machines will have access to any physical disks through Raw Device Mapping, native iSCSI software Initiator, or NPIV presentation.

All Virtual Machines running in the Virtual Desktop Infrastructure will have a single VMDK file for the operations system and applications to be installed on. All VMDKs provisioned for Template and Master Virtual Machines will be Thick Eager Zero provisioned.

VMFS Design

Templates Volumes

Volume names reference the vCenter Server managing these VMware Clusters, and the name templates.

This VMFS volume exists in the SAN to be the repository of Template Virtual Machines, Master Virtual Machines (one per desktop pool at a maximum) and ISO files (for installation of Windows Desktop Operating Systems).

This LUN in the SAN should be provisioned at 5-TB of space. This provides enough capacity to address between 30-60 Master Virtual Machines, if the need for that number of Master Virtual Machines arises. Virtual Machines here will be created with Thick Eager Zeroed Provisioned VMDK files.

Desktop Pool Volumes

Volume names reference the vCenter Server managing the VMware Clusters, and a two (2) digit identifier.

This VMFS volume exists in the SAN to be the repository for Virtual Desktop Pool Replica Virtual Machines (the base image for up to hundreds of Virtual Machines), as well as all desktops in the pool.

No manual creation of Virtual Machines is done on these volumes, as VMware Horizon View servers will automate creation and manage the desktop images that reside on these VMFS volumes.

These LUNs will be provisioned at 1-TB. The sizing of this LUN should be reviewed weekly, and alarms need to be configured in vCenter, to verify a minimum of 20% free space is available at any time. Sizing of these LUNs can be increased to 16-TB if required.

The performance of these volumes would needs to be reviewed regularly, as performance and workload metrics are available at ITAR.

LUN Size Recommendations

LUN sizing is recommended below.

Templates LUN is to keep Virtual Machine Templates, and Master Virtual Machines only.

All LUNs created on the 3Par will be Thin Dedup Provisioned.

All LUNs will be provisioned up front, as this array is dedicated to supporting only the VDI solution.

Table 49 - LUN Naming Convention, Purpose, & Sizing

VMFS Datastore	Type of Disk	Size of Disk	Expected # of VMs
vdivc01templates	All Flash Array	5-TB	5-55
vdivc01trend	All Flash Array	1-TB	32
vdivc01-01	All Flash Array	1-TB	50-100
vdivc01-02	All Flash Array	1-TB	50-100
vdivc01-03	All Flash Array	1-TB	50-100
04 -49	All Flash Array	1-TB	50-100
vdivc01-50	All Flash Array	1-TB	50-100

An example of one vCenter's ESXi LUN presentation is presented above.

Additional volumes can be created to support the workload requirements of the vCenter Server and its clusters.

As consumption of Virtual Desktops continues, review of these recommended setting may dictate changing the allocated size, or type of disk, supporting different feature or types of desktop users.

Design Justification

Sizing of LUNs is over-allocation, by default. Features in the HP 3Par 7450 allow up to 16-TB per LUN, if Thin Provisioning is used, on the SAN.

Allocation of one LUN per class allows for controlled utilization of array, and LUN.

All LUNs will be presented to all ESXi servers managed by a vCenter Server, even though 2 clusters will be created. This breaks the best practices rule of only presenting storage to all the nodes inside of a cluster. This decision was made to allow for any ESXi server in the VMware View Block to be moved between clusters as needed to accommodate any potential spike in workload requiring immediate CPU and Memory resources.

No more than 50 LUNs will be provisioned to ESXi servers being managed by a vCenter server. This provides resource limitations for each VMware Horizon View Block to address no more than 2,000 desktops per Block, a VMware Horizon View recommendation.

Not including the name of the Desktop Pool to the Datastore name allows for changes in desktop pools to LUNs, freeing up a one-to-one mapping of Desktops to LUNs.

Virtual Machine Design

Overview

Two types of Desktop Pools will be created in the VDI solution; one for the ITAR IT Team, and one for Students to access the curriculum environment. The IT Team will incur all of the restrictions imposed on the students, not for security, but to validate usability of the solution on a day-to-day basis.

Given the focus on keeping ITAR's data secured, and the use of these environments by students, certain options are explicitly prohibited.

Users will ability to print to any device, including within the ITAR facility. This is the current policy today. This policy is being enforced through Microsoft Group Policy Objects applied to the Virtual Desktops.

No Clipboard Redirection between the Virtual Desktop, and the end user access device will be allowed. This prevents a user from copy and paste functions being a method to take corporate data out of the Virtual Desktop Infrastructure.

No user will be permitted to utilize removable hard drives (portable USB Hard Drives, USB Thumb Drives, etc.). This restriction is in place, again, to prevent data from being removed from ITAR's datacenter. This policy will not be enforced for the ITAR IT Team.

Users will be given local administrative access (admin permissions), to enable installations that are required in classes.

Windows User Access Control (UAC) will be enabled.

Users be permitted to install applications to their Virtual Desktop. Applications can and will be published for the different users via Liquidware Lab ProfileUnity FlexApp software, for those classes not focused on installation of software.

Trend Micro Deep Security will provide Antivirus and IDS/IPS in an agentless configuration. This utilizes the vShield Endpoint drivers included in VMware Tools.

Virtual Machine Naming Conventions

Master Virtual Machines

A Master Virtual Machine can be the source for multiple Desktop Pools. ITAR expects to have no more than 20 different Desktop Pools, built from 2 Master Virtual Machines. To simplify ongoing operations, given that there would, at maximum, be only 20 Desktop Pools, each Desktop Pool could have its own Master Virtual Machine. Keeping Master Virtual Machines to a minimum will reduce the amount of systems to perform maintenance on, and provide a simpler deployment strategy.

If a Master Virtual Machine is deployed and built for a specific pool, it will be named based on the Desktop Pool that they serve. A breakdown of the naming convention is provided here, with the example Master Virtual Machine name being: w7m-poolA

All Master Virtual Machines will have the prefix: w7m-

This will ensure all Master Virtual Machine are easily searched, queried, and sorted in any management interface.

The next notation is an identifier of the Desktop Pool being serviced, between 2 and 7 characters (this must also be same name used in the next section to name the Desktop Pool Virtual Machines). In the preceding example, poolA is shown.

Though not possible at this time, given the separate networks per Desktop Pool requirement, if the Master Virtual Machine is deployed to support multiple desktop pools, it will be named: w7m-001

This allows for up to 1,000 variants of these multi-desktop pool Master Virtual Machines.

No other identifier would be required for Master Virtual Machines.

Linked-Clone (Non-persistent) Virtual Machines

Linked-Clones will be named in an automated fashion with parameters defined per Desktop Pool. A breakdown of the naming convention is provided here, with the example Virtual Machine name being: w7-poolA001

All Desktop Pools will have the prefix: w7-

This will ensure all desktops can be easily searched, queried, and sorted in any management interface.

The next notation is an identifier of the Desktop Pool, between 2 and 7 characters. In the above example, poolA is shown.

The reason for a 7 character maximum is to keep the full name of the Virtual Machine Hostname to a 13 character maximum, and avoid potential NetBIOS naming issues for any undiscovered requirements in the environment.

The final numeric section is a 3-digit identifier, starting with 001.

If the design is to have no more than 100 desktops per Desktop Pool, this allows for 1,000% of the desired maximum desktops, to allow for ongoing operations, such as recompose and refresh, without impact to the naming convention.

Using the Desktop Pool, IT Pool, as an example, the Naming Pattern to be used when creating the Desktop Pool would be: w7-it{n:fixed=3}.

Persistent Disk and Redirection to Disposable Disks

Windows operating systems can be broken into a few components, the Operating System (which is provided via Linked-Clones), the User Data and profile (which is maintained via Group Policy), and temporary scratch space and temporary files.

The User Data and profile, in a VMware Horizon View solution, can be managed through a utility that VMware provides, called View Persona Management. This will not be utilized, as all user data, and their profile, is completely managed through Liquidware ProfileUnity.

Redirection to disposable disk keeps certain Operating System files (such as temporary files or Paging file) on a VMDK that is deleted after a user logs off. This is achieved in our solution with Linked-Clone desktops, by defining a policy to refresh the desktop Operating System at each user logoff, achieving the same result, without additional tasks to perform.

Up Front and On Demand Provisioning

When a Desktop Pool is created, a number of desktops can be created at once (up front).

If a pool of desktops is allowed to have 100 desktops at a maximum, and 20 are needed today, you define a minimum of 20 desktops, a maximum of 100, and the number of 'Available' (or spare desktops) to be created when building the Virtual Desktop Pool.

In the case of Linked Clones, with auto-refresh, a number of spares should be created. 10%-25% is a normal range of extra desktops to have in the pool. In the example of 100 desktops being deployed, you may have an additional 4-10 desktops in the pool. This allows for users to log off, and immediately log back in to another available desktop, without waiting the 3-5 minutes for a desktop refresh to initialize and complete.

Computer Management via Active Directory

Computer Object management will differ slightly in a Virtual Desktop Infrastructure based on Linked Clones.

Master Virtual Machines will reside in an Active Directory Organization Unit (OU) that may have limited restrictions, so administrative configuration may be performed.

cn=Master Virtual Machines,cn=VDI,dc=itar,dc=priv

Linked Clones have automation that places all computer objects into a specified OU. This OU does not need the same level as management as traditional desktops have had. Configurations are maintained in the Master Virtual Machine. Inventory of the individual desktops is based on the Master Virtual Machine. Limiting traditional management tools to exclude the OU Linked Clones reside in can reduce license costs, and eliminate unnecessary administrative overhead and tasks.

cn=Win7 Linked Clones,cn=VDI,dc=itar,dc=priv

The specifics on Group Policy Objects are in the Appendix.

User Profile Management

Much of the user profile management can be performed using Group Policy Objects, and complemented by Liquidware Labs ProfileUnity.

End users require a consistent appearance for their day-to-day workflow. In a Virtual Desktop Infrastructure that is based on Linked Clones that have an auto-refresh policy, this would be impossible without some User Profile Management.

Native Microsoft Group Policy Objects provide some of what is required to make the end user experience acceptable, and its use is being minimized, as Liquidware ProfileUnity is providing much of these features, managing Linked-Clones, and the user profile.

vSphere VMs & Templates Hierarchical Design

Virtual Machine Folder Hierarchy within vCenter will have a base configuration that is kept simple. Top-level folders, such as shown in the exhibit, will be individual, master, or template Virtual Machines. A top-level folder of Desktop Pools will be created and will only contain sub-folders. As Desktop Pools are created, automation of VMware Horizon View functions will create folder structures underneath Desktop Pools that correlate to the name of teach Desktop Pool, and populated with the Virtual Desktop in the appropriate Desktop Pools folder.

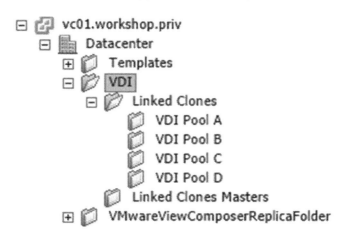

Figure 49 - VMs & Templates Hierarchy

Management Servers

All servers providing the VMware Horizon View functionality will run as Virtual Machines on the existing vSphere Infrastructure for servers. The only exception is vShield Manager, and the Trend Micro Deep Security Virtual Appliances that provide the vShield Endpoint protection for all Virtual Machines, which will run on the vSphere Infrastructure being built for VDI.

All servers being deployed follow standard ITAR naming conventions, and are backed up in accordance to standard ITAR practices.

All required databases will be hosted on the existing Microsoft SQL 2012 Cluster, sql2012it.itar.priv. This database server is considered highly available / always on.

vCenter Server – Per Block

Each Horizon View Block requires a vCenter Server, which will provide the capability to run up to 2,000 Virtual Desktops. vCenter will be installed on Windows, which allows for VMware Horizon View Composer to be installed alongside vCenter. Each vCenter will be installed to support a Medium Inventory (100-400 ESXi hosts and 1,000-4000 VMs).

- 2 x vCPUs
- 12-GB RAM
- 50-GB Hard Disk Drive
- 1 x Gigabit Ethernet Connection (VMXNET3)

VMware vCenter requires a database.

Databases are expected to be 5-GB for a VMware vCenter Instance. Sizing was performed using the vCenter Database sizing tool.

Databases for VMware vCenter are named based on the vCenter Instance ID (e.g. vdivc03 is the name of the database for vCenter Instance ID 3)

VMware vCenter Update Manager requires a database.

Databases are expected to be 200-MB for a VMware vCenter Update Manager Instance. Sizing was performed using the vCenter Update Manager Sizing Tool.

Databases for VMware vCenter Update Manager are based on the vCenter Instance ID (e.g. vdivc03um is the name of the database for vCenter Update Manager Instance ID 3)

vCenter Operations Manager – Per Horizon View Pod

A single instance of vCenter Operations Manager (vCOPs) is required per VMware View Pod. This will provide the metrics for all Virtual Desktops and Infrastructure required by Liquidware Labs Stratusphere UX. vCOPs is a deployed as a vApp, consisting of two Virtual Machines. This vApp will be sized according to an Extra Large Custom Balanced profile configuration.

- 16 x vCPUs (8 per VM)
- 47-GB RAM (26-GB for UI, 21-GB for Database)
- 7.2-TB Hard Disk Drive (Thin Provisioned from SAN, Thick Eager VMDK)
- 2 x Gigabit Ethernet Connection (VMXNET3)

vShield Manager – Per vCenter

vShield Manager is being installed to enable vShield Endpoint, and integration with Trend Micro Deep Security. This Virtual Machine is being sized per its system requirements.

- 2 x vCPU
- 8-GB of RAM (3 Reserved)
- 60-GB Hard Disk Drive
- 1 x Gigabit Ethernet Connection

VMware Horizon Composer – Per vCenter

This software provides the functionality of Linked-Clones, and requires a Windows operating System to be installed on. This software will be installed on the vCenter Server it will support, as the Windows vCenter installation will be used to support VMware View.

vCenter Server resources are defined above, and take into consideration VMware Horizon View Composer requirements.

VMware Horizon View Composer requires a database.

Databases are expected to be 1-GB for a VMware Composer Instance.

Databases for VMware Composer are based on the vCenter Instance ID (e.g. vdivc03composer is the name of the database for vCenter Composer Instance ID 3)

VMware Horizon View Servers

Physical (or Virtual Machine configuration) design, for this solution, focuses on the configuration and deployment of VMware Horizon View Connection Servers, and Security Servers. Each server has the ability to support 2,000 users per Connection Server (or Security Server). Blast Secure Gateway connections to remote desktops using HTML Access would reduce this count to 800 users per connection server, and will therefore not be used at this time.

One VMware Horizon View Connection Server (internal, internal paired with security server, and security server) is added for each VMware Horizon Block added to the VMware Horizon View Pod.

There will be two additional VMware Horizon View Connection Servers (internal, internal paired with security server, and security server) to account for application High Availability (keeping VMware Horizon View accessible during maintenance windows).

With the above two requirements, the first Horizon View Block being deployed will have a total of 3 x Internal Connection Servers, 3 x Internal Connection Servers (associated with Security Servers), and 3 x Security Servers.

The Virtual Hardware Configuration of these server instances should have:

- 4 x vCPU
- 10-GB RAM
- 70-GB Hard Drive
- 1 x Gigabit Ethernet Connection (VMXNET3)

This will allow for support of up to 2,000 users per Connection Server, regardless of type.

New DRS rules should be created on the cluster that will run the Connection Servers. This rule should "Separate Virtual Machines".

A rule for Internal Connation Servers should be created, and include all the Connection Servers poised for internal only functions.

A new rule for External Connection Servers should be created, and include all the Connection Servers paired with Security Servers, that handle external desktop users.

It is acceptable to allow for Internal and External Connection Servers to reside on the same node of a VMware High Availability Cluster, as these two types of servers address separate workloads.

A new DRS rule should be created on the cluster that will run the Security Servers. The same rule, and the same reasons apply here as well.

VMware Horizon View Events requires a database.

Databases are expected to be 5-GB for a VMware Horizon View Instance.

This will address all View Connection Servers across all vCenter Servers in the Pod.

Databases for VMware Horizon View Events are based on the View Namespace (e.g. mydesktop-itar is the name of the database for View Events Namespace)

Trend Micro Deep Security Virtual Appliance – Per ESXi Host

One Trend Micro Deep Security Virtual Appliance (TMDSVA) will be deployed per ESXi server in the VDI solution. This enables Antivirus, IPS/IDS in each of the Virtual Machines running in the solution, without agents.

The Virtual Hardware Configuration of the TMDSVA will require the following.

- 1 x vCPU
- 8-GB RAM
- 20-GB Hard Drive
- 1 x Gigabit Ethernet Connection (VMXNET3)

Trend Micro is in use today at ITAR, and policies for management of Desktops are in place at this time, and those policies will continue to be used in the VDI space.

F5 Big IP Load Balancer

While not a server, this functionality is critical to the VDI solution, to handle user requests for mydesktop.itar.priv.

Internal to the network, this will have policies that share the workload for Internal Connection Servers. External to the network, this will have policies that share the workload for Security Servers.

F5 is in use today at ITAR, for both internal and external resolution and load balancing.

Template Virtual Machines

In a Virtual Desktop Infrastructure, there are only a few Virtual Machine Templates that exist with a base Operating System, approved patches, and do not belong to a Windows Active Directory Domain.

Any Virtual Machine setting not explicitly called out here shall retain the default setting.

Virtual Machines settings will not be allowed to utilized COM Ports, LPT Ports, USB Ports (specifically portable hard drives or thumb drives), or any other peripheral which ties a Virtual Machine to a specific ESXi server or Thin Client.

Virtual Machine Templates are being built with a C:\ that is a 50-GB virtual hard disk. Additional space requirements may alter this size in the future for the Template Virtual Machine, or in specific Master Virtual Machines.

Virtual Machines hard disk drives should only have one (1) partition per hard disk drive, and the partition should consume the entire hard disk drive. All Virtual Machine Hard Disk Drives will be Thick Eager Zeroed VMDK files residing on a VMFS formatted Datastore.

Virtual Machines will only have one (1) Network Interface Card (NIC). Multi-Homed Operating Systems (two NICs, each connecting to a different network segment) are not permissible.

Virtual Machines Templates will have 2-GB of RAM. This is expected to meet demand for resources in some cases, and may be revisited per Desktop Pool.

Virtual Machines will have one (1) vCPU in the template. This is expected to meet demand for resources in some cases, and may be revisited per Desktop Pool.

Master Virtual Machines

Master Virtual Machines will be created from Virtual Machine templates, and then customized for users by the administrative staff. Printer drivers, applications required by a majority of users, Operating System patches, browser plugins, and other approved software are expected to be part of the Mater Virtual Machine.

Master Virtual Machines will be the Golden Image that all Linked Clone Virtual Desktops are provisioned from. A standard process, which includes documentation of any changes, for updating Master Virtual Machines are part of the operations documentation set.

Master Virtual Machines should have no floppy drive, nor present a CD-ROM drive to the end user. Floppy Drives will not be part of the Virtual Machine. CD-ROM presentation will be masked using tools available at ITAR (Microsoft Group Policy or Liquidware Labs ProfileUnity).

Desktop Pools

All desktop pools will be built as Linked-Clones (Non-Persistent Virtual Machines). No deviation is expected, or identified at this time.

A Linked-Clone Virtual Machine is created and automated based on the Desktop Pool Settings. All Virtual Machines in the Desktop Pool inherit the Virtual Hardware configuration of the Master Virtual Machine, upon which their deployment is based (memory assigned, number of CPUs, network connectivity).

A Non-persistent pool will 'refresh' Virtual Machines at user logoff, and can simplify ongoing management of Desktop Pools.

Creating an Automatic Desktop Pool with Floating Assignment allows for a user to simply receive the next available desktop from the pool. This removes the relationship of a user to a particular desktop. The desktop 'feels' like the user's desktop, as their profile customizes their desktop, and presents the user's data, through the tools provided in Liquidware Labs ProfileUnity.

Linked-Clones have their power policy set to always on.

Users will NOT be automatically logged off at disconnect, allowing for continuation of their work when they reconnect to their desktop.

Users will be allowed to reset their desktops through the VMware Horizon View Client.

Users will only be allowed one connection (prohibiting multiple connections to a single Desktop Pool).

Linked-Clone Virtual Machines will have Refresh at Logoff enabled, to simplify the maintenance required to a Desktop Pool.

Linked-Clone pools will only allow for PCoIP connectivity for a maximum of 2 monitors.

Desktop Pools will allow for PCoIP Hardware Acceleration, at a Medium Priority.

Desktop Pools will have adequate spare desktops per pool (defined in the VDI Pool Worksheets).

Providing users access to their Desktop Pools (Entitlements) will be assigned to Active Directory Groups that correspond to the Desktop Pools. If a user belongs to more than one of these Active Directory Groups, they will have access to more than one desktop. This is expected in a very limited scale in this infrastructure (such as IT Teams, or users who perform specialized operations requiring dedicated desktops).

Using 3D Graphics Applications

The software- and hardware-accelerated graphics features available with the PCoIP display protocol enable remote desktop users to run 3D applications ranging from Google Earth to CAD and other graphics-intensive applications.

Virtual Dedicated Graphics Acceleration (vDGA)

Available with vSphere 5.5 and later, this feature dedicates a single physical GPU (graphical processing unit) on an ESXi host to a single virtual machine. Use this feature if you require high-end, hardware-accelerated workstation graphics.

Virtual Shared Graphics Acceleration (vSGA)

Available with vSphere 5.1 and later, this feature allows multiple virtual machines to share the physical GPUs on ESXi hosts. You can use 3D applications for design, modeling, and multimedia.

Multimedia Redirection

The MMR (multimedia redirection) feature enables full-fidelity playback on Windows XP, Windows Vista, Windows 7, and Windows 8 client computers when multimedia files are streamed to a remote desktop.

With MMR, the multimedia stream is processed, that is, decoded, on the Windows client system. The client system plays the media content, thereby offloading the demand on the ESXi host.

With varied MMR settings required for each VMware View Client running on different Windows Operating Systems, MMR will not be used. Use of the Teradici APEX 2800 cards will provide this type of benefit.

Base Application Set

The base application set is applications that are common across all the desktops in the corporate environment.

Microsoft Office 2010
Adobe Reader XI
Adobe Flash
Google Chrome
Java
Legacy Application A

Custom Applications for Classes

Legacy Application A has already been captured as a ThinApp, and incorporated into the base VDI image (installed on the Master Virtual Machine via the ThinApp generated MSI). Legacy Application A has no further development and will not require updating. Legacy Application A will be required for the foreseeable future at ITAR.

It has been determined by ITAR to utilize FlexApp Packaging as the preferred manner for capturing applications needed by small sets of users that fall outside the scope of the base image software.

ThinApp will be used as an option to be utilized to capture and make available applications that are required by groups or departments, if necessary.

Desktop Pools Overview

For many configuration elements, including RAM, CPU, and storage sizing, requirements depend largely on the type of worker who uses the Virtual Desktop and on the applications that must be installed. These are actual Desktop Pools that will be deployed.

Table 50 - VMs & Templates Hierarchy

	IT Team	Standard Student	Power Student
# of Desktops Required	50	1,500	250
# of Spare Desktops	20%	20%	10%
Operating System	Windows 7	Windows 7	Windows 7
# of Monitors	2	2	2
vCPU	2	1	2
Memory	4-GB	2-GB	4-GB
HDD Size	50-GB	50-GB	50-GB
Disk IOPs	20-50	15-30	20-50
NIC Throughput (kbps)	100-125	100-150	150-250
Apps Required	Base	Base	Base
# of VDI Pools	1	15	4
DHCP Scope	x1	x15	X4
Dedicated / Floating	Floating	Floating	Floating
Linked Clone	Yes	Yes	Yes
Power Policy	Always On	Always On	Always On
Refresh Policy	At logoff	At logoff	At logoff
PCoIP H/W Acceleration	Highest	Medium	Medium
Folder Redirection	Liquidware Labs ProfileUnity	Liquidware Labs ProfileUnity	Liquidware Labs ProfileUnity
vSphere Cluster	Cluster1	Cluster2	Cluster1

IT Team Pool

The IT Team is migrating to VDI. This allows IT to use the solution they are supporting for the classrooms, and better understand and support the VDI solution. The IT Team Desktop Pool is sized for 50 IT Team Members, and its memory requirements are listed in the table below.

Table 51 - Power Student Desktop Pool

Task Worker Desktop	
Desktop	4-GB RAM
Average Memory Use	2.25-GB
Peak Memory Use	3-GB
Memory Overhead – VM	242-MB
Memory Overhead – Video	125-MB
RAM Required per Virtual Desktop	4.373-GB
# of Desktops Required	60
Total RAM 'required'	262.38-GB
Transparent Page Sharing Benefit	45-GB (750-MB of Common Windows & Apps)
RAM (with TPS Benefits) Required	213.38-GB

Standard Student Pool

Multiple Pools will be built with this configuration. Each pool deployed with this hardware configuration can use the following table to determine the memory required. This example is for 50 desktops required, with 20% of extra capacity (spare desktops).

Table 52 - Standard Student Desktop Pool

Standard Student Desktop Pool	
Desktop	2-GB RAM
Average Memory Use	1.25-GB
Peak Memory Use	2-GB
Memory Overhead – VM	138-MB
Memory Overhead – Video	36-MB
RAM Required per Virtual Desktop	2.174-GB
# of Desktops Required	70
Total RAM 'required'	152.18-GB
Transparent Page Sharing Benefit	52.5-GB (750-MB of Common Windows & Apps)
RAM (with TPS Benefits) Required	99.7-GB

Power Student Pool

Multiple Pools will be built with this configuration. Each pool deployed with this hardware configuration can use the following table to determine the memory required. This example is for 50 desktops required, with 10% of extra capacity (spare desktops).

Table 53 - Power Student Desktop Pool

Power Student Desktop Pool	
Desktop	4-GB RAM
Average Memory Use	2.25-GB
Peak Memory Use	4-GB
Memory Overhead – VM	242-MB
Memory Overhead – Video	125-MB
RAM Required per Virtual Desktop	4.373-GB
# of Desktops Required	55
Total RAM 'required'	240.515-GB
Transparent Page Sharing Benefit	55-GB (1-GB of Common Windows & Apps)
RAM (with TPS Benefits) Required	190-GB

Desktop Pool Refresh/Delete Policies

When designing a VMware Horizon View Virtual Desktop Infrastructure, a focus on avoiding repetitive administrative tasks, consistent monitoring requirements, and user disruption is a primary design goal.

When deployment of an Automated, Floating Desktop Pool is coupled with Profile Unity, or some other Persona Management, the Windows 7 desktop operating system becomes a replaceable component. No user specific data is tied to the Windows 7 desktop and the result is in an easy to maintain Desktop Pool. There are two options available for the automated maintenance of a Desktop Pool, Delete and Refresh.

Delete operations occurs when a user logs off their Virtual Desktop. The desktop the user was connected to is deleted from Active Directory, deleted from VMware vSphere Infrastructure, and is followed by the creation of a desktop to replace the recently deleted desktop. This puts an unnecessary strain on the vSphere Infrastructure, as well as causes the potential for creating issues with Microsoft Key Management Servers, in regards to tracking license consumption. Without the Delete operation, Active Directory is not taxed in resources by deleting and by recreating Active Directory computer object during recompose operations.

Refresh operations occur when a user logs off their Virtual Desktop. The desktop the user was connected to is Refreshed (or reverted back to its original state prior to the user connecting to and using the desktop). This is a simple operation for vSphere, Active Directory, and Key Management Servers, as this operation is performed at the vSphere Infrastructure, and is simply a revert to snapshot operation against the Virtual Machine, minimizing the maintenance operation of manual recompose or rebalance operations.

It is recommended to couple the Automated Floating Desktop Pool with a policy to refresh the desktop at each logoff by the user.

This will negate much of the day-to-day requirement for continuous monitoring of SAN volumes, Refresh operations, minimizing the Rebalancing operations of Desktop Pools, and user required interactions when patching occurs. These would be new operations that would be required for ongoing maintenance in the VMware Horizon View Administrator, and will be avoided by utilization of a Refresh At User Logoff policy.

Desktop Recompose Operations

While minimized through the use of Automated Floating Desktop Pools with Auto-Refresh enabled, a View Recompose operation will be required to updates to Virtual Desktops.

Master Virtual Machines being used for Linked-Clones, in an Automated Floating Desktop Pool, require snapshots. As updates and testing of the Master Virtual Machine occur when software and Operating System patches are release, final signoff that these patches and updates are approved for the environment. A Virtual Machine Snapshot is then taken.

A recompose operation is the transition of each desktop from one snapshot to another (from the original snapshot currently in use to the newly patched snapshot). This will automate the deployment of updated operating systems and application stacks to the end users. The users will get the new desktop and software stack that is in the newly updated Master Virtual Machine once they log off and log back into the system, with no additional administrative intervention or user instruction.

This operation occurs when delivering Operating System and application patches, as well as more significant changes to the desktop confirmation including entire Operation System changes.

Disaster Recovery and Business Continuity Design

Overview

While recovery, business continuity, and disaster recovery were not given a high priority in the design by ITAR, they are still important to address and outline.

Host Failure Protection

ESXi hosts provide availability to the VMware Clusters, through the use of VMware High Availability (HA). Host Profiles are used to initially configure, and validate weekly, the configuration of ESXi hosts has not changed.

If an ESXi hosts experiences a hardware failure, replacement of the server may take up to twenty-four hours (from initial discovery of the failure to returning to service). VMware Clusters were designed in an N+2 configuration, where up to two hosts can fail. This allows for failure of a node, to occur, and still have additional availability of +1 ESXi host.

Virtual Machines take advantage of the VMware HA feature, if they were running on the ESXi host that failed, and restart on surviving ESXi hosts. Desktop pools have 'spare' desktops as part of the pool design. The impact to the user is that the Desktop they were using 'rebooted.'

A single c7000 chassis would be considered a single point of failure for a VMware Cluster, and two c7000 chassis per VMware Horizon View Block are recommended.

Network Failure Protection

Network component failures, such as the core switches or the HP FlexFabric modules, have the potential to impact the operations and availability of the VDI solution.

Network core switches are redundant, and have support contracts with an SLA of 6 hour time to repair. If one of the two network core switches fails, there is a six hour window of 'risk' where redundancy is not available.

Each c7000 Chassis connects directly to the core network through the FlexFabric Modules. Two FlexFabric modules exist per chassis, and are connected redundantly to the network core switches. The HP c7000 chassis and its components have a support contract with an SLA of 6 hour time to repair. If a single FlexFabric module fails, there is a six hour window of 'risk' where redundancy is not available.

Storage Protection

The loss of a Storage Array has the potential to effect 2,000 users/students. The HP 3Par 7450 is a 2 x Node Storage Array, where the loss of a single node can be tolerated. The 3Par 7450 has a SLA of 6 hour time to repair. If one of the 3Par 7450 nodes failed, there is a six hour window of 'risk' where redundancy is not available.

It is possible to implement a 3Par 7450 in a 4 x Node configuration. This was not implemented due to the cost of the 4-Node 7450.

Loss of a drive shelf is a concern for ITAR, however small this risk is. HP 3Par offers Shelf Level Redundancy, at the cost of 25% RAW storage capacity, and requires 3 shelves to implement (2 add on shelves, plus the 7450 controller shelf).

Backups occur from the production backup services, and backup the Templates Datastore on each vCenter, which includes all Master Virtual Machines for each class. Backups of the individual Virtual Machines used by students is unnecessary, as the desktops themselves are disposable, and student data is kept on a separate DFS replicated back end file share.

vCenter / vSphere / Management Server Protection

vCenter and vSphere Component protection is covered in the vSphere Architecture and Design Guide, and has no variances here.

VMware Horizon View Connection servers provide redundancy amongst themselves. Each Block requires one Connection Server (one internal connection server, one external connection server, and corresponding security server). These are configured in a +2 solution, where if two Blocks are implemented, there are four connection servers (of each type). If there is a failure of one of the connection servers, no services are impacted, and recovery of the failed operating system can be performed.

Infrastructure Services Protection

Domain Controllers, DNS Servers, DHCP Servers, Load Balancers, NTP, and SQL Databases are redundant in their implementations.

A failure of any one of the servers hosting these infrastructure components does not affect production use, as they are capable of tolerating the loss of one of the operating systems providing these services. Recovery of the failed operation system can be performed.

Future – Site Protection

Creating a DR plan for the VDI solution is possible, though not practical without a DR plan for the balance of the infrastructure providing core services.

If at a later time a DR plan to address site failure is required, it is possible to extend the VMware Horizon View Architecture detailed here to incorporate an additional site, though the implementations chosen would vary based on many variables, such as RTO/RPO, site bandwidth, latency, and software features available at that time.

Appendix A: References

All reference material called out in the vSphere Architecture & Design Guide. Deviations are listed herein.

HP c7000 Architecture
http://h20195.www2.hp.com/v2/getpdf.aspx/4AA4-8125ENW.pdf?ver=2.0

HP 3PAR VMware ESXi Implementation Guide
http://h20565.www2.hp.com/hpsc/doc/public/display?docId=emr_na-c03290624

HP 3Par StoreServ Storage & VMware vSphere 5 Best Practices
http://h20195.www2.hp.com/v2/GetPDF.aspx/4AA4-3286ENW.pdf

HP 3Par
Teradici APEXTM 2800 Server Offload Card Administrator's Guide
http://www.evga.com/support/Manuals/files/PCoIP_APEX_2800_AdminGuide.pdf

Teradici Quantifying APEXTM 2800withLoginVSI
http://www.teradici.com/docs/default-source/resources/whitepapers/
qualifying-teradici-apex-2800-with-login-vsi.pdf?sfvrsn=2

Teradici APEXTM 2800: Addressing the next VDI bottleneck
http://www.teradici.com/docs/default-source/resources/whitepapers/
addressing-the-next-vdi-bottleneck.pdf?sfvrsn=2

Teradici APEX 2800 Tested & Certified on HP ProLiant Gen8 Blade Servers
http://www.teradici.com/resource-center/newsroom/latest-
news/2013/11/07/teradici-announces-general-availability-of-new-pcoip-
hardware-accelerator-(apex-2800)-tested-certified-on-hp-proliant-gen8-
blade-servers

VMware vSphere 5.5 Installation and Setup Guide
http://pubs.vmware.com/vsphere-55/topic/com.vmware.ICbase/PDF/
vsphere-esxi-vcenter-server-551-installation-setup-guide.pdf

VMware vSphere 5.5 Upgrade Guide
http://pubs.vmware.com/vsphere-55/topic/com.vmware.ICbase/PDF/
vsphere-esxi-vcenter-server-551-upgrade-guide.pdf

VMware vSphere 5.5 Server and Host Management Guide
http://pubs.vmware.com/vsphere-55/topic/com.vmware.ICbase/PDF/
vsphere-esxi-vcenter-server-551-host-management-guide.pdf

VMware vSphere 5.5 Virtual Machine Administration Guide
http://pubs.vmware.com/vsphere-55/topic/com.vmware.ICbase/PDF/
vsphere-esxi-vcenter-server-551-virtual-machine-admin-guide.pdf

VMware vSphere 5.5 Host Profiles Guide
http://pubs.vmware.com/vsphere-55/topic/com.vmware.ICbase/PDF/
vsphere-esxi-vcenter-server-551-host-profiles-guide.pdf

VMware vSphere 5.5 Networking Guide
http://pubs.vmware.com/vsphere-55/topic/com.vmware.ICbase/PDF/
vsphere-esxi-vcenter-server-551-networking-guide.pdf

VMware vSphere 5.5 Storage Guide
http://pubs.vmware.com/vsphere-55/topic/com.vmware.ICbase/PDF/
vsphere-esxi-vcenter-server-551-storage-guide.pdf

VMware vSphere 5.5 Security Guide
http://pubs.vmware.com/vsphere-55/topic/com.vmware.ICbase/PDF/
vsphere-esxi-vcenter-server-551-security-guide.pdf

VMware vSphere 5.5 Resource Management Guide
http://pubs.vmware.com/vsphere-55/topic/com.vmware.ICbase/PDF/
vsphere-esxi-vcenter-server-551-resource-management-guide.pdf

VMware vSphere 5.5 Availability Guide
http://pubs.vmware.com/vsphere-55/topic/com.vmware.ICbase/PDF/
vsphere-esxi-vcenter-server-55-availability-guide.pdf

VMware vSphere 5.5 Monitoring and PerformanceGuide
http://pubs.vmware.com/vsphere-55/topic/com.vmware.ICbase/PDF/
vsphere-esxi-vcenter-server-551-monitoring-performance-guide.pdf

VMware vSphere 5.5 Troubleshooting
http://pubs.vmware.com/vsphere-55/topic/com.vmware.ICbase/PDF/
vsphere-esxi-vcenter-server-551-troubleshooting-guide.pdf

VMware vShield Installation & Upgrade Guide
https://www.vmware.com/pdf/vshield_55_install.pdf

VMware vShield Administration Guide
https://www.vmware.com/pdf/vshield_55_admin.pdf

VMware vCenter Operations Manager vApp Deployment & Configuration
Guide
https://www.vmware.com/pdf/vcops-vapp-581-deploy-guide.pdf

VMware Horizon View Architecture Planning
https://pubs.vmware.com/horizon-view-60/topic/com.vmware.ICbase/
PDF/horizon-view-60-architecture-planning.pdf

Administering View Cloud Pod Architecture
https://pubs.vmware.com/horizon-view-60/topic/com.vmware.ICbase/
PDF/horizon-view-60-cloud-pod-architecture.pdf

VMware Horizon View Installation
https://pubs.vmware.com/horizon-view-60/topic/com.vmware.ICbase/
PDF/horizon-view-60-installation.pdf

VMware Horizon View Administration
https://pubs.vmware.com/horizon-view-60/topic/com.vmware.ICbase/
PDF/horizon-view-60-administration.pdf

VMware Horizon View Setting Up Desktops and Application Pools in View
https://pubs.vmware.com/horizon-view-60/topic/com.vmware.ICbase/
PDF/horizon-view-60-setting-up-desktops.pdf

VMware Horizon View Security
https://pubs.vmware.com/horizon-view-60/topic/com.vmware.ICbase/
PDF/horizon-view-60-security.pdf

VMware Horizon View Upgrades
https://pubs.vmware.com/horizon-view-60/topic/com.vmware.ICbase/
PDF/horizon-view-60-upgrades.pdf

VMware Horizon View User Profile Migration
https://pubs.vmware.com/horizon-view-60/topic/com.vmware.ICbase/
PDF/horizon-view-60-profile-migration.pdf

VMware Horizon View Integration
https://pubs.vmware.com/horizon-view-60/topic/com.vmware.ICbase/
PDF/horizon-view-60-integration.pdf

VMware Horizon View Direct-Connection Plugin Administration
https://pubs.vmware.com/horizon-view-60/topic/com.vmware.ICbase/
PDF/view-agent-60-direct-connection-plugin-administration.pdf

VMware Horizon vCenter Orchestrator Plug-In

https://pubs.vmware.com/horizon-view-60/topic/com.vmware.ICbase/
PDF/using-horizon-vco-plugin-10-guide.pdf

Obtaining SSL Certificates for VMware Horizon View Servers
https://pubs.vmware.com/horizon-view-60/topic/com.vmware.ICbase/
PDF/horizon-view-60-scenarios-ssl-certificates.pdf

Liquidware Labs ProfileUnity Product Documentation
https://liquidwarelabs.zendesk.com/entries/23327328-ProfileUnity-
FlexApp

Liquidware Labs Stratusphere UX Product Documentation
https://liquidwarelabs.zendesk.com/entries/38319968-Stratusphere

Trend Micro Agentless Security for VMware Virtual Data Centers and Cloud
http://www.trendmicro.com/cloud-content/us/pdfs/business/white-papers/
wp_agentless-security-for-vmware.pdf

Appendix B: TCP/IP Port Specifications

No deviations of the required TCP/IP ports for a vSphere Infrastructure are required from the vSphere Architecture and Design Guide for ITAR.

Additional TCP/IP port considerations are required for the VMware Horizon View software components, and are defined in this section.

TCP/IP Communication Ports

There are three sets of TCP/IP port communications in a VMware Horizon View solution. The assumption is there are front-end firewalls (from the internet to the DMZ), and back-end firewalls (between the DMZ and server VLAN). The third set will be from the Access Devices that exist on the internal corporate LAN to the Server and Desktop VLANs.

Front End Firewall Configuration

These rules must be in place to allow an external client (not in the corporate LAN) to connect with a VMware Security Server.

Source	Destination	Protocol	Port	Notes
Any	Security Server	HTTP	80	External client devices use port 80 to connect to a Security Server in the DMZ when SSL is disabled. Not recommended to open this port.
Any	Security Server	HTTPS	443	External client devices use port 443 to connect to a Security Server within the DMZ when SSL is enabled Recommended configuration (also the default)
Any	Security Server	PCoIP	4172	External client devices use TCP port 4172 to a Security Server within the DMZ when SSL is enabled, and also use UDP port 4172 in both directions

Table 54 - Front End TCP/IP Ports

Back End Firewall Configuration

To allow a Security Server to communicate with each View Connection Server Instance that resides in the corporate LANs. Similar rules must also be in place to allow the View Desktops to communicate with the View Connection Server instances.

Source	Destination	Protocol	Port	Notes
Security Server	View Connection Server	AJP13	8009	Security Servers use AJP13 to forward traffic to VMware Horizon View Connection Servers.
Security Server	View Connection Server	JMS	4001	Security Servers transmit Java Message Service (JMS) traffic to VMware Horizon View Connection Servers.
Security Server	View Desktop	RDP	3389	Security Servers use 3389 to transmit RDP traffic to View Desktops. For MMR, port 9427 is used alongside RDP. If no RDP access is allowed, this rule can be disabled. This rule should not be enabled.
Security Server	View Desktop	PCoIP	4172	External Client Devices use TCP port 4172 to a Security Server within the DMZ when SSL is enabled, and also use UDP port 4172 in both directions.
Security Server	View Desktop	PCoIP	32111	For USB Redirection, TCP port 32111 is used alongside PCoIP or RDP from the access device to the View Desktop.

Table 55 - Backend TCP/IP Ports

Appendix C: SSL Certificates

SSL Certificates must be used in a VMware Horizon View deployment. Multiple options exist for signing certificates, from using an internal Certificate Authority (CA) to purchasing a certificate from a Trusted Certificate Authority.

When using VMware Horizon View Security Servers to provide external access to VMware Horizon View, it is recommended to use an external Trusted Certificate Authority, so that devices outside of the control of administrative staff 'trust' the VMware Horizon View Connection server. This will mitigate a user clicking continue, when certificates are not trusted, or calling in for support to validate how to continue.

A public signed certificate will be required to allow for external users to automatically 'trust' the certificate that is provided from the VMware Horizon View Solution. This allows users internal to the corporate LAN, as well as those outside the corporate LAN where in house certificate cannot be managed, to 'trust' the connection to the VMware Horizon View Virtual Desktop Infrastructure.

The different types of certificates that can be utilized are listed here:

Single Server Name Certificate – You can generate a certificate with a subject name for a specific server. For example: dept.company.com. This type of certificate is useful if only one View Connection Server instance needs a certificate or if users access the View environment through a single URL, such as through a load balancer.

Subject Alternative Names – A Subject Alternative Name (SAN) is an attribute that can be added to a certificate when it is being issued. You use this attribute to add subject names (URLs) to a certificate so that it can validate more than one server. For example, a certificate might be issued for a server with the host name dept.company.com. You intend the certificate to be used by external users connecting to View through a Security Server. Before the certificate is issued, you can add the SAN dept-int.company.com to the certificate to allow the certificate to also be used on View Connection Server instances or Security Servers behind a load balancer when tunneling is enabled.

Wildcard Certificate – A wildcard certificate is generated so that it can be used for multiple services. For example: *.company.com. A wildcard is useful if many servers need a certificate. If other applications in your environment in addition to View need SSL certificates, you can use a wildcard certificate for those servers, too. You can use a wildcard certificate only on a single level of domain. For example, a wildcard certificate with the subject name *.company.com can be used

Appendix D: Security Configuration

All Operating System, server, storage, and network security requirements have been defined in the vSphere Architecture and Design Guide.

The following calls out additional settings that are required, primarily related to allocation of permissions to administrative teams.

Active Directory Groups

vSphere-Admins

This is an existing Active Directory group, with administrative permissions to vSphere Infrastructure (for Servers). This group will be provided administrative permissions to the vSphere Infrastructure for VDI, in order for the existing vSphere Administrators to assist VDI Administrators if the need arises.

VDI-Admins

This is a new Active Directory group, with administrative permission to the vSphere Infrastructure for VDI (not vSphere Infrastructure for servers), as well as the VMware Horizon View solution.

Administrators should be added to this group, as permissions are not assigned to individual user accounts. The AD group, vSphere Admins, will be added to this group as well.

It is recommended that all users in the VDI Admins Active Directory Group acquire a VMware Certified Professional-Desktop (VCP-DT) certification.

VDI-Support-Staff

This is a new Active Directory group, with administrative permissions in the VMware Horizon View solution (not the vSphere components).

Support staff will have operational permissions to perform administrative tasks related to managing the Virtual Desktop Infrastructure.

It is recommended that all users in the VDI Support Staff Active Directory Group acquire a VMware Certified Associate – Workspace Mobility (VCA-WM) certification.

Active Directory Service Accounts

itar\vdi-vcenter

Active Directory Service Account for vCenter Server functions related to the Virtual Desktop Infrastructure.

itar\vdi-vcops

Active Directory Service Account for vCenter Operations Manager functions related to the Virtual Desktop Infrastructure, and how it interacts with vCenter.

itar\vdi-vshield

Active Directory Service Account for vShield Manager (vCloud Networking & Security) functions related to the Virtual Desktop Infrastructure, and how it interacts with vCenter.

itar\vdi-view

Active Directory Service Account for VMware Horizon View functions related to the Virtual Desktop Infrastructure, and how it interacts with vCenter.

itar\trend-micro

Active Directory Service Account for Trend Micro functions related to the Trend Micro Deep Security solution, Virtual Desktop Infrastructure, and how it interacts with vCenter.

SQL Server Named Accounts

view

This provides DBO level access to the databases for VMware Horizon View Composer.

Each database is named for the vCenter Server related to the composer (i.e. vc01comp).

This one SQL account will have DBO level privileges to all SQL databases for View Composer functionality.

Appendix E: Monitoring Configuration

Monitoring configurations pertinent to the vSphere Infrastructure are defined in the vSphere Architecture & Design Guide.

Monitoring configuration pertinent to the Windows 7 Desktops are defined in the operational documentation for the Desktop Support staff, and must be maintained to identical levels in the Virtual Desktop Infrastructure as they have for the existing physical desktops. Use of Liquidware Labs

Stratusphere UX allows for extending the monitoring of physical desktops into the Virtual Desktop space, with no additional requirements to be delivered.

End User Profile Management will be required, to enable use of non-persistent desktops, consistent end user experience, and centralize user profiles in the above-mentioned Distributed File System. Separating the End User profile from the Windows Operating System will allow for non-persistent desktops, as it will maintain the customizations and data of the end users.

Liquidware Labs ProfileUnity is in use today, and is managing all user roaming profiles, folder redirection, and printer distribution at ITAR. This will continue to be used in the Virtual Desktop Infrastructure.

Appendix F: Group Policy Objects

Group Policy Objects have made managing Microsoft Active Directory easier by providing policy based management. One of the negative sides about Group Policies, is that you can have GPO sprawl, or a large number of Group Policy Objects, that can be difficult to determine the end result. In a Virtual Desktop Infrastructure, rethinking Group Policy Objects can drastically reduce the number of Group Policy Objects, and how they link to Organization Units in Active Directory.

Computer Applied Group Policy Objects

Computer based Group Policy Objects have been used to distribute software, collect inventory, configure setting based on variable hardware, variable operating systems, and manage certain machines differently based on geographical location, Operating System, and productivity software versions deployed.

When managing VDI based desktops, a redesign should be performed to rethink computer object Group Policy Objects.

Managing the OU that contains Master Virtual Machines may have limited Group Policies, to allow administrators to modify operating systems and applications. Managing the OU that contains the Linked Clones should have very few GPOs associated with them, as most of the configuration is known (all VMware virtual hardware), the Operating System is known (it is exactly what is in the Master Virtual Machine), and the applications are know (whatever is in the Master Virtual Machine).

Given the controls and consistency, a Linked-Clone Virtual Desktop is a standard desktop that an end user can consume, and this allows for a limited number of Group Policy Objects to be defined, and still accomplish complete computer management in the environment.

These settings are applied to the Organizational Unit where Linked-Clone Virtual Machines are deployed.

cn=Master Virtual Machines,cn=VDI,dc=itar,dc=priv

cn=Win7 Linked Clones,cn=VDI,dc=itar,dc=priv

User Applied Group Policy Objects

Similar to computer based Group Policy Objects, User have been assigned GPO to distribute software, configure setting based on variable hardware, variable operating systems, and manage certain machines differently based on geographical location, Operating System, and productivity software versions deployed.

When managing VDI based users, a redesign should be performed to rethink user object Group Policy Objects. Much of the same strategy mentioned for Computer Objects can be applied here to the user objects.

These settings are applied to the users logging in to a Virtual Desktop Infrastructure to consume a Virtual Desktop.

Exercise

For these exercises we will use the blueprint based design review checklists found in Appendix C. Remember the scoring considerations.

1. Use the Blueprint Based Design Review Checklists (BBDRC) to analyze the design presented in this chapter. What areas were
   a. Missing? (0 rating)
   b. Weak? (1 rating)
   c. Good/MQC? (2 rating)
   d. Great/Exceeds MQC? (3 rating)
2. Add up the points for each of the checklists to see how you compare against an MQC rating?

Additional lab exercises are in the chapter, Building A Design Lab.

Though not detailed, they provide the actions that should expose the conditions and situations that that must be taken into consideration during the design of a Virtual Desktop Infrastructure.

CHAPTER 7

ANALYSIS

*"When you want to know how things really work,
study them when they're coming apart."*
— *William Gibson, Zero History*

Ever heard of the Socratic Method? As the authors of this book, we had all heard of it, though as we wrote this chapter of analysis, we unknowingly used the Socratic Method. What is this Socratic Method? It is (paraphrased here, of course) a way of asking questions and creating discussions between people that stimulates critical thinking. It focuses the discussion around defending one's point of view, and the discussion between individuals can strengthen (or weaken) either point of view. Why bring this up? As you read this chapter, you can see that we provide many questions, and not exactly specific answers. IT Architecture always involves an "…it depends…" answer. Given that each design 'depends' on different circumstances, it is imperative that an architect has the ability for critical thinking, and can dig into the details to provide the best design possible.

This chapter provides both design and operational pattern analysis. We will look at areas of the example design documents and provide critique from an architect perspective. Where appropriate we will also show alternatives. We will identify strengths and weaknesses in the example design documents to help understand the approach your customers, or even panelists in a review board, take in evaluating a design.

As you review this chapter, remember that we provide a subset from our analysis of the example design. Our goal is to teach how to think like an architect versus a deep dive on the technological aspects, especially physical design components. Our goal is to help you learn framework, methodology, process, and higher order thinking. To do this we hope to invoke your thoughts about the design, risk, technology, and operations. We will NOT teach details on technical solutions as the justification for design decisions.

This chapter also highlights one of the reasons for use of what is perceived to be older designs in this book, namely vSphere 4 in the Server Virtualization chapter, and vSphere 5 / VMware View 6 in the Desktop Virtualization chapter. One, it shows that the design and architecture is important, and that the physical design (namely the version of vSphere) is just a component of the overall design. Two, it allows us to pose questions for you regarding how components or areas of the design can change as portions of the physical elements change. Although the physical architecture is the final outcome, the steps leading to the final physical design decisions will be grounded in the conceptual and logical models, which typically will have a longer life than the physical model.

This chapter is comprised of two major sections to review the Datacenter Virtualization design and Desktop Virtualization design in the preceding chapters. Within each of these sections we will also call out considerations for the other design documents included in Chapter 5.

For the analysis we will factor in design characteristics (availability, manageability, performance, recoverability, security), considerations for design (requirements, constraints, risks, assumptions), supporting details (justification, impact, risk analysis), and technology (compute, memory, storage, network, graphics, and others as appropriate).

Server Virtualization Analysis

This section focuses on analysis of Chapter 4 in relation to server virtualization. The choice of vSphere 4 was intentional as we seek to use this for discussion on designing for upgrades and changes as business demands evolve.

Storage Design

When reading the design, a description of using Profile Driven Storage was given, with practical consumptions of a Storage Profile. The downside here, is that the design stated that the storage being used was a single array subsystem, with a single disk type, making this feature of little perceived use.

- But what if this was enabled, even though a single tier of storage was available at the time of implementation? Think through all the possibilities of enabling that option, and what the impact would be if you called this initial tier of storage Tier 1, and if you called it Tier 3 (how would this affect adding storage in the future?). Could Profile Driven Storage been used to simplify placement of Virtual Machines needing SAN based Replication with a user defined tag?
  - ○ Profile Driven Storage, or Storage Profiles, could advertise capabilities that an array provides (replication, thin provisioning, de-duplication, etc.). Using these capabilities to create policies that could automate placement of virtual machines on the appropriate tier of storage, with the required capabilities of the array. This may be more effort to stand up initially, but the ongoing benefits would be worth this effort.
- How could this have changed the process for deployment of Virtual Machines?
  - ○ Without policy driven placement of virtual machines, an administrator must be aware of what the capabilities of each Datastore is. Sometimes this is achieved through complex naming conventions of the actual Datastore, which would reflect its capabilities. Using Storage Profiles could simplify the placement of virtual machines onto storage that provides the capabilities required by the business.
- What would happen in the future of operations if another higher (or lower) tier of storage was utilized to address capacity or performance requirements?
  - ○ Imagine calling this Tier 1 storage. While it may actually be Tier 1 storage during this deployment, in the future, another storage tier could be added, which has more performance capabilities. This would require modifications to the original Tier 1 storage labels. Would this impede operations? Probably not, but it would require

some effort to apply new labels, which would create some additional configuration work at some point in time.

Storage Clustering and Availability was discussed in this section as well, though no clear path to utilize or not utilize this feature was provided.

- Was this perhaps unfinished, not addressed, or simply providing information to the consumer of this design?
  - Review any design you create, and look for missing items, such as this. It is acceptable to call out that you will not utilize a feature, but not dictating how to consume a feature such as this could leave the reader of your document to different interpretations of your design.
- Did you have a reason to not make a decision?
  - That is acceptable too, IF you can capture the reason you did not make this design choice when submitting the design. It is critical for the customer to understand the reasoning behind NOT making a design decision that would utilize a feature or function of the system. Perhaps there was a requirement or constraint that led to the decision, but more importantly is there a risk that is created from this decision.

What additional considerations would need to be documented regarding the full automation of VMware Storage DRS?

- What schedules would be allowed for automating these actions?
- How often would a rebalancing operation occur?
- What impact could this have on the back-end networks, storage and Ethernet?

We also must review the Storage Presentation to Hypervisors. Definition of LUN sizes, potential maximum sizing, and justification for maximum real world sizing is provided.

- What is the maximum number of Virtual Machines we would like to have on any one particular LUN, and why? What impact would exceeding that 'maximum' number have on our solution?

- What if we had a requirement for larger than 2-TB LUNs? How could we address this? Is 2-TB a theoretical limit, practical limit, or a guideline for our LUN sizing?
- What about non-consecutive LUN Identifiers from the storage array, and what impact would that have on our implementations?

In the design, it was noted that the Hypervisor would utilize internal hard drives, in a RAID 1 configuration, to eliminate a hard drive failure from causing an HA event. There are different methods available for configuring an ESXi Hypervisor to boot. Each of these methods has implications, costs, risks, and operational differences.

- What if this utilized Boot from SAN? How would this impact zoning, and presentation of LUNs to ESXi servers that are members of the same cluster?
- What if a USB/SD Card was used to boot the ESXi Hypervisor? What other considerations would then have to be made for ongoing operations and troubleshooting? Is there an impact to your availability using USB/SD?
- What if Auto Deploy was chosen as the means to manage the ESXi Hypervisor? How could this impact the operational processes of the solution as a whole? Would you create a separate management cluster that provided base functions, including AutoDeploy? How will Auto Deploy change the availability and recoverability requirements of the components required to make Auto Deploy function (i.e. DHCP, TFTP, etc.)?
- What if Auto Deploy was used in conjunction with USB/SD Card/ Hard drives? What risks could be mitigated, and what could that provide the solution during any type of maintenance window? What additional skills are required to enable the Auto Deploy feature?

What other uses could there be for internal hard drives in a vSphere Solution?

- Would you use it for VSWP files?
- Would Virtual Machines dedicated to a particular host reside on local VMFS volumes, and if so, how would this impact startup order, HA, DRS, and other ongoing operations processes?

- Are there virtual machine workloads, such as Active Directory Domain Controllers, where data is replicated by the application for availability, which could run on local disk? While the VM would not recover from an HA event, the application itself would still be available (assuming you have more than one AD DC).
- What if you had a read intensive application, and wanted to enhance its performance. Would SSD drives and configuration of Virtual Fast Cache be appropriate? What if you had a write intensive application? Would SSD in Virtual Fast Cache provide the same benefit?

In terms of the design decisions, justifications, and implications, it appears that the design would meet the needs of the requirement, so let us explore "…what if…" scenarios….

If a Fiber Channel SAN did not exist, how would this impact the choice of the storage provided in terms of capacity? Performance? Growth? How would this impact additional skills required to administer and maintain?

Would a different product have been chosen if the FC SAN did not already exist in production? If so, why would you choose a different array?

Would an iSCSI solution even be considered here, if no existing FC SAN existed? Why or why not, and what impact would that have on this design? The same questions can be asked of NFS storage solution.

How could new technologies/features/architectures be utilized to create a better solution than what was available at the time the older design was done? For example, would VMware Virtual SAN or other hyper-converged solution be a good fit? How would it impact the other aspects of the proposed design solution (compute, networking)? How would it impact the design qualities of availability, manageability, performance, recoverability, and security? Are you gaining greater manageability at greater cost? Will your performance or recoverability be impacted? Will the security of data be jeopardized in any way?

Summary

A Fibre Channel design has the advantage of providing a clearly defined administration demarcation point. As Fibre Channel is its own topology it does not have an impact on the IP networking. But with a mix of Fibre Channel and IP Storage, like iSCSI, that management demarcation becomes a bit more blurred unless a dedicated set of IP switches is used for the IP storage network. Architects must identify the advantages and disadvantages of different storage technologies (FC, iSCSI, NFS, VSAN) and map those findings to the impacted design qualities. After which they can suggest a design that most closely matches the important design qualities and respective requirements.

Network Design

Configuration of Virtual Standard Switches (vSS) of Distributed Virtual Switches (vDS) is an important part of any vSphere design. Is there more than one way to design the network? Absolutely, so consider alternatives as you read through this set of questions...

- How would this design change with 10-GbE? Would you design with 2 x 10-GbE or would you suggest 4 x 10-GbE?
- How would virtual switching be modified if 10-GbE was implemented?
- What if licensing dictated use of vSS only? Would this pose any risk to the accomplishment of the requirements?
- How could new technologies/features/architectures be utilized to create a better solution than what was available at the time the older design was done? For example, would network and security virtualization with VMware NSX be a good fit? How would it alter the logical design and physical design? How would it impact the design qualities of availability, manageability, performance, recoverability, and security?
- How could a different physical network architecture, like spine/leaf, impact the proposed design and associated design qualities?

Compute Design

The design was constrained to a particular vendor, Dell, and specifically Dell rack mount servers.

- What if this constraint was removed?
- How would the design change if the compute platform was open for any vendor, any form factor?
- What would be the impact of using blade servers?
- Would the impact be reflected in the conceptual design, logical design, and/or physical design?
- Is physical real estate in the data center a concern?
- Is there a requirement for rack density?
- Does the data center have the proper power and cooling infrastructure to support you selected compute platform?

Summary

Designing a compute infrastructure with today's abundance of hardware choices is a complex decision. Architects must identify the advantages and disadvantages of different and new hardware platforms like rack mount servers, blade servers, converged infrastructure, and hyper-converged infrastructure. Only by thorough inspection of each platform's characteristics will an architect be able to identify which one will best fit the solution architecture. You must remember that choosing a platform must meet any suggested business and technical requirements while also adhering to overall design quality requirements.

Resource Design

The current design did not utilize Resource Pools in the DRS cluster. Be careful, however, not to jump too quickly into using resource pools as an "organizational management" tool. They are "resource management" tools, not folders to be used for organizing virtual machines.

- Is this a risk? Is it wrong not to use Resource Pools?
- There may be valid arguments that support either position: that use of resource pools is good, and that use of resource pools is bad. If the project does not include business drivers or technical requirements for a feature then there is no sense using it. As mentioned previously you should never use a technology just for the sake of technology as doing so could have a negative impact on design qualities. You should however take the opportunity to think about scenarios where Resource Pools are appropriate. Does the project have a need to control memory and CPU resources to groups of virtual machines?
  - In this particular design there was no requirement defined to control, whether to limit or guarantee, CPU or memory resources for virtual machines. If this requirement existed, then resource pools would have been one way in which to meet this requirement.
- Do you forecast that the current or future workload profiles will increase enough to cause contention?
  - If you anticipate that contention for resources could arise then you might consider using resource pools as a means of establishing resource allocations to establish a performance baseline that will be consistent over time. Imagine how application owners will react when the performance of their systems exceeds expectations on day of the new roll out and then think about how those feelings will change in 8, 12, or 16 months when contention for resources has brought performance down. Even if the performance is still meeting defined service level agreements (SLAs) it will still be perceived as a drop and therefore frowned upon.

Summary

Designing a solution for controlling resources relies on many factors and can be difficult to create due to the numerous available options. Resources can be controlled at a higher level through designated clusters or at more granular levels through resource pools. Separate clusters can be a more simple design, but also more costly. Resource pools are a more complex solution but don't require a financial investment.

Management Layer Design

Do you agree with the concept of a management cluster?

- Do you disagree with vCenter Server running on a cluster that is managed by that vCenter Server?
- What types of business requirements would drive you to eliminate the "management from within" design?
- Is there a risk in this design that would support an alternate design where two management clusters would each host a vCenter Server that managed the other?
- Does the design properly address the operations management requirements?
- Is Role-based access control used to ensure the principle of least privilege or is there an unnecessary risk of human error due to lack of permissions applications?

Summary

Using separate clusters as boundaries for workloads is a great way to prevent contention between virtual machines that are consumed by the end user and those, which help to make up the virtual infrastructure. This isn't a mandatory part of a design as it is certainly possible that cost could play a factor in the inclusion of a management cluster. Without a management cluster the virtual data center constructs of resource pools become the foundation of resource allocation.

Virtual Machine Design

The customer workloads identified in this project were stable, static, and predictable.

- What elements of the design would change if the workloads were more dynamic in their resource utilization?

Summary

In an ideal world designs would be prefaced with a capacity planning report or a set of application requirements that facilitate the initial configuration specifications for a virtual machine. If those are not available then template configurations for small, medium, large, and x-large virtual machines will allow you offer prescriptive guidance on virtual machine density, resource consumption, and scale.

Monitoring Design

The business processes and workload profiles in this project simplified the scaling process for the data center. Think about how the design would be different if the business processes and workload metrics were not easily quantifiable.

- How would you implement a monitoring solution to measure the performance characteristics of the system?
- What metrics would you want to keep a close eye on?
- What thresholds would you define for these metrics?
- How would you react to crossing these defined thresholds?

Summary

Monitoring of an IT infrastructure can sometimes be overlooked. Designing a solution without accurate definition of workload profiles will lead most architects to err on the side of caution and consequently over configure resources. It is in the cases of unknown or undefined workload profiles where monitoring is especially critical. A good monitoring solution will identify key metrics of both the physical and virtual infrastructure across all key resources compute, storage, and networking.

There a wide variety of tools, from open source to vendor provided, that can be used to provide granular monitoring of the environment. You can choose from protocol-based solutions like NetFlow, syslog, SNMP or you can find a vendor solution from companies like Splunk, Solar Winds, and VMware. In some cases your vendor solution will simply provide a value add to an open solution perhaps offering a better interface or easier installation.

Security Design

The given design had minimal security requirements due to the nature of the workloads.

- Should there have been more stringent security requirements around management and access to applications and services what would have changed in the design?
- Would stronger security requirements have impacted any of the other design qualities? Availability? Manageability? Performance? Recoverability?

Summary

You shouldn't be surprised to learn that in some cases the security design on an IT infrastructure is not only the most time consuming but also the most expensive, not just financially but also in terms of tradeoffs with manageability and performance. IT designs with regulatory compliance requirements increases the complexity of the design. Do not expect that any design were security is a priority is going to be an easier design, a more manageable design, or a cheaper design.

The IT security industry changes rapidly with the advancement of hardware, software, heuristics, algorithms, and platform. Security postures for workload might remain consistent but the manner in which we implement that posture will certainly change over time. You don't have to look too far to find a good example of how the security solutions are evolving and therefore offering more design choices. It wasn't long ago that many IT architects were sold on the requirement for an air gap between production, dev/test, and DMZ. Nowadays this isn't seen as the only option for enabling isolation between these data center silos.

In today's enterprise experts are beginning to understand new security architectures like micro-segmentation, which can radically transform the way data centers are designed. Using a security platform like VMware NSX solutions can be designed that provide new levels of integration between hypervisors, network-based firewall, identity firewalls, and third-party products that offer antivirus, antimalware, intrusion detection, intrusion prevention, and advanced L4 through L7 services.

Availability and Recoverability Design

The design included does not utilize site failover technology like VMware Site Recovery Man-ager (SRM).

- How would SRM with array-based replication affect the design?
- Datastore to VM placement considerations. How would SRM with vSphere Replication affect the design?
- What are the current risks to the design without a geo-failover solution?
- Are there other things that can be done to support recoverability in the event of a local disaster?

The workloads identified in this design were a good fit for the use VMware High Availability. At the same time due to the short-term nature of the virtual machines recoverability of anything outside of infrastructure services was not a strong concern.

Summary

It is important to understand that the workloads of any solutions architecture directly impact the availability and recoverability design. In the existing case the workloads consumed by the end users are transient in nature.

The virtual machines are created and destroyed on a weekly basis leaving little need to design complex availability and recoverability solutions. Workloads that are long-term tenants with dynamic data sets will require much more attention.

There is also a budding trend in infrastructure design that deals with workloads that some are calling "cloud ready" or "scale out" applications. These applications are designed to leverage many instances of the application running across a distributed compute platform. In these cases, where the hardware becomes even more commoditized, infrastructure architects are leveraging this distributed application architecture (and deployment) to minimize the need for designing availability and recoverability solutions. The mentality here is that availability of hardware and application is handled by the existence of n number of additional instances that can fulfill requests in the event of failure. These types of workloads are most commonly seen running on data center designs that leverage a combination of open source solutions like KVM on Ubuntu with OpenStack. However, with the increase in popularity of the "open" mindset there is an emergence of solutions that are vendor-driven. For example, VMware Integrated OpenStack (VIO) is a VMware generated OpenStack deployment built to leverage the VMware infrastructure components like VMware ESXi, VMware VSAN, and VMware NSX.

Desktop Virtualization Analysis

In the Desktop Virtualization chapter, much of the vSphere Design was omitted from the actual document to save space in this book, and prevent redundant reading. If submitting a VDI design, it would incorporate both chapters, as you WOULD need to address both the VDI components as well as the vSphere Infrastructure that power the VDI components.

In the analysis section, many of the same analyzed points apply to the Desktop Virtualization chapter. Take those same analysis points, and apply them to this design.

Additionally, we will ask you to consider whether the solution presented has components that might have been approached differently.

Storage Design

In the Virtual Desktop Infrastructure, inheritance of many of the vSphere Storage Design objectives are the same, though there are different design goals expected to be realized for this type of solution.

The storage used in this section is different than the storage used in vSphere Design. Though this may contradict the case study, it was done to show that the physical components used in a design do affect the solution as a whole when being implemented. The manner in which vendors' storage arrays are implemented, as well as the resources they provide, effect the solution you are designing.

References are seen in vendor documentation for VMware View that state IOPs requirements will dictate placement of Replica disks, as well as Linked Clone disks, though no specific back end requirement is made in this book, as the storage used is an SSD array.

- What if this solution did not have inline de-duplication, thin provisioning, and reclamation of free disk space?
  - This would impact the selection of components, as it would require additional capacity, and create additional efforts to perform reclamation of storage space no longer in use.
- In an all SSD array, would the cost be prohibitive to add the required capacity?
  - Budgets are always something to be concerned about. It that were the case, then this might drive you to the next discussion point...
- What if this solution did not have the luxury of using an all SSD array?
  - You would be required to consider placement of Virtual Machines on different types of datastores, each with their own performance characteristics. This is considered tiered storage. An assessment of the VDI workload would provide you with the types of workloads, and their back end requirements for disk performance. Alignment of replica disks, and linked-clone disks, to the appropriate

storage tier meeting that performance characteristic, would be required.

- ◦ How would this impact your daily operations, if at all? Additional configurations would be required, additional training of the staff managing the VDI solution would be required, and a monitoring solution would need consistent review of its metrics to validate that performance is what the end user requires.
- What if this solution used NFS instead of block-based storage?
  - ◦ You are now required to have all the considerations of the previous 2 points, and then you would be required to incorporate a sound network design component to deliver the NFS in a reliable way.
  - ◦ This would change the physical components used as well, as you no longer would need FC-HBAs, and now need at least 2 additional network ports.
- What if the storage used had auto-tiering of disks (the ability for the array to move blocks between FC and SSD disks based on utilization)?
  - ◦ This in theory could provide the performance required of a VDI solution. This could provide a simplified design (one type of Datastore vs replica and linked-clone datastore), the same way an all-SSD array does.
  - ◦ This may bring in additional cost to the array, as this may require some software licenses to use this feature. Now, analyzing the cost of this new feature, we must consider the budget. Will the budget support this?
- What if the storage was all FC based disk (no SSD in the array), but each ESXi host had SSD disks for Virtual Fast Cache or some other form of Datastore caching?
  - ◦ This could meet the requirements for performance. Many offerings exist from many different vendors, which can use SSD or RAM from an ESXi hypervisor as a read (or sometimes even write) accelerator.
  - ◦ This would require licensing, potentially additional cost (SSD drives, software licenses), and additional knowledge of the team managing the solution.

○ This could even impact your selection of hardware. What if there was no supported way to add SSD drives to your selected hardware platform (unlikely, but possible)? Another reason why physical components are among the last item defined in a design.

Summary

The example design shows that consideration was given to address the performance characteristics required of the VDI solution. Focus on this area of the solution is extremely important, as desktops have very different requirements for IOPs than servers do.

Something not defined well enough is the external dependency on a file share for the repository of user profiles and published applications. You could build a very resilient VDI solution that has great performance, but if it were unusable because of a bottleneck at the file share, this whole project could fail.

Remember to consider the external dependencies and THEIR storage requirements, both capacity and performance. Your solution's success may depend on it.

Network Design

There were network isolation requirements defined to keep each classroom isolated from other classes. Subnets and VLANs were used to meet that requirement.

• In this design, HP FlexFabric was used, and each of the two onboard NICs were split out to 4 separate NICs to separate different types of traffic. What if just 2 10-GbE cards were used, without the ability to physically separate the traffic? Would use of Network IO control help?

   ○ In the Design, this leads to creation of 3 Distributed Virtual Switches, each with a specific pair of NICs. It would simplify the configuration if a pair of 10-GbE NICs were used, as this would only require a single Distributed Virtual Switch.

- ◦ What if the deigns called for a single Distributed Virtual Switch? That may simplify one aspect of the design, but it could lead to complicated configurations if 6 NICs were members of that Distributed Virtual Switch, and different port groups used different NICs as active, standby, and/or unused.
- What if VMware NSX (network virtualization) was used to meet this requirement?
  - ◦ VMware NSX introduces an entirely new set of features for networking and security in the software-defined data center. NSX would radically change this design. The physical networking would become less dynamic and less reliant on the consistent configuration of VLANs by leveraging a VXLAN overlay for newly required networks. In addition, leveraging micro-segmentation would ensure that consumers are able to access only their prescribed workloads.

Summary

With 10-GbE networking present in many datacenters now, some of us might assume that designs with 1-Gbp/s networking might be showing their age...they are not.

The desktop design used a vendor technology to separate the different traffic types. It could have been 2 x 10-GbE NICs that met this solution, with logical separation of traffic through the use of VLANs. Neither way is right, and neither way is wrong. They would both use the tools, hardware, and configurations required to separate the different types of traffic, and provide guaranteed bandwidth.

As this book ages, 40-GbE and 100-GbE will become prominent in the data center. Will the concepts you learn here, about 1-Gbp/s versus 10-GbE, still apply? Absolutely....you will just have more bandwidth to utilize.

Compute Design

HP blades servers were used in the desktop virtualization design, versus rack mount servers in the server virtualization design.

- How would this be implemented differently if Dell blade servers in the design?
  - ○ Dell chassis use switches for external connections, while in this design FlexFabric was used. This creates a different implementation of the network portion of this design, from the blades to the upstream physical switches connecting the chassis.
  - ○ This could impact the management tools used to monitor and deploy the compute hardware that is part of this design.
- What if rack mount servers were used instead of blades?
  - ○ Rack mount servers would each require networking and storage connectivity. This may lead to more cabling to deliver the solution, increasing the number of ports required quite a bit.
  - ○ Rack mount servers do not suffer from over-subscription the way that blades in a chassis do. If bandwidth was a concern, you could consider the use of rack mount servers instead as one manner to meet that requirement.
  - ○ What if there was a need to place high performance graphics cards in servers to deliver a great user experience? This is typical in some solutions, and perhaps the only way to deliver it would be through rack mount servers, as they can accept add on cards not typically available to blade servers.
- What if a hyper-converged solution was chosen to deliver compute and SAN instead?
  - ○ A hyper-converged solution can drastically alter the compute and the SAN components of a solution. Many different offerings exist, and each vendor will have their own requirements to deliver a hyper-converged solution.
  - ○ Many of the same considerations mentioned in previous two bullets will be required, and will extend in to

considerations for network design as well as the storage design.

Summary

The compute resources used in the solution used a blade chassis. This simplified cabling, IPMI management, and connectivity of network and storage resources. Adequate consideration for adding bandwidth was given, and called out when discussing the configuration of interconnect used in the solution.

No mention of the oversubscription of resources was considered in the design. While many of us know that a blade chassis solution is oversubscribed, it should have been called out as part of the risks associated with the design.

Management Layer Design

The management layer in a VMware Horizon View solution has the traditional VMware vSphere components, such as vCenter and ESXi. It also has the VMware Horizon View management interface. Add to that, the configuration requirements of the VMware Horizon View Connection Servers, load balancers, and certificates required to complete the solution, you can see that there are many components that must be addressed as part of the design.

- Why would you not just use an existing vCenter to manage the VDI solution?
    - A reason that is often given is that VDI software could have different requirements from the vSphere solution used for servers. Simplifying the ongoing maintenance would be one reason to do this. Bringing them all under one vCenter, and hence one management pane, may sound good until you need to upgrade one component in either environment (server or desktop environments), and

find conflicting levels of support that prevent you from implementation of a new feature.

○ The vCenter used for VDI has a different maximum number of virtual machines than vCenter used for managing your virtual servers.

○ Internal politics may drive this requirement as well. Perhaps the team responsible for virtual desktops has nothing to do with the team responsible for virtual servers. Having a separate vCenter could meet this requirement.

• Would you use the same vSphere Single Sign-On domain as the vSphere Infrastructure that provides server virtualization?

○ This could be a solution that works well. Reducing the number of Single Sign-On domains to manage would be good. In the previous bullet, we talked about separation of vCenter to provide environments that simplify, or remove, interdependencies. Having one VMware Single Sign-On domain (meow) could create potentials for ongoing maintenance and upgrade to have complexities in the same manner as a single vCenter could.

○ This could simplify the management required if all vSphere environments, servers and desktops, were in the same VMware Single Sign-On Domain. One place to manage permissions, roles, tags, licensing. Just remember to consider if this would impact operations and maintenance going forward.

• Why was vSphere 5 used for this design, when the case study asked to use the same version of vSphere for the server AND desktop infrastructures?

○ This was a requirement that was given as part of the design, yet the design used vSphere 5 for the VDI solution. Another requirement was that the end user must have a great desktop experience. The reason this was done in THIS design, was to take advantage of better performance of the PCoIP capabilities in the new version of VMware vSphere and VMware Horizon View.

○ Not every requirement can always be met in a design, and some requirements conflict with each other. It is your job as an architect to identify the requirements, and provide the leadership required to successfully architect a solution that delivers on all the requirements possible, while identifying and resolving conflicting requirements.

- Are different tools used to manage a VDI environment from a VMware vSphere environment?
  - Some of the tools are identical, such as the vCenter server. Some of the tools would be new, such as the VMware Horizon View Portal. This is one of the additional tools required to manage this environment. Additional skills are now required to use this new tool effectively, and manage the VDI solution.
  - End user profile management is an additional set of management responsibilities. This is true, regardless of physical or virtual desktop deployments, and critical if a linked-clone solution is being deployed (where a desktop is destroyed and provisioned at user logoff). Imagine if these tools were not in place, and every day when a user logged in they got a new desktop that needed full configuration. This would lead to a poor user experience, and potentially, a failed design, since the users would not be able to perform their duties.
  - Being able to monitor and understand the performance an end user has when interacting with the VDI solution will be of great importance. Given the anywhere, anytime access to a desktop, the support staff managing this solution must be able to quantify the end user is having a good experience. Specific tools have been created to monitor this, and can provide the support teams with a full view of performance from the end users point of view, as well as all the way through the vSphere Infrastructure that supports the VDI solution. Finding a tool that meets this requirement should be a part of the project, and can simplify the identification and remediation of problems that exist in the environment.

Summary

Separation of the VDI environment from the vSphere environment for servers provides solid boundaries of operational maintenance, upgrades, and design patterns. A limitation of this is that it creates two environments to manage separately, which can add to the burden of the day-to-day administrator of these environments. Best practices are to keep them separated, though you may find a small VDI solution where you are required to mix these environments under one vCenter server. Make sure you understand the implications of this for design, deployment, maintenance, and scaling of both environments.

Bringing two separate vSphere Infrastructures under one VMware Single Sign On domain can simplify much of the licensing, roles, permissions, and tags that are created. This still leaves you with separate vSphere and vSphere for VDI environments, but you now share a common VMware Single Sign On. Be sure to highlight and discuss with your customer the impact, strengths and weaknesses of making this choice, or avoiding this choice.

In a VDI environment, we may sacrifice additional administrative work for the sake of keeping the end user happy. A VDI solution is all about the end user, making their life better (by providing anytime anywhere access to the desktop), and making sure that their computer experience meets or exceeds what a physical desktop could deliver. Every VDI project is eventually evaluated for success...if the user is happy, then the project is a success. As you design any VDI solution, consider how a user works, what they need to have on their computer (applications, printers, their data, even their background JPG that they need). If you consider it from this perspective, and design around happy end users, you will always succeed.

Virtual Machine Design

Why not use one master image to deliver to all users?

- When virtual machines are used as masters for a linked-clone desktop pool, all desktops are identical in their configuration. With different desktops required for the different classes, and the hardware configurations being different between them, it would be impossible to have only one master image for each configuration.
  - Applications differ between the classes as well. Even though application delivery has been defined, it may be a requirement for the student to install the application, while in other instances, the application may be already provisioned to the student. This would also be a consideration to how you configure master images, and maintain them going forward.
- What if the sizing of the C:\ was 50-GB instead of the 25-GB mentioned in the design? How would this impact Virtual Machine density per VMFS volume?
  - When using linked-clones, the virtual machines used by users are all thin provisioned. If the drive space allocated to users increased from 25-GB to 50-GB, this provides the potential for users to create that much more data, and require that space form the back end SAN. This in turn could reduce the number of VMs per VMFS volume the back end LUNs were increased in size.
  - With inline de-duplication available, would the real capacity needed from the SAN change? It might if each desktop were deploying different types of software. The inline de-duplication may make this additional capacity given to each VM a non-issue. No definitive answer can be given here, but it highlights that you must understand how the desktops are used, and what the requirements would be for storage capacity, as you build a VDI solution.
- Use of ProfileUnity Flex-App is called out to deliver applications to users. Are there any other ways to deliver software to desktops?
  - You could install applications into the master image. This would be a practical approach if all users needed to use the same software. Unfortunately, this is not going to cover every application.
  - Another approach could be to use VMware ThinApp to virtualize an application. This has helped countless people

in situations where one critical application was preventing an upgrade to a new operating system. ThinApp abstracts the application from the operating system, and makes the virtualized application portable across operating systems. Again, this may not be a solution that can resolve every problem.

○ Published applications are still a valid way to deliver applications. This can deliver applications to physical or virtual desktops in exactly the same way, and may be a solution that will work for you, though again, it may not be the solution for every application required.

Summary

Linked-clones were used to meet the requirement of easy to maintain desktops. They are always deleted at the end of each class, and a new batch of desktops is deployed and ready to use by the next set of students. This greatly simplifies the amount of effort required to maintain the infrastructure, as maintenance is implemented through policy.

ProfileUnity Flex-App was used in this design to capture applications, and make them available to a large number of users. This simplified the management of applications required by the students, as it did not require creating new desktop images each time an application was updated. It made the desktops independent of the actual applications required by each class.

Details on how to analyze, plan, design, and deploy applications was not part of this book. There are many tools available that can assist with this requirement. The design should have addressed in more detail how the decision to use a single tool to virtualize applications was made, beyond the statement "...it is already in use.".

Analysis Conclusion

Analysis of the material included in chapters 4-6 has covered good, bad, and neutral design decisions. For some of the questions raised we have provided answers or guidance for further analysis by the reader. Remember that these example design documents are for learning good, weak, and bad characteristics of design choices and alternatives.

It is critical that an architect do a detailed review of all design documents, not just the ones focused on the architecture. Operations, validation, implementation, and other documents help complete a full solution for a project. All documents should factor in traceability, accountability, and linkage to each other.

Further commentary and feedback is provided in the accompanying location on the IT Architect Series web site. If there is something in any of the designs that you want to start a dialogue on, covered in this this book or not, join us at the website, and let's continue the analysis!

## CHAPTER 8

PRESENTING AND DEFENDING THE DESIGN

"Infrastructure designs should be based on problem solving solutions for critical and non-critical business requirements. The designed solutions should be agnostic from products and proprietary technology perspectives and focused around currently available capabilities for solving the presented problems. This design approach would allow the design of all architectures the ability to stand the test of time and evolve as the requirements evolve over time. Enterprise infrastructure designs should never be dictated by any one particular proprietary technology or capability as it can become outdated and obsolete in a short period of time."
— *Rawlinson Rivera, VCDX-086*

Design Presentation

Once a design is complete, the next step is presenting the solution to the sponsors and stakeholders of the project. This includes a presentation and supporting information. It is important to know the audience you are presenting to and it is not uncommon to deliver multiple presentations to different audiences. The presentation given to a C-level audience should be very different than the one given to more tech savvy stakeholders. For example, the executives are generally more interested in vision and business goals than in configuration specifications of the technology solution. Once the presentation(s) is (are) complete, the project is then scheduled for deployment.

This section will discuss the process of developing your design presentation and creating it using some tools we have developed and found useful for this purpose.

Goal of Presentation

The goal of the presentation is to educate the audience about key elements of the solution developed. This should provide information on the project, the team, the key aspects of the design, and the plans for installation, validation, and operation.

Utilize Tools for Storyboarding

The tools we use in this book can be the basis for storyboarding the project and ultimately to develop the presentation. Each of these tools is defined in an Appendix, with the exception of the example Table of Contents, which can be found in chapter 2, Infrastructure Design Methodology and Documentation.

- **Discovery Phase Survey (DPS)** - provides the inputs including requirements, constraints, risks, and assumptions. [Appendix A]
- **Design Decisions Workbook (DDW)** - provides the documentation of key elements of the design. [Appendix B]
- **Design Review Readiness Assessment (DRRA)** - is used for evaluation the readiness of you and your design materials. [Appendix C]
- **Example Table of Contents** - can be used to frame the discussion areas.

For those not familiar with storyboarding, this is a way to develop a visual representation and flow of events to convey a story. Think of the movie industry and what they may include as an extra when you purchase a movie. One of the extras might be the storyboard showing you a high level view of how a story progresses. This is a critical part of the planning for something that is later turned into an actual movie.

When presenting a design, you can take a similar approach in developing your presentation to tell the story of both the project and the design.

Design Presentation Workflow

The design presentation can use the following, or a modified version based on the project. The deck proposed here includes several key components.

- **Credentials** – who you are, qualifications, and role on project
- **Project detail** – includes requirements, constraints, risks, confirmed assumptions, and key design areas with design considerations and design patterns. The choice of what you include in the main part of the presentation and the Appendix is up to you. We show one way in the example presentation slides within this book.
- **Appendix** – extra reference material that can be used in support of questions on the design. This is where you can include diagrams and tables in support of the design presentation. The appendix should include configuration specification details about the technology. Basically, anything that can facilitate diving deeper into the design, should that be necessary.

When developing your presentation consider built-in hyperlinks as follows. The following has proven to be efficient for both customer presentations and for VCDX design defense sessions.

- **Presentation Index** – This slide has one link to the Master slide index and one link to the Appendix slide index.
- **Master slide index** – This slide has a list of links to each slide in the main presentation, and then a link to the Appendix Table of Contents.
- **Appendix slide index** – This slide has a list of links to each slide in the appendix, and then a link back to the Master index slide.
- **Back reference** – Each slide will have a link back to the relevant slide index. This is to simplify movement within the presentation, especially as questions are raised.

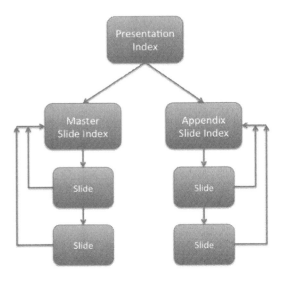

Figure 50 - Slide Preparation

When developing slide ordering with an index, consider what headers to use for readability.

Design Presentation Slides

We are including examples here that show how one project might be represented. This is tied to the example designs included in the book.

1. **You** – Include your name, title, company, skills (education, training, certification), and role on the project.
2. **Project Overview** – Include the project title and an abstract of what the project covers. Where appropriate, cross-reference the detailed project "Statement of Work".
3. **Inputs** – Include the most important Requirements, Constraints, and Risks used to develop the design. Don't list every item here, only the critical inputs. A full list will be in the design documentation. Use of a Business Problem section has been useful to describe the business drivers where you can list out specific requirements

influencing your design decisions. The rest may be included in the supporting reference slides. Assumptions must be confirmed and then are placed under the requirements and constraints, or are listed separately. Risks and Assumptions are best included in the main part of the presentation while requirements and constraints can be placed in the Appendix. The choice is based on the project, the audience, and the architect.

a. **Requirements** – Include details on key requirements for the project. These should be indexed sequentially and align with the requirements section in the documentation. Many architects will have a letter code and a sequential number code. The letter code for this section might be 'R' or 'REQ' followed by a 2-digit or 3-digit number. When creating this section, anticipate questions that may come up from the audience. Also consider discussions related to changes made between the beginning and end of the project that affected the requirements. You do NOT have to include all the project requirements if there are many. Consider the most critical requirements.

b. **Constraints** – Include details on constraints that were not changeable for this project such as vendor, technologies, budget, timelines, and other influencing factors. Ensure this slide matches the documentation. The letter code for this section might be 'C' or 'CON' followed by a 2-digit or 3-digit number. Describe how the constraint impacted the design.

c. **Risks** – Include details on significant risks to the project. These could be geographic, technical, operational, financial, and training in nature. To avoid conflict with the requirements list, this section might utilize a prefix for each item of 'RISK' or 'RI' followed by a 2-digit or 3-digit number. When listing risks, be sure to include the likelihood of the risk occurring and prepare to discuss risk mitigation. Likelihood can be represented in many forms. One example is to use 'rare', 'moderate', 'likely', and 'almost certain'. In areas prone to natural disasters, designs typically will list the relevant natural disaster as 'almost certain' to occur. Examples of natural disasters include hurricanes, tornados, earthquakes, wildfires, and others based on the location.

4. **Workload Analysis** – Include an **overview** of the workloads that will be placed on the infrastructure. This may include new versus existing workloads with the operating system, application name(s), dependencies, resource requirements, and other information that may influence the design. Remember this is a summary of what is included in the design document. Do not include too much detail in the slides. Instead, highlight the analysis of the critical applications that were included as part of the project, and summarize the rest.

5. **Technology Components** – For each of the following, be sure to include both text and topology diagrams to simplify explanation. For each of the technology areas for compute, networking, and storage, there will be some overlap in how we explain what is described in the slides.

    a. **Compute** – Include the compute resource information with a topology diagram. This can include the type of servers and associated clusters. When there is a mix of hardware platforms, describe how they are grouped into clusters and if CPU compatibility mode is utilized. Consider the questions that may be asked, including traceability back to the project requirements and constraints. Identify unique points you wish to cover, including risks, alternative options, and the tradeoffs. Were any assumptions made during the assessment of the workloads and the infrastructure platforms?

    b. **Networking** – Include the networking components and associated topology diagram identifying connectivity. Detailed diagrams can be included in the Appendix. Remember that a detailed diagram may not be viewable in one piece and may require extra diagrams that show a zoom-in view of each section. Include both physical and virtual networking components (such as VMware NSX). Be prepared to answer questions on traceability back to the project requirements and constraints and the other points listed under the Compute slide description. This may include items such as physical and virtual switch configurations, firewalls, and routers.

c. **Storage** – Include the storage components and associated topology diagram identifying connectivity. As explained in the two previous items for Networking and Compute, consider putting detailed diagrams in the Appendix with extra diagrams showing a zoom-in view. Again, consider the traceability, unique points, risks and tradeoffs, and any assumptions made. This may include items such as multi-tiering of storage and specific features or capabilities of the storage devices (iSCSI, NFS, FC SAN, and VSAN).

6. **Design Areas** – These are the top-level design areas of Availability, Recoverability, Manageability, Performance, Security, and Risk Management. What physical and virtual components are utilized for this project? Show traceability back to the project requirements and constraints, showing the key points you want to describe, the risks, the tradeoff to alternative choices, and any assumptions. *VCDX Note: You have flexibility on naming for your particular project, but when using the presentation for a VCDX defense, these are the key areas used in scoring a candidate's skills (in the VCDX Blueprints).*

a. **Availability** – In many ways this can be closely tied to recoverability and performance. This focuses on how a resource or workload is made available and can include technologies like VMware DRS, VMware HA, and VMware FT. These technologies reduce the downtime and/or increase availability. This design area should also include 3rd party technologies if they are part of the normal business work process. Other things for consideration may include stretched metro clusters and OS clustering for application level protection.

b. **Recoverability** – Show what needs to be recovered such as virtual machine, operating system, application, component, and system level items. This focuses on how the infrastructure components or workloads can be recovered and can include things like VMware HA, VMware FT, backup/recovery, and VMware Site Recovery Manager. Include 3rd party backup technologies in this area.

c. **Manageability** – Show the management topology. What is managed and how? Are there multiple vendors handling manageability and if so, how are they integrated? This may include VMware vSphere technologies like VMware vCenter, VMware vRealize Operations or 3rd party management tools. In many cases, regulatory compliance and corporate governance will drive change control management through people, process, and technology.

d. **Performance** – Show how the design manages and handles the performance of both the infrastructure and the workloads. How are SLAs met? What happens if SLAs are at risk? How do you use specific technologies like VMware vRealize Operations, VMware DRS, and other tools to manage performance to meet the defined SLAs. Remember to include key performance metrics.

e. **Security** – Show the governance that the project must adhere to? Is it affected by internal regulations, or government/industry regulations such as PCI or HIPAA. How are roles and responsibilities of accounts handled? What security technologies or configurations are utilized and what do they protect against? When do you use manual responses versus automated responses? Are there specific security validation tests run? How frequently?

f. **Risk Management** – Show the risks to the project and how they are addressed. This can include the likelihood of the risk occurring and the budget required for mitigation. As the project develops, new information will usually be revealed. Were there specific risks identified by the stakeholders? Were additional risks identified during the project? Were any risks identified outside of the stakeholder list? What risks exist that have not been addressed by the business? What are the financial analysis and cost tradeoffs for risks, including risk of failure, cost of failure, and cost of risk mitigation? What technologies were specified for each risk mitigation step listed? Were there alternative risk mitigation steps, and, if so, why were they not used?

7. **Appendices** – This section includes supporting slides with tables, graphics, and diagrams. This is used as a reference to answer questions raised during the main presentation. Diagrams may vary in size. Complex diagrams should be used for context with enlarged sections showing the details in a readable form. If you find yourself thinking that you don't have material for the Appendices, you have placed too much detail in the previous sections!

Validating Your Presentation

When creating your presentation, be sure to test it out before you see the stakeholders. Review the design and the presentation with project team members. Test the presentation on several projectors to ensure readability. A good book on developing slides can be found in *slide:ology: The Art and Science of Creating Great Presentations*, by Nancy Duarte through O'Reilly. Some common mistakes the authors have seen are:

*   Too much detail in a diagram to be readable.
*   Too many words or lines of text on a slide.
*   Bright text on bright background or dark text on bright background. To see a good example of bad color choices, create a slide with a white background, then create a text box with yellow text and a green background. We've seen people do this before. This is another aspect of the art of design; how you present.
*   Low quality images, unreadable when shown on a projector.

A design presentation should have a logical flow that is easy for the audience to follow but at the same time should be organized enough to support dynamic movement through the presentation. Ideally you would move through your presentation from slide 1 to slide N, but reality suggests that you will likely move forward and backward through your slide deck as the audience's questions ebb and flow through design topics. As we have suggested previously, you should utilize hyperlinks in the presentation that support jumping through various stages and topics of the design. The sample presentation shown in this chapter includes hyperlinks in the table of contents, appendix, and even in text and images of slides that detail design solutions.

For readers that are creating designs for their own company or for a client of their company, you may be using standardized design templates. As with any templates, these will be starting points to provide a basis for the design and will need to be customized for the project. These are typically used to ensure branding continuity.

Once you are comfortable that the content is accurate, appropriate, and organized, you should perform multiple test runs of your delivery. This will help you build fluency with your presentation and, if used, the location and direction of the hyperlinks. When testing your presentation, spend a maximum of approximately 1 to 3 minutes per slide. If questions arise, respond appropriately but be clear and concise in your answers. If you are presenting to a 'test audience', have them evaluate the following:

- Your presentation skills
- The primary and supporting material from the deck
- Your responses to questions
- Alignment of the requirements and constraints with the final design

Here are some open-ended questions that many customers and VCDX panelists ask during a design presentation or design defense.

- What would you change in your design if you could? Consider changing/removing a requirement or a constraint.
- What challenges did you face and how did you work through them?
- Were there issues that could not be resolved? If yes, what would be needed to address the issues?
- How could risks be mitigated? How should risks be mitigated?

Example Design Presentation

We have included an example design presentation here in the following pages. This is based on the design shown in chapter 4. This example includes hyperlinks to allow for quick navigation. These are not functional in this book format but are simple to set up within your presentation using your presentation tool's functions for hyperlinking.

This presentation has 71 slides, though this book has only a small subset of those slides. This was done to keep the content short, yet still remain relevant, for the purpose of providing you an example of a presentation within the book.

The full presentation, of all slides in this deck, will be available online for you to use as a template.

VCDX NOTE: The presentation you use for your defense will need to be presented within a fixed amount of time.

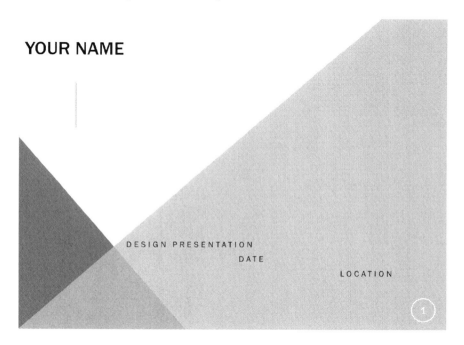

Figure 51 - Presentation Title

TABLE OF CONTENTS

Figure 52 - Table of Contents

EXECUTIVE SUMMARY

As IT Architect Resource (ITAR) has acquired the Authorized Training Center (ATC) status they required a remote training environment to support storage and virtualization training products.

ITAR was contracted to create the ITAR Services Virtual Datacenter (ITAR VDC) to support these training needs.

Figure 53 - Executive Summary

294

Your presentation should begin with an introduction of yourself (especially if there are new people in the room) and a short executive summary about the project. Some folks feel like it is a good idea to cover requirements, constraints, and assumptions while others feel like it is unnecessary. The best idea might be to ask the customer if they would like to review a numbered list or if it is ok for these to be drawn out as part of the presentation and discussion.

CONCEPTUAL DESIGN

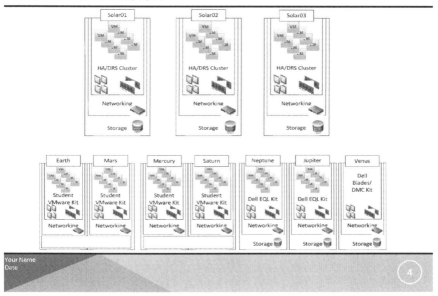

Figure 54 - Conceptual Design

Rather than jumping straight into deep technical conversations you should begin with a high level perspective by focusing on the conceptual design and work your way down through the logical design and finally into the details of the configuration specifications of the technology deployment.

LOGICAL CLUSTER DESIGN

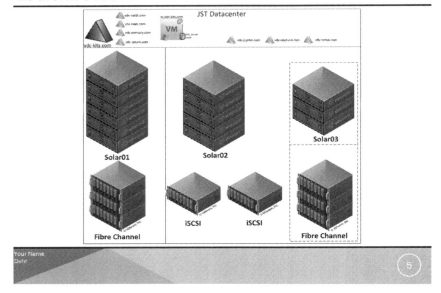

Figure 55 - Logical Cluster Design

LOGICAL NETWORK DESIGN

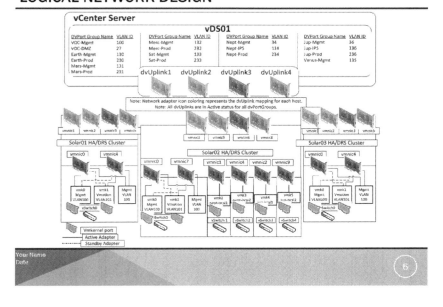

Figure 56 - Logical Network Design

PHYSICAL NETWORKING DESIGN

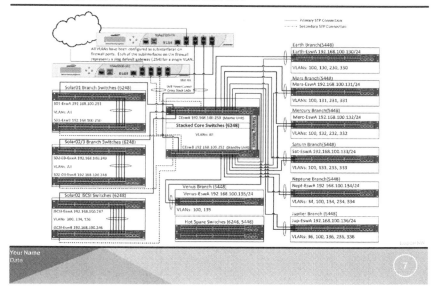

Figure 57 - Physical Networking Design

SOLAROX LOGICAL STORAGE DESIGN

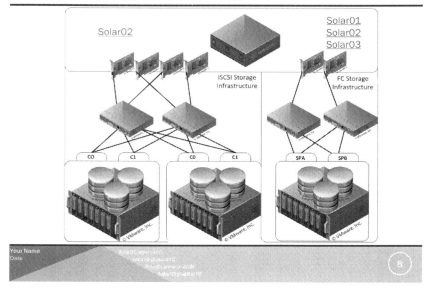

Figure 58 - Solar0X Logical Storage Design

FIBRE CHANNEL SWITCH DESIGN

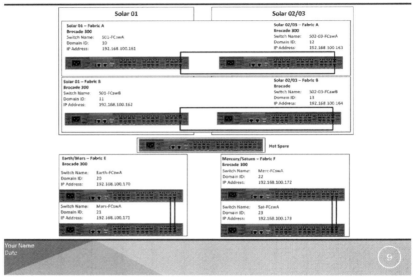

Figure 59 - Fibre Channel Switch Design

SOLAR01 VMFS DESIGN

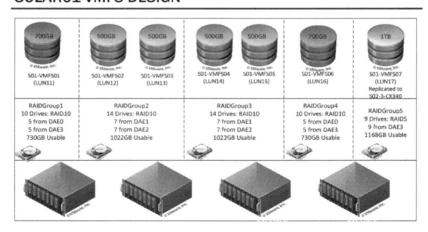

Figure 60 - Solar01 VMFS Design

SOLAR03 LOGICAL VDI DESIGN

Your Name
Date
11

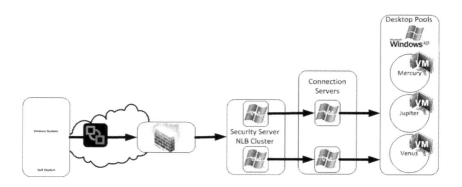

Figure 61 - Solar03 Logical VDI Design

DISASTER RECOVERY/BUSINESS CONTINUITY

Component	BC/DR Notes
ESXi hosts	Host profiles, vicfg-cfgbackup (vMA)
vCenter	vDR, Clone, SQL backups (full, differential, log)
Infrastructure services	Redundant DCs, DNS, DHCP
FC/iSCSI Storage	N+1 on switches, none for array data*
Network	N+1 switch, TFTP switch config backup
VM Templates	OVF export, vDR, replication

Your Name
Date
12

Figure 62 - Disaster Recovery / Business Continuity

This slide is the end of the planned presentation. You will notice that the slides, thus far, are all logical, conceptual, or high-level information. Any details on configuration specification have been avoided. This is intentional to follow allow each part of the presentation lead into, and support, the following slides and create a logical flow from conceptual, to logical and physical design phases.

"This is intentional as it eliminates 'rat holes' and allows you to focus on the main presentation and flow. Obviously, the audience will take you down other paths, but you don't want to encourage it too much, especially when you are pressed for time." – Doug Baer, VCDX-019

At this point the high level points of the design have been addressed. The information given thus far identifies how your design addresses the requirements. From here on the appendix includes slides with more details. The slides that make up the appendix include:

- Configuration specification slides that provide details about how the infrastructure is configured.
- Physical designs that provide details on hardware make and model, IP addresses, and cabling.
- Information collected from customer (i.e. requirements, constraints, assumptions).

These should be included so that your presentation is flexible enough to address multiple audiences. The audience you are presenting to will determine whether you dive into any of the content in the appendix. If the presentation is targeted towards a more technical audience, you should plan on proceeding to the appendices that were created with the next level of detail. If you are targeting higher level stakeholders or executives you will probably stop and ask if there are any questions or any areas they would like to have additional discussions on.

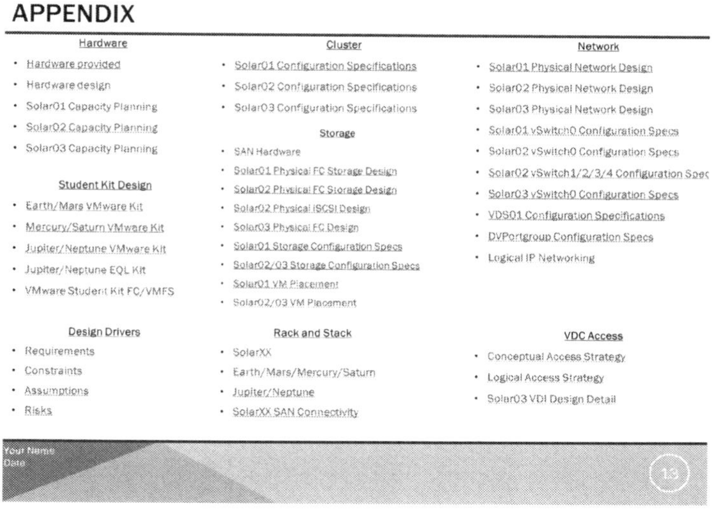

APPENDIX

Figure 63 - Appendix header slide with links to individual reference slides

The first part of the appendix details the hardware decisions and capacity planning that formed the basis for these decisions. Capacity planning is key component to a design but is not always available. Even if you don't have metrics derived from capacity planning tools, it is still a good idea to create a capacity plan that can identify the scalability of a solutions' architecture.

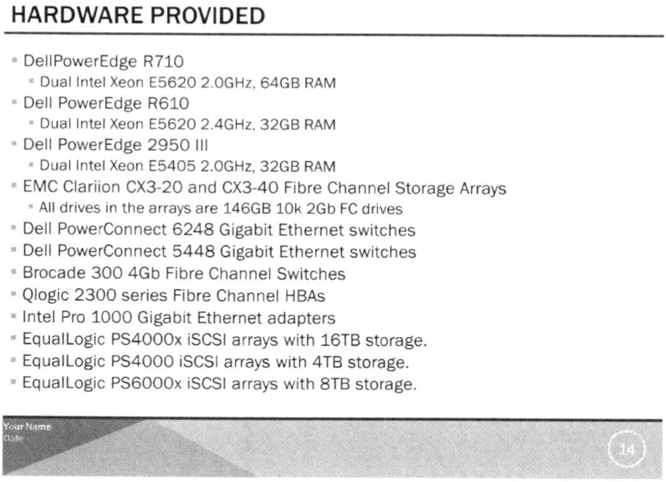

HARDWARE PROVIDED

- ⁎ DellPowerEdge R710
  - ⁎ Dual Intel Xeon E5620 2.0GHz, 64GB RAM
- ⁎ Dell PowerEdge R610
  - ⁎ Dual Intel Xeon E5620 2.4GHz, 32GB RAM
- ⁎ Dell PowerEdge 2950 III
  - ⁎ Dual Intel Xeon E5405 2.0GHz, 32GB RAM
- ⁎ EMC Clariion CX3-20 and CX3-40 Fibre Channel Storage Arrays
  - ⁎ All drives in the arrays are 146GB 10k 2Gb FC drives
- ⁎ Dell PowerConnect 6248 Gigabit Ethernet switches
- ⁎ Dell PowerConnect 5448 Gigabit Ethernet switches
- ⁎ Brocade 300 4Gb Fibre Channel Switches
- ⁎ Qlogic 2300 series Fibre Channel HBAs
- ⁎ Intel Pro 1000 Gigabit Ethernet adapters
- ⁎ EqualLogic PS4000x iSCSI arrays with 16TB storage.
- ⁎ EqualLogic PS4000 iSCSI arrays with 4TB storage.
- ⁎ EqualLogic PS6000x iSCSI arrays with 8TB storage.

Figure 64 - Hardware Provided

HARDWARE DESIGN

The server hardware provided by ITAR was allocated to the ITAR VDC according to the table below.

Server Models in Cluster	CPU Models in Cluster	Total CPU Capacity in Cluster	Memory per Host	Total Memory in Cluster	vSphere Version	Cluster Name	# of Hosts in Cluster	Storage Access Technology
PowerEdge 2950 III	Dual Intel Xeon E5405 (2.0)	96GHz	32GB	192GB	4.1 U2	Solar01	6	Fibre Channel
PowerEdge R710	Dual Intel Xeon E5620 (2.4)	96GHz	64GB	320GB	4.1 U2	Solar02	5	Fibre Channel, iSCSI
PowerEdge R610	Dual Intel Xeon E5620 (2.0)	48GHz	48GB	144GB	4.1 U2	Solar03	3	Fibre Channel

Figure 65 - Hardware Design

SOLAR01 CAPACITY PLANNING

VMs	# VMs	RAM	Total RAM	HD	# cpu	CPU count	vCPU GHz	Avg CPU Use %	Avg CPU Use GHz	Peak CPU Use %	Peak CPU Use GHz
Earth vCs	7	2	14	30	2	14	4	0.1	2.8	0.25	7
Mars vCs	7	2	14	30	2	14	4	0.1	2.8	0.25	7
Mercury vCs	8	2	16	30	2	16	4	0.1	3.2	0.25	8
Saturn vCs	8	2	16	30	2	16	4	0.1	3.2	0.25	8
DCs	8	1	8	30	1	8	2	0.01	0.16	0.01	0.16
DHCP	5	1	7	30	1	7	2	0.01	0.14	0.01	0.14
File Servers	2	2	4	130	2	4	4	0.25	2	0.15	1.2
UDAs	15	1	0.5	15	1	5	2	0.05	0.5	0.1	1
vCenter	1	8	8	145	2	2	4	0.1	0.4	0.3	1.2
Totals/ Mode	61	2	88	30	2	86	30				34
Mode		2		30	2						

Cluster	# Hosts	Ram/ Host	Total RAM	HA % Free	Usable RAM after HA	Sockets/ Host	Cores/ Socket	CPU Speed	Total CPU	Usable CPU after HA
Solar01	6	32	192	20	153.6	2	4	2	96	76.8

Memory Configured	88	
Total Memory Available	154	66
Peak CPU Usage	34	
Total CPU Available	77	43

CPU Use	VM	RAM
8	vCenter x 8	16
0.02	DC	1
0.02	DHCP	1
0.2	UDA	0.5
8	SUM	19
43/8		66/19
5 kits	Estimated Additional Capacity	3 kits

Figure 66 - Solar01 Capacity Planning

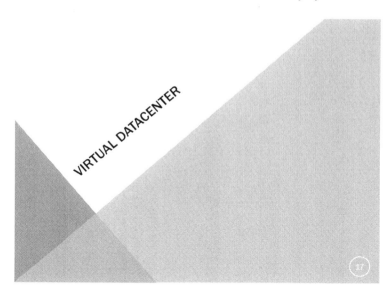

Figure 67 - Virtual Datacenter - Section Title Slide

This section is specific to a VMware solution. Your design may vary. This section of the appendix details the VMware vCenter Server design and how the VMware ESX Clusters are configured for VMware vSphere HA and VMware vSphere DRS.

SOLAR01 CLUSTER CONFIGURATION

Cluster Features	Setting	Value	
	HA	Enabled	
	DRS		
vSphere HA			
	Host Monitoring	Enabled	
	Admission Control	Enabled	
	Admission Control Policy	Percentage of cluster resources reserved as failover capacity	20%
	Advanced options	Das.isolationaddress1	192.168.100.254
		Das.isolationaddress2	192.168.100.253
		Das.failuredetectiontime	20000
	Virtual Machine Options	VM Restart Priority	Medium
		Host Isolation Response	Leave powered on
	Virtual Machine Settings	VM Restart Priority for vCenter	High
		VM Restart Priority for FS01	High
	VM Monitoring	Enabled	Medium
	Virtual Machine Settings	VM Monitoring for vCenter	High
		VM Monitoring for FS01	High
vSphere DRS			
	Automation Level	Fully Automated	Default
	DRS Groups Manager		
	Rules	Anti-affinity for DCs	
	Virtual Machine Options		
	Power Management		
Vmware EVC	Vmware EVC Mode	Intel "Penryn" Gen. (Xeon 45nm Core 2)	
Swapfile Location	Default		

Figure 68 - Solar01 Cluster Configuration

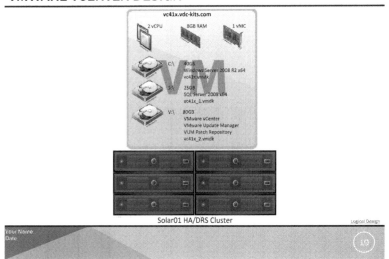

Figure 69 - VMware vCenter Design

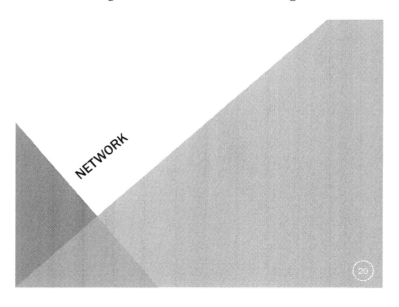

Figure 70 - Network - Section Title Slide

The Network section of the appendix offers details of network cabling, IP addresses, and the makes and models of the networking gear. For many customers these details will be important discussions as networking is the integration point between physical and virtual.

Especially when preparing designs that leverage virtualization, it is important to provide clear diagrams for the physical and virtual networking. Be sure to include:

- Sample physical cabling diagrams
- Physical and virtual switch configurations (VLANs, port groups, etc.)
- Any proprietary protocols

SOLAR01 PHYSICAL NETWORK DESIGN

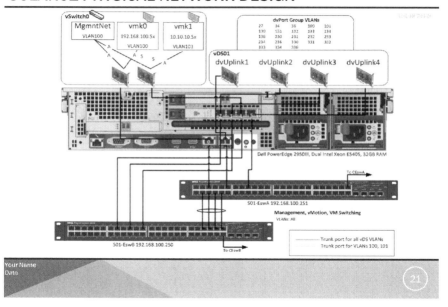

Figure 71 - Solar01 Physical Network Design

SOLAR01 VSWITCH0 CONFIGURATION

vSwitch0 Properties			
vSwitch	General	Number of ports	120
		MTU	1500
	Security	Promiscuous Mode	Reject
		MAC Address Changes	Accept
		Forged Transmits	Accept
	Traffic Shaping	Disabled	
	NIC Teaming	Load Balancing	Route based on the originating virtual port ID
		Network Failover Detection	Link status only
		Notify Switches	Yes
		Failback	Yes
VDC-Mgmt	General		
		Network Label	VDC-Mgmt
		VLAN ID	100
VMK-Mgmt	General	Network Label	VMK-Mgmt
		VLAN ID	100
		vMotion	Disabled
		Fault Tolerance Logging	Disabled
		Management Traffic	Enabled
	IP Settings	192.168.100.5x/24	
	NIC Teaming	Override switch failover order	Enabled
		Active Adapters	vmnic0
		Standby Adapters	vmnic4
		Unused Adapters	empty
VMK-vMotion	General	Network Label	VMK-vMotion
		VLAN ID	101
		vMotion	Enabled
		Fault Tolerance Logging	Disabled
		Management Traffic	Disabled
	IP Settings	10.10.101.5x/24	
	NIC Teaming	Override switch failover order	Enabled
		Active Adapters	vmnic4
		Standby Adapters	vmnic0

Your Name
Date
22

Figure 72 - Solar01 vSwitch0 Configuration

VDS CONFIGURATION

vDS01			
Properties	General	Name	vDSO1
		Number of uplink ports	4
	Advanced	MTU	1500
	Discovery Protocol	Enabled	
	Type	CDP	
	Operation	Listen	

Cluster Hosts	vmnic	Location	dvUplink
Solar01	vmnic1	On board	dvUplink1
	vmnic2	PCI	dvUplink2
	vmnic3	PCI	dvUplink3
	vmnic5	PCI	dvUplink4
Solar02	vmnic3	On board	dvUplink1
	vmnic5	PCI 2	dvUplink2
	vmnic6	PCI 2	dvUplink3
	vmnic8	PCI 4	dvUplink4
Solar03	vmnic1	On board	dvUplink1
	vmnic2	On board	dvUplink2
	vmnic3	On Board	dvUplink3
	vmnic5	PCI	dvUplink4

dvPortGroup Name	VLAN ID	dvPortGroup Name	VLAN ID
DMZ	27	Sat-Mgmt	133
VDC-Mgmt	100	Sat-Prod	233
Earth-Mgmt	130	Sat-vMotion	333
Earth-Prod	230	Nept-Mgmt	34
Earth-vMotion	330	Nept-Mgmt-IPS	134
Mars-Mgmt	131	Nept-Prod	234
Mars-Prod	231	Nept-vMotion	334
Mars-vMotion	331	Jup-Mgmt	36
Merc-Mgmt	132	Jup-Mgmt-iPS	136
Merc-Prod	232	Jup-Prod	236
Merc-vMotion	332	Jup-vMotion	336
		Venus-Mgmt	135

Your Name
Date
23

Figure 73 - VDS Configuration

DVPORTGROUPS CONFIGURATION

dvPortGroup				
General	Name	insert name		
	Number of ports	128		
	Port binding	Static		
Policies	Security	Promiscuous Mode*	Reject	
		MAC Address Changes	Accept	
		Forged Transmits	Accept	
	Traffic Shaping	Ingress	Disabled	
		Egress	Disabled	
	VLAN	VLAN type	VLAN	insert VLAN ID
	Teaming and Failover	Load Balancing	Route based on physical NIC load	
		Network failover detection	Beacon Probing (*Link Dependency enabled)	
		Notify Switches	Yes	
		Failback	Yes	
		Failover order	All dvUplinks Active	
	Miscellaneous	Block all ports	No	
	Advanced	Allow override of port policies	Enabled	
		Configure reset at disconnect	Enabled	

Figure 74 - dvPortGroups Configuration

LOGICAL IP NETWORKING

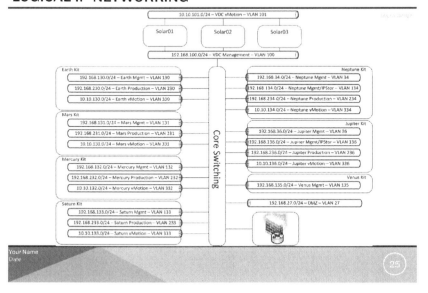

Figure 75 - Logical IP Networking

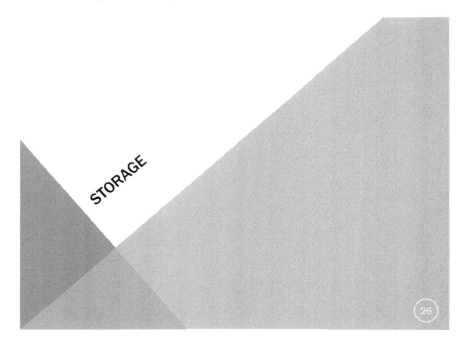

Figure 76 - Storage - Section Title Slide

A detailed section on storage, like networking, should provide hardware and configuration specifics for both the physical and virtual environment. With a variety of options available for storage solutions, the appendix could be used to identify the pros and cons of various storage options; fiber channel, iSCSI, NFS, and converged. In situations where you are recommending a storage solution, customers are often interested in understanding the driving factors.

STORAGE AREA NETWORK HARDWARE

Hardware	Make and model	Qty	Notes
FC Array	EMC CX3-40	2	4G
FC Array	EMC CX3-20	4	4G
FC DAE	EMC Ultrapoint DAE4	7	15 x 146GB 10K RPM
FC Switches	Brocade 300	9	24 port, 4G
FC HBAs	Qlogic QLE2460	22	Single port 4G HBA
FC HBAs	Qlogic QLE2462	3	Dual port 4G HBA
ISCSI Array	EqualLogic PS4000x	2	16 x 500GB 7200RPM, Dual Controller 1Gbps
Ethernet Switches	PowerConnect 6248	9	48 port, 1Gbps
	PowerConnect 5448	8	

Figure 77 - Storage Area Network Hardware

SOLAR01 PHYSICAL FC STORAGE DESIGN

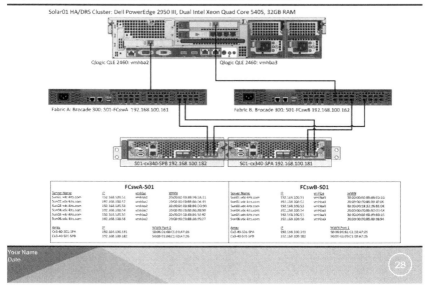

Figure 78 - Solar02 Physical FC Storage Design

SOLAR02 PHYSICAL ISCSI STORAGE DESIGN

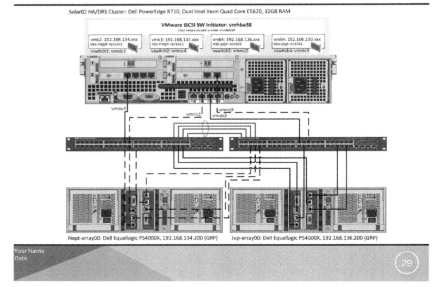

Figure 79 - Solar02 Physical iSCSI Storage Design

SOLAR01 FC STORAGE CONFIGURATION

RAID Group	# of Drives	RAID Type	Notes	Space	LUN IDs	LUN Size
RAIDGroup1	10	10	Use 5 disks from DAE0 (non-Flare) and 5 disks from DAE3	730GB	11	700GB
RAIDGroup2	14	10	Use 7 disks from DAE1 and 7 disks from DAE2	1022GB	12,13	500GB
RAIDGroup3	14	10	Use 7 disks from DAE1 and 7 disks from DAE2	1022GB	14,15	500GB
RAIDGroup4	10	10	Use 5 disks from DAE0 (non-Flare) and 5 disks from DAE3	730GB	16	700GB
RAIDGroup5	9	5	Use the remaining 9 disks from DAE3	1168GB	17	1TB

LUN	Datastore	Block Size	Capcity	PSP
LUN 11	S01-VMFS01	8MB	700GB	Round Robin
LUN 12	S01-VMFS02	8MB	500GB	Round Robin
LUN 13	S01-VMFS03	8MB	500GB	Round Robin
LUN 14	S01-VMFS04	8MB	500GB	Round Robin
LUN 15	S01-VMFS05	8MB	500GB	Round Robin
LUN 16	S01-VMFS06	8MB	700GB	Round Robin
LUN17	S01-VMFS07	8MB	1TB	Round Robin

Figure 80 - Solar01 FC Storage Configuration

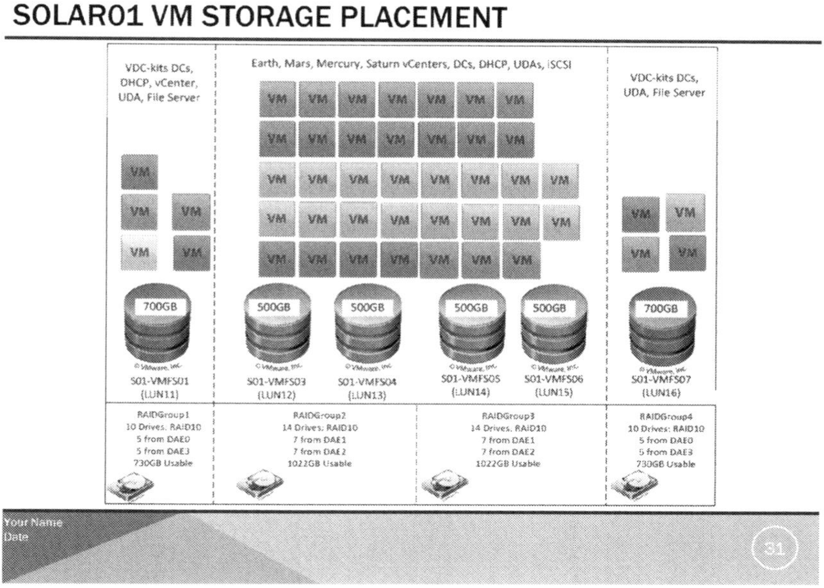

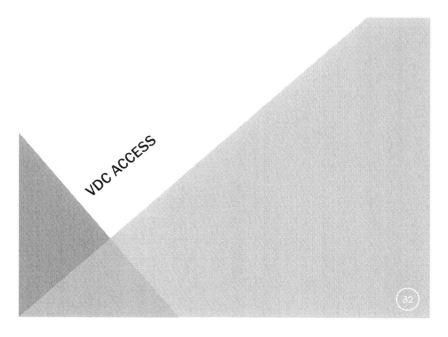

Figure 81 - Solar01 VM Storage Placement

Figure 82 - VDC Access – Section Title Slide

CONCEPTUAL ACCESS STRATEGY

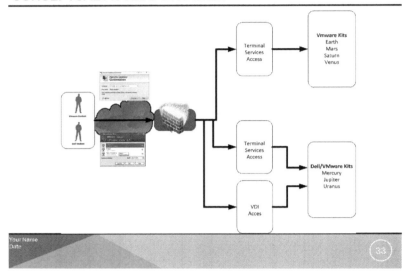

Figure 83 - Conceptual Access Strategy

LOGICAL ACCESS STRATEGY

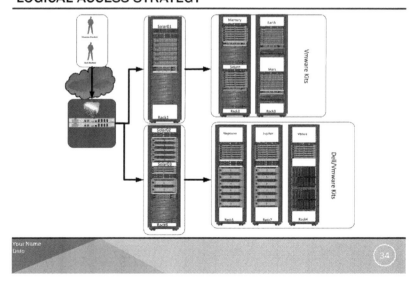

Figure 84 - Logical Access Strategy

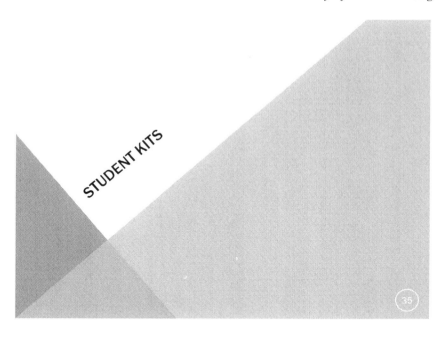

Figure 85 - Student Kits – Section Title Slide

EARTH/MARS VMWARE KIT DESIGN

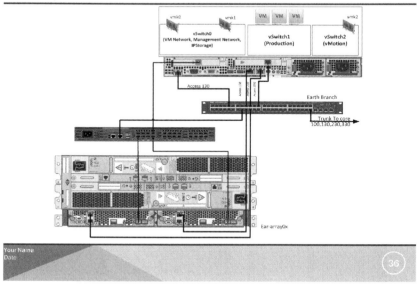

Figure 86 - Earth / Mars VMware Kit Design

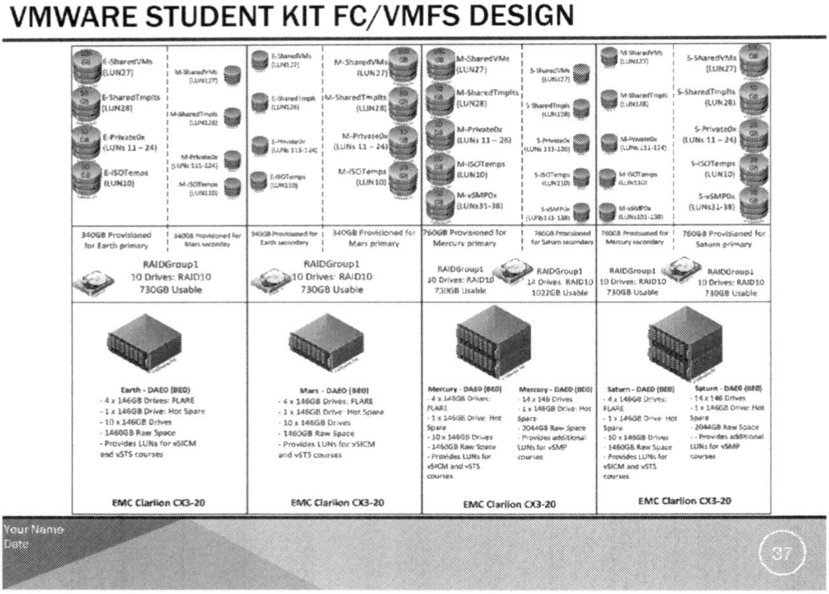

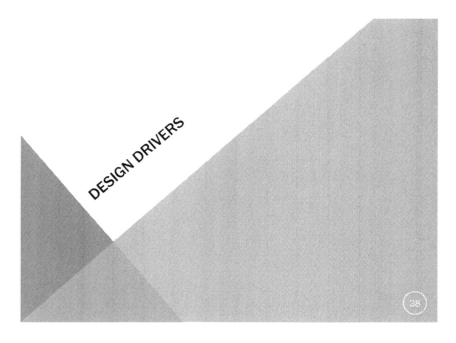

Figure 87 - VMware Student Kit FC/VMFS Design

Figure 88 - Design Drivers – Section Title Slide

Many people believe that the information in this section should be included in the presentation. There really isn't a right or wrong answer. Keep in mind, however, that the folks you are presenting to spent hours and hours in meetings answering your questions to give you this information so that you can make design decisions. Do you think they need you to read it back to them?

If you stop to think about it, this information will all come out during your discussions about the proposed solution. You don't need to read it from slides when you can deliver the same information in a more natural and organic manner. Rather than saying "let's review your requirements," you will have ample opportunities to say, "we decided on this in order to satisfy your requirement for _____." This approach maximizes efficiency of your presentation and keeps the time you spend regurgitating things they already know to a minimum.

We would NOT suggest omitting this information because a customer could ask to see it in this format. Rather, as it is done here, it should be included in the appendix with the idea that it likely will not be used.

INTRODUCTION

ITAR Services Team
* xxxx– Senior Director
* xxxx– Infrastructure Manager
* xxxx– Enterprise Storage Product Manager
* xxxx– Partner Manager
* xxxx– Partner Manager
* xxxx– Senior Trainer
* xxxx– Senior Trainer

ITAR Design Team
* xxxx– Lead architect
* xxxx– Consulting architect
* xxxx– Consulting architect
* xxxx– Systems Engineer, Consultant
* xxxx– Network Engineer, Consultant

Figure 89 - Introduction

DESIGN PHILOSOPHY

It is our due diligence to ensure that the design elements we work with to create this solution are all justifiable in the eyes of ITAR and our design team. Our efforts must focus on providing sound technical solutions that solve problems without undue complexity.

This is not an exercise or demonstration in implementing or using technology just for the sake of the technology.

Figure 90 - Design Philosophy

REQUIREMENTS (1 OF 3)

*   Customer experience should remain above average as determined by post-class customer evaluations.
*   Customer access to the VDC must use standard ports 3389 and/or 443.
*   ITAR VDC must meet/exceed the VATC setup guidelines and ITAR course specifications for respective products.
*   Support must be provide beginning one hour before the start of class and ending one hour after on each day of class for the respective time zone where the class is being delivered.
*   Support request must be responded to within 15 minutes.
*   Disruptions to VDC access must not exceed 2 hours, unless the root of the problem is failed student hardware for which ITAR knowingly has not provided the hardware required to achieve an N+1 redundancy. Under these circumstances the disruption time is determined by the ITAR business critical support contract.
*   Disruptions to the VDC caused by complete storage array failure do not qualify for repair under the two hour time constraint. A complete storage failure should be reported immediately to the instructor, ITAR management team, and ITAR infrastructure team. In this case a best effort will be made by the ITAR team to restore class to its normal operating environment.

Figure 91 - Requirements (1 of 3)

REQUIREMENTS (2 OF 3)

- VMware class compute workloads should not impact ITAR EqualLogic and/or ITAR Blades and DMC training. An overlap in networking is acceptable.
- Student access to VDC kits should be limited to only the class for which they are enrolled and last only for the duration of the class.
- Class setup and configuration is expected with as little as 2 business days' notice.
- The VMware VDC, ITAR EqualLogic VDC, and Blades/DMC VDC should be modularized to support partial decommissioning upon request by ITAR .
- The infrastructure must scale to accommodate the projected growth of the ITAR education products assembled for the ITAR specific training. VMware training was expected to remain stable but not require scaling beyond the initial infrastructure.
- Due to the potential impact of resource contention on customer experience CPU and Memory resources should not be overcommitted.

Figure 92 - Requirements (2 of 3)

REQUIREMENTS (3 OF 3)

- The infrastructure design and management must be limited to technologies/features available to ITAR IT team. Any third-party products used to develop the infrastructure must be approved by the ITAR infrastructure team.
- Design changes must be approved by the ITAR infrastructure team
- Beyond the core infrastructure, failures in management infrastructure should be isolated to impact only one of the training product lines.
- The infrastructure must support a simple and easy remote management as the principle engineers and support technicians are not local to the Johnstown, PA datacenter. This requirement was self-imposed and not suggested by the ITAR team.

Figure 93 - Requirements (3 of 3)

DESIGN QUALITY PRIORITIZATION

After mutually agreeing to the design quality definitions ITAR Education Services ranked the design qualities according to the following table.

	Rank	Design Quality
Most Important	1	Availability*
	2	Performance*
	3	Manageability
	4	Recoverability
Least Important	5	Security

Figure 94 - Design Quality Prioritization

CONSTRAINTS

- Hardware is limited to hardware that can be provisioned by ITAR and can be accomplished within the budget for the project. Additional hardware purchases are limited beyond what is directly required for the direct customer facing student VDC lab infrastructure.

- Any required support for the VMware VDC beyond what can be provided by the existing infrastructure management team will be submitted to the ITAR Support Services.

- The vSphere troubleshooting class has strict requirements on the ESX /ESXi and Powershell version for the configuration of the student servers and damage scripts to operate correctly. The version required is 4.0 with no update for vSphere and Powercli 4.0, however, the ITAR R610 with the H700 SCSI controller is not supported on this version of vSphere. It is supported on ESXi 4.0 Update 2

- The VDC design must not include solutions or configurations for which the ITAR infrastructure team is not prepared or able to manage.

Figure 95 - Constraints

ASSUMPTIONS

- ITAR assumes all financial, legal, and logistical functions of the VMware Authorized Training Center agreement.

- The VMware class requirements as outlined by the VMware created VATC setup guides are sufficient for achieving performance levels that result in adequate customer experience (CE) ratings.

- Hardware provided by ITAR will scale to meet the ITAR training demand.

- All hardware and software (VMware) issues can be resolved by the local datacenter staff or the ITAR Support Services.

- ITAR customers will be able to accommodate the VDC access strategy (on ports 3389 and/or 443).

- Internet bandwidth in the datacenter is sufficient to handle remote connections to the VDC.

- The power and cooling infrastructure at the physical datacenter is constructed with redundancy to ensure continued operations.

Your Name
Date
46

Figure 96 - Assumptions

RISKS

- Initial hardware specifications may not scale to educational demand.
- Multiple hardware failures exceeding an N+1 redundancy design.
- ITAR Support Services is unable to resolve a VMware issue.
- No protection for complete site failure.
- ITAR Blade class is delivered on two blade chassis. Loss of a Blade chassis incurs a loss of infrastructure for 50% of the class population.
- The evolution of the class requirements outgrows the hardware provided resulting in a negative impact to the CE.
- Loss of a ITAR EqualLogic iSCSI array that is part of the student infrastructure would be susceptible to the ITAR 4 hour business critical support contract.
- The VMware vSphere Troubleshooting student kits must be modified to use vSphere 4.0 Update 1. The PowerCLI will be updated accordingly.
- The EqualLogic VDC for Neptune and Jupiter have a dedicated IP storage network that is the same network as the Management and IP Storage network for the VMware VDC for Neptune and Jupiter. If EQL and VMware classes run simultaneously the two classes will share the same networks. In addition if the Neptune or Jupiter kit is used for a concurrent VMware and ITAR class it will push the EQL class to using a non-VMware supported nested ESXi solution. ITAR has acknowledged the risk and will try to avoid this scenario.

Your Name
Date
47

Figure 97 - Risks

Of the slides in this section of the Appendix the risks slide is the one for which we could be convinced to move into the presentation so that it is purposefully shown and addressed. This is especially true if the design included imminent and potentially detrimental threats to the environment as a result of a requirement or constraint.

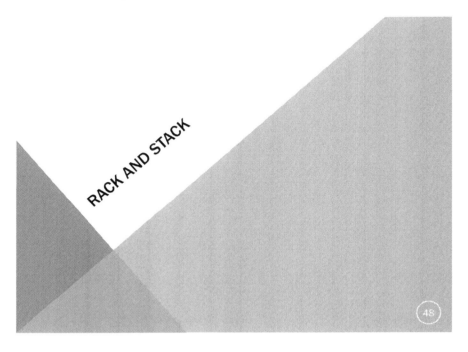

Figure 98 - Rack and Stack – Section Title Slide

SOLAR01/02/03 RACK AND STACK

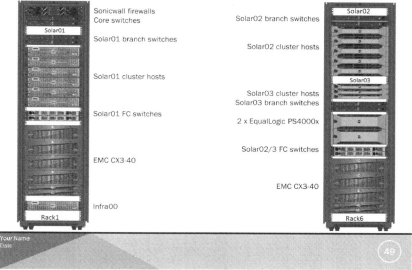

Figure 99 - Solar01/02/03 Rack and Stack

EARTH/MARS RACK AND STACK

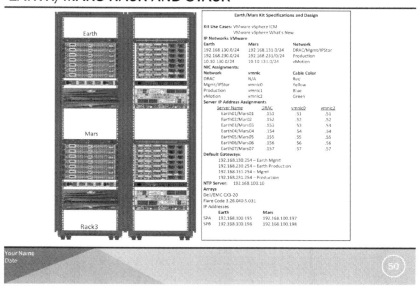

Figure 100 - Earth / Mars Rack and Stack

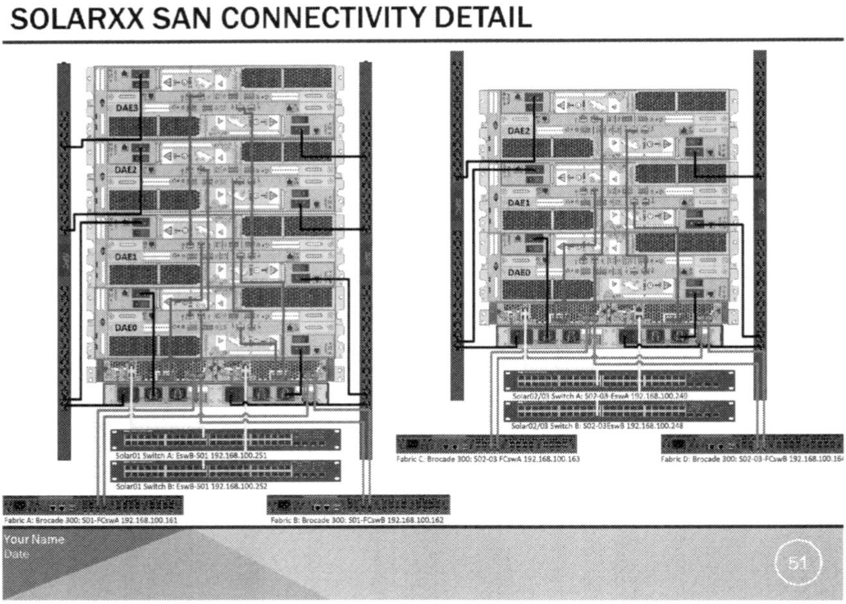

SOLARXX SAN CONNECTIVITY DETAIL

Figure 101 - SolarXX SAN Connectivity Detail

Exercises

1. Create a presentation in support of your design.
   a. Consider the flow of information.
   b. Consider quality over quantity by focusing on key items for the presentation and providing supporting information in the reference section.
2. Consider the use of animation where appropriate to reinforce what you are covering. This should never take priority over the actual content.
   a. For the example slides and for your presentation, what do you consider valuable to animate? Examples include data flow, processes, and zoom-in effects of specific details you will cover in your discussion.

## CHAPTER 9

DESIGN IN PRACTICE – SUMMARY, RECOMMENDATIONS, AND NEXT STEPS

"At the heart, infrastructure design is the building of a home for dynamic and static applications and data to live and function. Similar to building a home, infrastructure design helps to provide the foundation, structure, and flow for applications and data throughout their lifecycle based on business requirements, constraints, and assumptions (when lacking data or insight). Like a home, an infrastructure design should allow for current and future needs in a manner that is efficient, minimizes risk, and manages initial cost, and cost over time. And to help meet those goals the overall infrastructure design should be kept as simple as possible, while still meeting the requirements of the business."
— *Lane Leverett, VCDX-053*

Design in Practice

The goal of this book was to educate on infrastructure design principals and methodology. There are many overlaps with the best practices used by architects focused on building infrastructures ('cities') when compared to servers ('buildings'). There are complexities in developing both, including integration of multiple components from multiple vendors in both software and hardware. The complexities grow greater in infrastructure design due to sizing and potential for disparate solutions that must be integrated, validated, and maintained successfully.

A secondary goal was to provide a reference with example architecture design documents for server and desktop virtualization, including more than just the architecture material. The inclusion of other example documents (installation, configuration, validation, operations, etc.) fills a gap in the industry for those getting started in infrastructure design needing a reference on creating this material.

This is the first in a series of books titled 'IT Architect Series'. Subsequent books will provide additional examples in other areas such as Software Defined Networking (SDN), Software Defined Storage (SDS), and Hybrid Cloud. These will also include reference material and exercises.

Summary and Recommendations

Here we summarize what we've covered with recommendations

Design Phases

We have identified an iterative process for design that spans the four phases used as part of the design process.

- We discover the inputs to create the conceptual model based on the owner's perspective.
- We develop the solution, creating a logical design that includes concepts and structure without specifying products or configurations.
- We design the architecture where we show the physical design with specific vendors, products, and configurations that set the time clock for deployment based on the products specified.
- We determine success criteria and create a test plan that will prove the design, as implemented, meets requirements.

Although the project may end, at some point there will be changing business requirements, application workloads, and technologies that will require review, refinement, and evolution of the design and related materials.

Design Characteristics

We reviewed the key design characteristics present in most infrastructure designs. These include availability, manageability, performance, recoverability, and security.

Considerations for Design

We covered how requirements, constraints, and risks are used to drive the solution and why it is critical to evaluate and confirm assumptions.

Documentation Set

We covered the inputs driving the design and the documentation set created for a project. The core documents we recommend are the following.

- **Architecture Design** – includes functional and technical design consisting of requirements, constraints, assumptions, risks, out-of-scope items, conceptual/logical/physical design components, design considerations, and design patterns.
- **Installation Guide** – how to install and configure the solution.
- **Implementation Plan** – details on project schedule, training, required skills, roles, responsibilities, and deployment guidance.
- **Validation/Test Plan** – provides the testing required to ensure a successful solution. The validation/test plan can include unit-level testing, system-level testing, integration-level testing, performance/stress testing, and others as appropriate.
- **Operating Procedures** – provides guidance on performing the activities required by the administration and support teams, both for recurring regularly scheduled activities and during special circumstances.

Design Decisions

We provide the reason why design decisions should be included in the design, calling out the justification, impact, and risk of the choices made. This is also an area where alternative choices can be described and the reasons they were not selected for the design.

Exercises

Exercises have been included to help with teaching the concepts and to allow for further exploration and learning by the reader. Not all will include answers. Some are open-ended questions to invoke thinking like an architect.

Tools

The four appendices include tools that the authors have found useful, crafted in a way to allow customization by the reader. These are examples of tools. You are likely to find or create other tools to help you as you work on design projects.

The discovery phase is the starting point to build a conceptual model of the requirements, constraints, and relationships. It is also a phase where initial risk considerations are factored in. The Discovery Phase Survey provides a starting point for your questions. As discussed previously, use of the Socratic Method has shown to be very beneficial in qualifying and strengthening design considerations and design decisions.

The second phase is the logical design where a solution is created without choice of specific vendors, technologies, or configurations. This is used for discussion with the business owners and project team to clarify alignment with expectations. We have included a Design Decision Workbook, broken into several categories, which can be used for documenting design considerations and design decisions for both the logical and physical design phases. It is expected that the reader will adapt this to the type of design they are developing.

The third phase is the physical design which includes the where vendor, technology, and configuration are specified for the appropriate logical design areas. This also uses the Design Decision Workbook.

Once the initial design is completed, use the example design presentation from Chapter 8 as a reference for your design presentation.

After the above are complete, you can then use the Design Review Readiness Assessment as one method to determine readiness to defend the design based on your material, your presentation, and yourself.

The final tool, Building a Design Lab, is a reference to helping you create an environment to evaluate designs that you have developed. This is specifically tied to VMware technologies based on the experience of the authors but can be modified to use other technologies. It can be used to both learn and to help in developing and testing a design.

Next Steps

We recommend several courses of action to help you in developing skills in infrastructure design, both for new and experienced architects.

1. **Understand the different phases in design and utilize the examples we provide as well as the reference documents we list.** As you do this, recognize that the examples provided were based on the skills and experience of the authors, and the capabilities of the technologies to match the case study.
2. **Using the Socratic Method, review the designs provided and question the design considerations and design decisions.** What questions would you ask for clarification? What questions would you ask to reveal more information that confirm or reject specific decisions that were made?
3. **Review other designs.** Apply the Socratic Method as you review the material. Did they include the same documents (separate or grouped) that we use in the book examples? If not, why were they not included? Ask questions to understand decision points that were driven by industry verticals, business scenarios, application types, deployment models, and specific named applications.
4. **Reverse engineer an existing infrastructure and develop a design to match.** Again, apply the Socratic Method to further expound on the reasoning behind decisions made. As you do this, consider alternative approaches to improve the qualities of the design you are creating. Explore the factors that influence your choices such as your experience, available technologies

and operational practices, and governance such as regulatory compliance guidelines. Don't forget the customer experience too. They can provide feedback that identifies constraints or risks based on their infrastructure.

5. **Be creative.** Use the learning process to experiment and apply agile principles such as 'fail fast'. Agile methodology helps development through incremental and iterative work segments called iterations or sprints, and is an alternative to waterfall methodology, which is a traditional, sequential development process. Do NOT use 'Water-scrum-fall'. If you try to mix agile and waterfall approaches you risk failure.

6. **Share your experience.** Mentoring and teaching others is a great way for you to also learn. Professional discussions that dive into the 'why' behind decisions open your eyes to new solutions.

7. **Have fun.**

Focus on creating quality in what you produce within the timeframes and budgets you have as constraints. Focus on alignment of the solution with the needs and expectations of the business, but understand that there may be specific things that require discussion and potential changes in the requirements and constraints that you start with. When developing the solution, remember that the business will rely on this design for production to support business objectives and income. Ensure that you reduce the risk of failure. Where, due to external circumstance you have risk that cannot be addressed, be sure to document this in the design and in the presentation. Risks must be covered in the discussions with the business and project team to ensure clarity and to provide an opportunity for corrective action.

We wish you the best on your journey and in the projects that you tackle. We are open to questions online and typically use Twitter for this. Our handles are included in the Front Matter of this book. We will not be able to support you on developing your design but are happy to clarify questions on methodology and what we have included in this book.

DISCOVERY PHASE SURVEY

During the discovery phase of a design project there are questions that must be asked to ensure sufficient information is obtained for a successful design. This appendix includes a set of survey questions that can help in understanding details of the project as well as the existing infrastructure, applications, operations, and existing challenges.

Project

Are there any expectations around the time-to-market from project funding approval to the infrastructure online for business workloads? Are these reasonable or will you have to negotiate expectations vs. reality?

- How is the current procurement process set up?
- Does the solution include integration of many vendor products? If so, how is this integration done?
- Do the current procurement timelines and logistics have an impact on products and services they deliver?
- What workloads could benefit from consolidation with virtualization?
  ◦ Consider both production and dev/test environments.
- Are there any sole-supplier agreements you must follow?

The following provide areas to expand on project related questions.

- Business Objectives
  ◦ Server Consolidation
  ◦ Business Continuity
  ◦ Virtual Lab Automation
  ◦ Desktop Management

- Lifecycle Objectives
  - Build, Deploy, Update, Monitor, Recover, Retire
- Business Continuity and Compliance
  - Data Protection
  - High Availability
  - Disaster recovery
  - Compliance
- Data Center Locations
  - Enterprise In-house
  - Enterprise Extranet
  - Service Provider
  - Remote and Branch Office
- Operations
  - Provisioning
  - Consumption
  - Issue Resolution
- Requirements, Constraints, Risks, and Assumptions for
  - Availability
  - Manageability
  - Performance
  - Recoverability
  - Security

The following sections provide additional example questions that could be used during the discovery phase. Choose from these items but also consider questions customized to the specific project you are designing for.

Existing Infrastructure

The following are example questions for the existing infrastructure. Anything that may be a dependency with the design should be covered. These questions include business, technical, and operational items. Do not ignore the current infrastructure's capacity and performance metrics that should be considered and validated for the success of project decisions.

1. What are the business expectations of the infrastructure operations team?
2. What are the current uptime requirements?
3. Are the current systems delivering the desired uptime? If not, why?
4. What are the uptime expectations for this project (100% or less)?
5. Are critical business services documented with dependencies?
6. How much time does the infrastructure team spend maintaining current environments versus implementing changes for business requirements?
7. Where would the business like to see improvements in the infrastructure? (availability, manageability, performance, recoverability, security)
8. How well documented is each environment?
   a. Is there an accurate inventory of the equipment in service and out of service at each site?
      i. Understanding what is available may allow equipment to be repurposed by being put into service, replacing even older equipment.
   b. Do site topology diagrams exist?
      i. A high level MS Visio documenting environments at each site will allow an architect to repurpose equipment or replace older equipment if needed.
9. Is there a current business continuity plan and disaster recovery plan? If so, when was the last test? Was it successful?
10. Are there any change control procedures in operations?
11. What is the technology refresh rate over 3, 4, or 5 years? Include considerations related to depreciation/amortization purposes.
12. How are assets tracked and monitored?
13. A high level blueprint (MS Visio or OmniGraffle image) documenting environments at each site.
14. Does the staff see any outstanding issues that need to be addressed (hardware, software, etc.) and the timelines they should be addressed by? Are any outstanding for an extended time period?
15. Does the staff see any products, hardware or software, that they feel would be an enhancement to their existing environment?

Applications

1. Is there a list of applications considered for deployment on the new infrastructure based on this design?
2. Has an application review been conducted for resource requirements?
3. Is application performance considered a benefit to the business or a problem?
   a. Do SLAs exist? Are SLAs being met?
   b. What are perception issues versus technical or operational?
4. Are there hardware dependencies?
5. Are applications suited for deployment on this new infrastructure?

Security

1. Are existing security policies and procedures documented?
2. What governance rules apply to security policy? Consider the perspective from the industry the business is in and from other corporate security considerations.
3. Are there regulatory compliance guidelines that must be followed?
4. What roles, responsibilities, and access controls must be enforced?
5. Are there specific current gaps that must be addressed by new designs?
6. Are there existing environments that can be considered a 'model' for desired governance/security implementation?
7. What are the applicable regulatory requirements for the environment? (DISA, HIPAA, SOX, etc.)
8. Is there a regular audit schedule? Penetration testing?

Availability

1. Are there multiple sites involved in the design?
2. What are the business recovery and disaster recovery expectations: (RTO, RPO, expectation vs. reality)?

3. Does a data retention policy exist with the tools to ensure compliance? Does a policy need to be created?
4. Does the IT team have the tools to insure compliance with BCP/ DR/data retention policies?

Manageability

Identify aspects of the project and infrastructure tied to manageability.

1. What management tools are currently in place? Do they support a scalable architecture?
2. Are there any gaps in the current toolset?
3. Are there any regulatory requirements for IT today or coming in the future? Are current systems compliant?
4. How is maintenance managed for software and hardware?
5. Are hardware and software support contracts co-termed so that they may be paid in an orderly fashion?
6. Is there old hardware being supported that should be upgraded or replaced?
7. Is there a reliance on old software that can be upgraded or replaced?
8. Do they see any outstanding (hardware, software, etc.) issues that need to be addressed? What are the timelines that they should be addressed by?
9. Do they have any hardware which are not covered under Warranty by the vendor?
10. Are there any products/hardware that they feel would be an enhancement to their existing environment?
11. Is additional training required?
12. Is the current staff sufficient to support the infrastructure? Is there a need for any subject matter expertise in-house or through strategic partner resources?
13. Do staff need/want training in any special areas that would improve their work performance or make their jobs more efficient?

Identify Staffing Skills & Gaps

Though not a technical or direct business requirement, this is an important responsibility of any consultant, architect, or team leader.

Bringing new hardware, software, processes, and solutions into the standard operations of a business is a normal activity. After the architect and implementers are done, the teams that will own and operate the infrastructure will need the skills and confidence to take ownership of the solution. This is critical for success of the project.

The architectural lead has a responsibility to address all the business, continuity, compliance and operational objectives of the project. While engaging the business to gather requirements, and develop the solution, you are developing a relationship with those team members who are helping you gather the requirements and their details. Not every team member will have all the skills required to use and maintain the solution. As the architect responsible for developing the solution, it is also your job to identify any gaps in skills that exist, and create a plan to address these gaps.

How can you address gaps in the skills required to maintain the solution?

There are many ways to do this. You could recommend that people acquire certifications, or that they take classes, or perhaps even lead them through a workshop on how to utilize the solution. Operational guides will make the transition easy, but sharing that knowledge, and giving confidence to the team can produce much better results.

One of the more difficult parts of enabling the teams that own the solution, is articulating the importance of training to leadership. Not all leadership teams believe that training is an important component of the whole solution. If that is the case, it will be something you as the architect can be the champion of.

It may be expensive to have your team trained, but what is the cost of having an untrained team managing your environment?

Exercises

1. Create a traceability matrix (text or spreadsheet) to hold the questions and data.
2. Create a presentation
   a. Identify the primary questions and answers that drove major design decisions.
   b. List key requirements, constraints, validated and non-validated assumptions, and risks. Include indexing. For example, you could us C001 to represent the first constraint used to drive a major design decision.
   c. Include related, and indexed, design decisions.

DESIGN DECISION WORKBOOK

> *"Infrastructure design is about the actualization of targeted business requirements through alignment with the architectural capabilities of an IT solution. This actualization should occur through a top-down approach to design, ensuring business requirements drive architectural infrastructure design decisions within each layer of a design as you move through the creation of conceptual, logical and physical design elements."*
> — *Wade Holmes, VCDX-015*

This example workbook is designed for tracking design decisions and patterns. It can also be adapted for operational decisions and patterns. Although there are many design workshops and architecture courses that a candidate can take, nothing beats experience. This is why designs based on an actual project created for an organization build strong skills on top of the educational foundation of an architect.

When developing a design, this workbook can be used to create visualization of each phase of design. At the deployment phase, visualization can show how the current state of the environment (the "as-is") moves to the implementation of the design (the "to-be"). The diagrams used allow for clarity when reviewing and using the design. This may include vision statements, objectives, design methodologies, implementation, operational service models, and key goals as the visualization moves from "as-is" to "to-be".

The following table encapsulates the VCDX design approach in showing the checklist of items that are evaluated for each design decision. It shows the **Design Decision** being made, the combination of options, and the choice taken. It shows the matching **Justification**. The chosen **Design Pattern** is described. The **Impact/Implications** to other areas of the design are identified. Finally, the associated **Risk** is identified for the chosen design pattern. A risk should have a probability and an impact, and be as quantified as possible. Mitigations should also be listed.

We will provide examples of these in the design examples.

Table 56 - Design Decision Information

Design Option	What choice must be made based on the options available?
Design Choice	What choice was made?
Justification	Why must it be made?
Design Pattern	How will it be instantiated?
Impact/Implications	How does this impact other areas of the design in a positive or negative way?
Risks	What are the risks and likelihood of occurrence? Are assumptions validated?

A simplified version of this can also be used as shown in the following table.

Table 57 - Design Decision Information simplified

Design Decision	What design decision was made?
Justification	Why must it be made?
Impact/Implications	How does this impact other areas of the design in a positive or negative way?
Risks	What are the risks and likelihood of occurrence?

As an architect works through a design project and new information is learned through development of the solution, new decisions may come up. Each of the items listed in the Design Decision Information table should be tracked for traceability. If there are specific items that require signoff, this is typically handled in a separate document from the design.

The following workbook has been created for use in projects and in architecture design workshops. Information in the workbook also includes project related details. As you fill in this workbook remember that not all information provided by customers is complete or accurate. As an architect, it is your imperative to make decisions based on reality, not perception, and to validate both the information gathered and assumptions made.

Examples are provided in the tables in this appendix.

Project Overview

Team Name: **Company, Organization, or Working Team**

Team Members: **Name, Company, Contact information, Skills**

Project Description: **Use Case Scenario**

Requirements

Provide the business requirements driving the design.

R001 – All tenants have a requirement for security boundaries due to governance.

R002 – Financial reporting (chargeback or showback) should cover both the provider and the consumer.

R003 – Demonstrated Return on Investment (ROI) including investment, return, and payback window.

R004 –

R005 –

Constraints

Provide design constraints based on the project/scenario and assessment information provided.

C001 – Limited IP address space of Internet use.

C002 – Must meet PCI and compliance guidelines.

C003 – Must determine how SOX may influence design decisions.

C004 –

C005 –

Assumptions

Provide assumptions based on information provided but not specifically listed. Assumptions can be inferred from requirements, constraints, and assessments.

A001 – Training will be scheduled for administrators.

A002 – Designers understand the features and capabilities of individual products and the scalability of the supported configurations.

A003 –

A004 –

A005 –

Risks and Risk Mitigation

Provide risks associated with the project, the design, and the design patterns as appropriate. Typically this area would include major risk items. Minor risk items may be included in the appropriate areas of the design document, but can also be included in this section.

RI001 – Primary datacenter is located in an area that has experienced frequent weather issues that have resulted in power outages.

RI002 –

RI003 –

RI004 –

RI005 –

Topology

Draw topologies used to create the design. These will include logical, conceptual, and physical design diagrams. These topologies will include vSphere technologies and other technologies related to the design. These diagrams will also include non-VMware components.

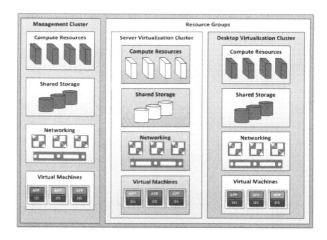

Figure 102 - Example Topology Diagram 1

Clusters

Provide a set of design decisions for the vSphere clusters used for management and resource groups. Consider what type of clusters, sizing/ scalability, and segmentation will be used.

Table 58 - Cluster Design Decision

Design Option	Do we map vCloud Resource Groups to vSphere clusters or to resource pools?
Design Choice	vCloud Resource Groups are mapped to vSphere clusters.
Justification	To support SLAs at the vCloud layer, all the resources of the underlying vSphere cluster must be made available. If vCloud Resources were mapped to resource pools, it is possible that a conflict will arise that may negatively impact vCloud layer SLAs.
Impact/ Implications	The vSphere clusters used must be dedicated for the vCloud Resource Group usage only. May impact budget.
Risks	May impact scalability of infrastructure. Identify risk, and probability (high, medium, or low) and define the impact that this would have on the solution. Also include potentials for remediation.

Network

Provide the networking design decisions. In many large infrastructures, converged networking will mean an overlap with storage design decisions.

Table 59 - Network Design Decision Template

Design Option	
Design Choice	
Justification	
Impact/ Implications	
Risks	

Storage

Provide the storage design decisions. Remember that business requirements, application SLAs, and infrastructure technologies may require hybrid solutions.

Table 60 - Storage Design Decision Template

Design Option	
Design Choice	
Justification	
Impact/ Implications	
Risks	

Allocation Models

Provide design decisions on how allocation of resources will be handled when there are different allocation models required. For example, how do you ensure dedicated resources do not get mixed with shared resources in supporting production versus sandbox workloads?

Table 61 - Allocation Models Design Decision Template

Design Option	
Design Choice	
Justification	
Impact/ Implications	
Risks	

Monitoring

Provide the monitoring related aspects of the design and how they relate to other areas of the design. For example, does monitoring require the triggering of a failover workflow? Monitoring could trigger VMware Site Recovery Manager (SRM) engine in the event of data center failure to start the recovery process at an alternate site.

Table 62 - Monitoring Design Decision Template

Design Option	
Design Choice	
Justification	
Impact/ Implications	
Risks	

Governance

Provide design decisions based on governance. This includes availability, business continuity, disaster recovery, and security.

Table 63 - Governance Design Decision Template

Design Option	
Design Choice	
Justification	
Impact/ Implications	
Risks	

vApps (Virtual Appliances)

Provide design decisions based on the workloads that will be run. These workloads may be virtual machines or applications.

There may be dependencies within a multi-tiered application. How do you handle supporting these dependencies?

Table 64 - vApps Design Decision Template

Design Option	
Design Choice	
Justification	
Impact/ Implications	
Risks	

Service Catalog

A service catalog can mean two things. It can be a set of services that can be consumed. It can also be a set of vApps that are used by a business to support the set of services.

Table 65 - Service Catalog Design Decision Template

Design Option	
Design Choice	
Justification	
Impact/ Implications	
Risks	

Workflow Considerations

Provide design decisions on areas that require workflows, and on the workflows themselves.

Table 66 - Workflow Design Decision Template

Design Option	
Design Choice	
Justification	
Impact/ Implications	
Risks	

Desktop Considerations

Provide the design decisions related to desktop solutions.

Table 67 - Desktop Design Decision Template

Design Option	
Design Choice	
Justification	
Impact/ Implications	
Risks	

Roles and Responsibilities

Provide the design decisions related to the roles and responsibilities of those installing and maintaining the solution.

Table 68 - Roles & Responsibilities Design Decision Template

Design Option	
Design Choice	
Justification	
Impact/ Implications	
Risks	

Validation Testing

Provide the design decisions related to what needs to be validated in the implementation of the design. This includes the following types of tests:

Unit level

System level

Integration level

Some designs may also require additional tests in the areas of security, performance, recoverability, availability, and manageability.

Validation should also consider the customer use cases are validated based on the design created. When dealing with industry requirements, such as healthcare, validation has specific meaning. The testing with these industry requirements may be called validation or verification. It is up to the reader to determine the implications on the design based on subject matter experts. Here we are covering design validation, not regulatory compliance validation or verification. Each type of industry has its own set of unique requirements that must be met.

Table 69 - Validation Design Decision Template

Design Option	
Design Choice	
Justification	
Impact/ Implications	
Risks	

CUSTOMER PRESENTATION PREPARATIONS

"The world of IT has been driven by the need to meet all needs and expectations of not just the business owners but also of the end users. To design the perfect infrastructure is a combination of technological prowess, business acumen and a psychology understanding of the people that will consume this technology. This is how great Infrastructures are designed."
— Brad Maltz, VCDX-036

This Appendix is a reference that is primarily for VCDX candidates and is based on a combination of VCAP and VCDX blueprints. It also includes checklists for design documents and for assessing readiness of an individual to conduct a design review.

All VCDX candidates should ensure alignment with the related track blueprints. This section provides an example of a checklist used to validate the completeness, but not necessarily the accuracy, of the material submitted. This set of checklists will change with subsequent releases as the tracks and programs evolve. The actual blueprints can be found at: www.vmware.com/go/vcdx.

In each of these checklists there will be a checkbox used to verify you have reviewed this area within your design. If a checkbox item is selected, you would then identify a ranking based on readiness level. We are using a ranking of 0 through 3 as defined below.

- 0 = missing information in the submitted materials
- 1 = are not sufficiently covered and will result in less scoring opportunities

- 2 = good coverage and meets minimally qualified candidate (MQC)[7] level
- 3 = good coverage that exceeds MQC level

Remember that this review is based specifically on the submitted material. It does NOT represent the scoring rubric, nor does it provide a final evaluation of whether a candidate will pass. That is done during the in-person defense session. Tips for the next step can be found in the VMware Press book, VCDX Boot Camp[8].

Application Checklist

Before covering the blueprint-based checklists, we will provide the checklist for the application that must be completed and submitted along with your VCDX design submission. The design submission requires a specific set of design documentation from the project you are using for your defense.

The application should contain pointers to areas within the documentation, including document name and section or page numbers, pointing out important areas for scoring opportunities. For example, if you have a creative approach to address a challenge in the requirements, constraints, or risks, that would be good information to point out in the application. Key business requirements, design patterns, and operational patterns are valuable, provide scoring opportunities, and lead to discussions in the defense that increase your chances for success.

- Section 1 – Candidate Information
    - Candidate Name
    - VCP Number
    - Company Name
    - Title
    - Business Email
    - Alternate Email

---

[7] A Minimally Qualified Candidate (MQC) is considered ......

[8] http://www.pearsonitcertification.com/store/vcdx-boot-camp-preparing-for-the-vcdx-panel-defense-9780321910592

- ◦ Business Address
- ◦ Home Address
- • Section 2 – Employment Experience
  - ◦ Current Position
  - ◦ Previous Employment Experience
- • Section 3 – Candidate Biography
- • Section 4 – Project References
  - ◦ Project Name
  - ◦ Company Name
  - ◦ Company Contact Responsible for Internal Management of the Project
  - ◦ Company Contact Responsible for Implementing/ Supporting the Design
  - ◦ Contacts that Provided Additional Inputs in this Design
  - ◦ Project Start Date
  - ◦ Project End Date
  - ◦ Assessments Used
    - ▪ Virtualization Assessment
    - ▪ Health Check
  - ◦ Deliverables Provided
    - ▪ Architecture Design
      - • Conceptual
      - • Logical
      - • Physical
      - • Technology Areas
        - ◦ Monitoring
        - ◦ vCenter
        - ◦ Host
        - ◦ Storage
        - ◦ Networking
        - ◦ Update Management
        - ◦ Virtual Machines
        - ◦ Security
        - ◦ Business Continuity
        - ◦ Disaster Recovery
        - ◦ Backup/Recovery

- Installation and Configuration Guidelines and Procedures
- Operational Verification (Test Plan)
- Operating Procedures
- Next Steps
- Other _____
- Other _____
  - Project team members
    - Other _____
    - Other _____
- Section 5 – Design Development Activities
  - Other _____
  - Other _____

The handbook and application include additional details on what to include. Conceptual, logical, and physical design components are important and can benefit from the inclusion of diagrams. Point these out in the application.

Documentation Checklist

The following objectives checklist includes the high level areas that should be included. This is to ensure completeness within the major areas of scoring. These are not necessarily a recommendation for specific documents or sequencing of content, but should be considered when reviewing the design for completeness.

- Customer Requirements
  - Availability
  - Manageability
  - Performance
  - Recoverability
  - Security
- Solution Architecture
  - Availability
  - Manageability
  - Performance

- ○ Recoverability
- ○ Security
- Engineering Specifications
  - ○ Virtual Data Center Management
  - ○ Virtual Machines
  - ○ Compute Resources
  - ○ Network Resources
  - ○ Storage Resources
- Implementation Plan
  - ○ Plan to go from Hardware and Software Components to a Deployed System
  - ○ Training Guidance
  - ○ Project Plan Schedule for Implementation
  - ○ Special Considerations
- Installation Guide
  - ○ Installation Procedures
  - ○ Integration Procedures
  - ○ Special Considerations
- Operational Procedures
  - ○ Routine Procedures
  - ○ Infrequent Procedures
  - ○ Special Case Procedures
- Test/Validation Plan
  - ○ Unit Level Tests
  - ○ Systems Level Tests
  - ○ Integration Tests
  - ○ Operational tests
- Risk Management
  - ○ Risk Identification
  - ○ Risk Mitigation
  - ○ Validation of Risk Management
- Design Phases
  - ○ Conceptual Model
  - ○ Logical Design
  - ○ Physical Design
- Discovery
  - ○ Requirements
  - ○ Constraints

- Assumptions
- Validation of Assumptions
- Risk Considerations

The following checklists go into more detail and are grouped by track. It is important for a candidate to use these checklists as a starting point. The current blueprints on the VMware site will provide the latest information for each track. These can be found at www.vmware.com/go/vcdx.

VCAP-DCD Blueprint Checklist

- Create a Conceptual Design
  - Gather and Analyze Business Requirements
  - Gather and Analyze Application Requirements
  - Determine Risks, Constraints, and Assumptions
- Create a vSphere Logical Design from an Existing Conceptual Design
  - Map Business Requirements to the Logical Design
  - Map Service Dependencies
  - Build Availability Requirements into the Logical Design
  - Build Manageability Requirements into the Logical Design
  - Build Performance Requirements into the Logical Design
  - Build Recoverability Requirements into the Logical Design
  - Build Security Requirements into the Logical Design
- Create a vSphere Physical Design from an Existing Logical Design
  - Transition from a Logical Design to a vSphere Physical Design
  - Create a vSphere Physical Network Design
  - Create a vSphere Physical Storage Design
  - Determine Appropriate Compute Resources
  - Determine Virtual Machine Configuration
  - Determine Data Center Management Options
- Implementation Planning
  - Create and Execute a Validation Plan
  - Create an Implementation Plan
  - Create an Installation Guide

VCAP-CID Blueprint Checklist

- Create a Conceptual Design
  - Create a conceptual design based on business requirements
  - Identify and categorize business requirements
  - Determine capacity requirements
  - Determine availability requirements
  - Determine security and compliance requirements
  - Create service definitions
- Create a vCloud Logical Design
  - Determine catalog requirements
  - Determine organization structure
  - Define and size components for a management cluster
  - Define and size resource groups
  - Determine virtual data center structures
- Create a vCloud Physical Design
  - Create a physical vCloud network design
  - Create a physical vCloud storage design
  - Create a physical vCloud compute design
- Create a vCloud Security Design
  - Create a directory authentication structure for a vCloud
  - Design a vCloud for multi-tenancy
- Create Extended vCloud Designs
  - Design a Hybrid vCloud
  - Design a multi-site vCloud Solution
- Determine Availability Requirements for a vCloud Design
  - Incorporate availability requirements into a vCloud design
- Determine Metering and Compliance Requirements for a vCloud Design
  - Determine isolation requirements
  - Determine logging requirements
  - Determine management policy requirements
  - Determine chargeback policies and metrics
- Create a vApp Design
- Define a vApp network topology
- Determine remote access requirements for a vApp

- Determine shared infrastructure requirements for a vApp
- Determine requirements for multiple vApp instances

VCAP-DTD Blueprint Checklist

- Create a Conceptual Design
  - Identify business requirements for a View design
  - Identify technical requirements for a View design
- Create a View Desktop Pool Design
  - Create a desktop virtual machine design
  - Determine session integration requirements for a desktop pool design
- Create a View Pod and Block Design
  - Create a View component infrastructure design
  - Determine the database architecture for a View component infrastructure design
  - Create a ThinApp repository architecture design
- Determine VMware vSphere Infrastructure Requirements for a VMware View Design
  - Integrate a View design with vSphere
  - Integrate View design with infrastructure services
- Create a Physical View Storage Design
  - Create a physical design for View infrastructure storage
  - Create a physical design for View pool storage
  - Create a physical design for desktop application storage
  - Determine performance requirements for a View physical storage design
  - Create a tiered View physical storage design
- Create a Physical View End User Design
  - Create a physical View client design
  - Determine session connectivity requirements for a View client design
  - Determine management requirements for a View client design

Design Review Preparedness Checklist

It is important to be honest here. The only person you can hurt is yourself – it is much better to understand your weaknesses so that you can work on them before being tested in the defense. Whenever possible, have a colleague provide answers to these questions.

- Do you have a concept of enterprise architecture strategies?
- Did you provide a complete solution to meet the business requirements?
- Can you identify and understand all business requirements and demonstrate how they are addressed in the design?
- Can you explain each decision and defend the choice you made?
- Can you discuss other possible options and justify why you made your specific choice?
- Do you have experience in all areas and technologies that the design covers? If not, are you ensuring you learn them?
- Have you selected a design that matches the requirements of the blueprint and the application?
- Did you use best practices? Do you understand why they are the best practices for the project you are working on?
- Can you identify areas where you deviated from best practices and explain why you did so?
- Can you identify the constraints imposed?
- Can you identify the inherent risks in the solution and in the design patterns used? What is the likelihood of risk and the mitigation required?
- Have you validated all decisions? Are they sound? Do you understand the impact on other design areas? How do they affect budget, skills, timelines, technologies, and configuration?
- Can you answer questions on everything you have submitted to a customer or to the VCDX defense panel?
- Have you had others review and provide feedback on your design? Have you run a study group to ask deep-dive questions on your design material?
- Have you created a presentation to outline the project, the design inputs, and the design outputs?

APPENDIX D

BUILDING A DESIGN LAB

"The difference between an infrastructure designer and a infrastructure admin or builder is not the ability to meet and exceed the requirements for the project. The difference is the ability to effectively communicate the 'why' to both technical and non-technical audiences. It is as much art, experience, psychology, and writing, as it is technical understanding."
— *Matt Cowger, VCDX-052*

This appendix provides some guidance on building a design lab, on a very tight budget, to be used for developing a design and integrating new technologies. It also provides many tasks that an administrator or architect must have familiarity with when they are working with this technology, or making design choices during the architecture of a solution.

No personal design lab will be able to cover every scenario but it can definitely provide a workspace to develop a starting point. Your creativity can enable you to integrate other technologies through discussions with vendors, friends, and coworkers.

If you are looking to invest a bit more, there are quite a few ways you can build a lab at home. One example is provided by Michael Webster online at http://longwhiteclouds.com/2011/08/24/my-lab-environment

A quick search on the web will provide even more details on some of the extreme lab designs that people have. Also, consider using some of the older, retired equipment you can find at your office. Just because the equipment is 'retired', doesn't mean you cannot use it for your lab environment.

Once you get through the building of your home lab, we have exercises listed here that you should be well versed in. Going through these, repeatedly, will make sure you are aware of many of the decisions required during the workflow of developing a design.

Building A Home Lab

Some of us have the luxury of excess resources at our offices that are dedicated sandboxes for us to play in. Most of us striving to expand our skill sets do not have this luxury, and hence this content.

Many people are looking to build a home lab environment in order to practice and keep up with evolving virtualization technologies. This is not always an easy question to answer, given all the potential variables in hardware and software, as well as the need to stay within a budget for most people. Fortunately, technology prices are always going down.

Keep in mind, that this is a scenario based on a US $2,000 budget. This is not the ONLY solution that can work, but it takes you through the thought process to develop this lab, picking specific hardware components, and combining them to make a home lab, capable of providing the resources to learn and develop solutions with. Take the framework from here, and make it work with your needs and your budget.

Home Lab Explained

Mark Gabryjelski has a home lab presentation on YouTube consisting of five (5) videos of 75 minutes total. By watching the presentations, you can see what parts were used and how they were integrated. The goal of these videos is to provide you with validated compatibility, and some guidance if you are just starting out in the virtualization space.

Go to YouTube, and look up the MarkGabbs channel and search for "How To Build A Home Lab For Hypervisors for ~$2,000". You will find the five video playlist.

Network

Start with the network, as it binds all things together.

With a focus on a small budget, the switch used has eight (8) network ports available. There are 8, 16, and 24 port versions of the switch used in the video presentation. If you have another switch you would like to use, please do. Keep in mind that along with budget, additional considerations used in selecting a switch are Layer 3 routing, LACP, QoS, and advanced features that are normally seen in a production network infrastructure.

Pick a network switch that you like and that conforms to typical industry standards, but make sure to take into account the ability to route at the switch and other advanced features. If you have the luxury, make sure the switch is quiet. This sounds like a silly thing, but when you have many cooling fans, they can become a great distraction.

Could you utilize a virtual machine as a router? Absolutely, though this may detract from your understanding of the physical networking devices, and how they relate to the infrastructure you are building. Once you have the skills to understand how physical networking devices integrate in your environment, feel free to move on and use a virtual machine as a router in your environment.

Remember to build VLANs, and corresponding subnets. The example home lab keeps things very simple for networking. Each VLAN is one broadcast domain, and has one private class C subnet (255.255.255.0 or /24 as the mask) available in it.

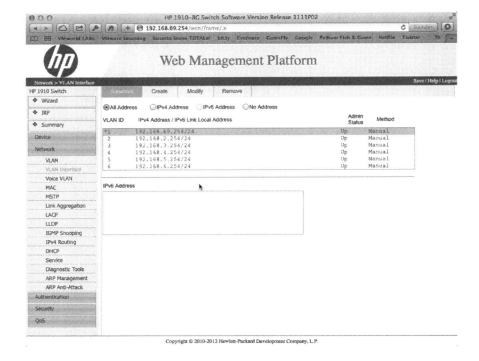

Figure 103 - VLAN Example

Define the purpose of each VLAN / subnet. Separate ESXi management from vMotion, Fault Tolerance, NFS, and normal Virtual Machine traffic (put them on separate VLANs / subnets).

Test the network before you layer on the virtual infrastructure you plan to build. Making sure the foundation is in place and working correctly (to route traffic in and out of your home lab) is essential, and you should validate it before you move on to building the other components.

The Lab Ethernet Storage

The storage used was chosen based on budget. It provides two (2) network ports and four (4) hard disk drive bays. There are many options available to build the storage component.

My key consideration here was to have both iSCSI and NFS storage from the same device. While it may not have dual redundant upstream switch resiliency, it is a home lab. As such we look for the features and function available to it, such as VAAI compliance, and focus less on the ability for a home lab to provide redundancy.

Again, pick a device that you like, but do your best to get both iSCSI and NFS functions in the home lab. Do you see how each Ethernet connection in this example serves either iSCSI or NFS, and exists in its own VLAN? You can do this over a single port on some systems. On other systems, it is not an option.

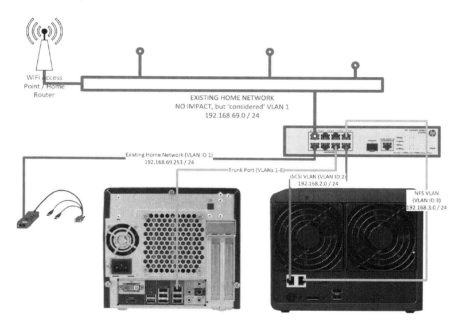

Figure 104 - Home Lab Layout

Although Fiber Channel SANs are possible, for home use this may exceed most budgets.

Build an NFS Datastore for templates and an iSCSI Datastore for use by Virtual Machines.

Remember to build reasonable size LUNs. You are learning how to deploy storage, and sizing the Datastore LUNs to 'normal' production sizes will not be within the budget of your home lab. The functionality of managing, presenting, and securing the LUNs will be within scope. If looking for suggestions, keep a template Datastore at 100-GB and other Datastores at 250-GB. You will be able to grow these later if required.

KVM at Home on a Budget

When watching the presentation on YouTube for building a home lab, you will notice one 'Luxury Item', which is an IP accessible KVM.

This has been included based on the belief that when learning about enterprise class deployments, you should be familiar with the tools available to most system administrators. If you are a seasoned veteran, you already know the benefits of the iLO / DRAC / IPMI functionality of server hardware, and expect it for most of your systems. The item mentioned provides the same functionality for any desktop or server you may have available.

The Lab Hypervisor Host

Finding low cost hardware that has Intel-VT built in, AND has the ability to support 32-GB of RAM is a challenge (at the time of this writing). Current price points as of this writing is approximately US $600 for a motherboard and 32 GB of RAM.

Don't worry too much about anything being a single point of failure when building a home lab system.

We recommend 2-4 TB of storage to start with, ideally in a RAID 1 (mirroring – only 50% of storage is usable) or RAID 5 (only 20% loss of usable storage) configuration.

While the list of parts shows two NICs, the system comes with one NIC.

Build out the vSwitches on this system as highlighted in the presentation. This will allow running both ESXi and nested ESXi servers on this hardware. Nested ESXi servers are run as virtual machines.

Configured successfully, you can have 4-6 hypervisors running as nested ESXi on this hardware. This should provide you with lots of running hosts and VMs to play, manage, and use for learning.

Configure the vSwitch to support connectivity to your home network, as well as a TRUNK to support using VLANs in the nested hypervisors. Make sure to allow all security settings to pass traffic through the physical ESXi host, as shown in the next figure, otherwise the nested hypervisors will not function as intended.

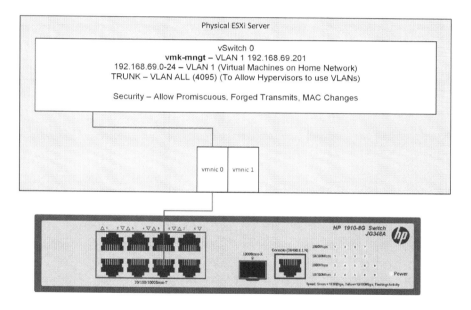

Figure 105 - Physical ESXi Networking

The Virtual (Nested) Hypervisor

Now that the physical system can run Virtual Machines, create the nested ESXi hypervisors.

365

Using a virtual hypervisor, and getting the networking right, is a bit of a challenge initially, but once you have done it, it will make sense. The Port Group TRUNK will be how all the NICs in your nested ESXi hypervisor connect. This allows for the use of VLAN tags within the nested hypervisor.

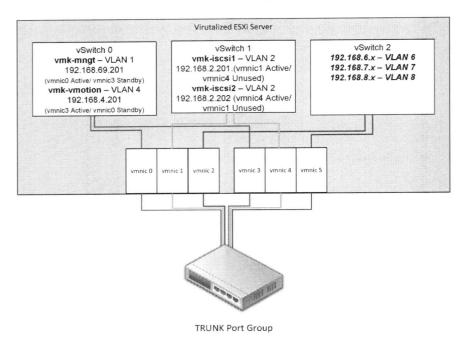

Figure 106 - Nested ESXi Networking

In the example configuration you have 32 GB of RAM to work with. Four nested ESXi servers with 8 GB of RAM will use all of this memory. Now consider what Transparent Page Sharing will do for you. You will be able to run up to 6 Nested ESXi servers. The nested guest virtual machines will benefit as well, so 32-GB will go surprisingly far in a lab setting.

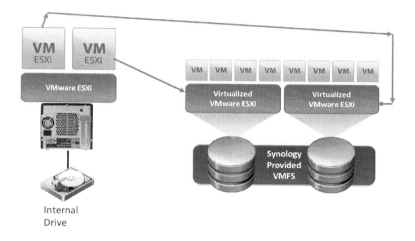

Internal
Drive

Figure 107 - Lab Environment Fully Deployed

Self-paced exercises

The purpose of these exercises is to nudge you into creating documentation, design plans, implementation guides, and the application of critical thinking as you make decisions in the design of your infrastructure.

Some of these labs may seem elementary if you have been working with the products for any length of time. Do not take these for granted, as each of these items exposes a skill (or set of skills) that will be required to better understand how the environment works as a whole.

None of these self-paced exercises give you specific guidance, though they do focus on areas that administrators and architects of Virtual Infrastructures focus on during their ongoing support of an infrastructure, and how they create new infrastructure. They address areas that you should explore, learn to understand, and comprehend the impact that they would have on your infrastructure. The goal would be for you to challenge yourself to understand how each choice you could make, in each of the areas highlighted as a task, could change the outcome of a design and impact standard operating procedures..

There are many sections contained here. Most are related to Datacenter Virtualization (DV), and some are related to Desktop Virtualization (DT), If you are looking for tasks in the realm of Desktop or Cloud, getting the Datacenter Virtualization foundation will support those additional skill sets.

Build The Hardware For Your Lab

1. Build out a managed network environment
   a. Draw the logical design blueprint
   b. Draw the physical network configurations you need for the hardware chosen
   c. Use multiple VLANs and subnets (keep it simple with all Class C networks) – you can use 10.X.X.X networks with Class C subnets also
   d. Validate the ability to route bi-directionally with your new networks
2. Build the hardware for your iSCSI / NFS shared storage
   a. Validate hardware against the VMware Hardware Compatibility List (HCL)
   b. Purchase the hardware required
   c. Assemble the hardware
   d. Configure NFS and iSCSI Storage
   e. Determine security/masking/authentication for your shared storage
3. Add KVM functions as appropriate
   a. Use features familiar to you in the datacenter (iLO, DRAC, IPMI, etc)
   b. Learn features of Remote Media and Remote Management if you are not familiar with it
4. Build the hardware for your home lab hypervisor
   a. Validate against the VMware HCL
   b. Purchase the hardware required
   c. Assemble and configure the hardware for ESXi (physical implementation)
   d. Install ESXi software for the physical hosts

e. Configure all settings in the ESXi host
f. Integrate NFS with the ESXi host
g. Integrate iSCSI presentation to the physical hosts

Build Network Services & Active Directory

Whenever you build or modify any environment, you must have a plan to follow. This allows you to identify any deviations (scope creep) from your plan and know when you have reached your success criteria. Creating the documentation to support your plan usually comprises a majority of the time spent on any project. Don't forget about a test plan and use it!

At every point moving forward, consider all the information required to deploy software in your environment. Every piece of information that you are required to enter to deploy the software *must* be in your documentation set. As you build your documentation, you will realize how much you take for granted, and that your documentation set will grow as you add more features and functionality to your infrastructure. Remember, as you are required to enter information you did not call out as part of your plan, go back and update your documentation. This takes time and effort, but will lead to creating great documentation. If you are not comfortable that you can give your documentation to an intern, and that they can successfully complete the project, your documentation is not yet ready.

If you would like to build a full set of documentation to learn more on what an architect typically creates, refer to the example Table of Contents in Appendix E of this book, as well as Chapter 5, which covered the installation processes and validation of configurations of a small subset of VMware vSphere components.

Here we provide a recommendation on what to include.

1. Document Your Network Core Services Strategy
   a. IP Address Ranges & VLANs
   b. NTP Server
   c. DNS
   d. DHCP
   e. SNMP Communities

f. SMTP Mail Relays

g. SQL Server

h. Domain Controllers

i. Active Directory Organization Unit (OU) Layout

j. Naming Conventions

k. vCenter Configuration

l. vSS / vDS configurations

m. Storage Presentation

n. Directory Based Service Accounts

o. Active Directory Groups for Administrators (do not use Domain Admins)

p. Certificate Services

q. Backup Strategy

2. Implement NTP Strategy

3. Implement Active Directory

a. Create two Domain Controllers

b. Tune the PDC Emulator Domain Controller registry according to your NTP Server Strategy. One preferred method is having this one virtual machine sync via VMware Tools on the ESXi host(s) that is getting its time from an NTP Server.

c. Create Organization Unit configuration

d. Create Service Accounts

e. Create Administrator Management Groups and permission allocations

f. Create 'secure' Group Policy Objects to enable server settings via Policy

i. Firewall enabled plus RDP and ICMP allowed

ii. Adding Service Accounts to local Administrators group as needed

4. Tune DNS Infrastructure

a. Configure replication partners for DNS Servers

b. Configure security around DNS Zone Replication

c. Create all Forward & Reverse Lookup Zones

d. Create 'A' records and 'CNAME' records according to your documentation

5. Create, tune and authorize DHCP Services with reserved static IP addresses for your virtual servers
   a. Create DHCP scopes according to your documentation
   b. Control multiple scopes, reservations, and scope options
   c. Enable IP Helper addresses in the network devices
6. Create SMTP Servers (You can use Exchange, Sendmail, a virtual appliance, or any other solution to provide you with SMTP services)
7. Create a centralized Syslog Server
   a. vCenter Syslog Server is one way to collect logs from ESXi hosts. ESXi hosts can send logs to more than one syslog server
   b. Have a dedicated Syslog Server for collecting and all other Syslog capable device logs into a centralized infrastructure
8. Setup the SQL Server
   a. Configure Mixed Mode Authentication
   b. Create named SQL Server accounts
   c. Create databases required for infrastructure
   d. Assign DBO permissions for the SQL Account for appropriate databases. Never use the SA account. Learn how to manage SQL permissions.
9. Create Certificate Services Server

Build a vCenter Server

Practicing deployment and configuration of vCenter Server multiple times. Use self-signed certifications and then repeat with signed certificates. It is best to use signed certificates for production use, but unsigned certificates will be fine for a home lab. Follow the settings defined in your documentation. If modifying the settings from what was specified, ensure you update the documentation.

1. Deploy a Microsoft Windows virtual machine dedicated to core vCenter services
2. Deploy vCenter and its core components
   a. Install Single Sign On
   b. Install vSphere Web Client
   c. Configure the default search domain for Single Sign On

d. Install Inventory Service
e. Install vCenter Server
f. Install vCenter Update Manager
g. Install vCenter Syslog Collector (vSphere Integrated)
h. Install vCenter ESXi Dump Collector (vSphere Integrated)
3. Configure vCenter Server
   a. Tune vCenter Server settings
      i. Statistics Levels
      ii. Runtime settings
      iii. Mail
      iv. SNMP
      v. Logging options
      vi. Database (number of connections)
      vii. Database retention policy
      viii. Reboot for Runtime settings to take effect
   b. Verify all services started appropriately
   c. Create a vSphere Datacenter
   d. Create a VMware Cluster (Do not enable HA or DRS yet)
   e. Create virtual machine & templates folder layout
   f. Create Virtual Distributed Switches
      i. Enable Health Check
      ii. Define LACP policy
      iii. Define CDP / LLDP policy
      iv. Define MTUs
      v. Enable Network I/O Control (or not…)
      vi. Configure Security Policies
      vii. Configure Load Balancing Policies
      viii. Configure TCP Segmentation Offload support
      ix. Configure VLAN based Port Groups
      x. Create PVLAN
      xi. Create backup of Virtual Distributed Switches
   g. Create Custom Roles (Permissions) for your infrastructure
   h. Integrate SYSPREP files
   i. Create Customization Specifications (answer files)
4. Configure Update Manager
   a. Configure download sources
   b. Configure notification schedule
   c. Configure download schedule

d. Configure cluster & virtual machine default settings

e. Create baselines & baseline groups

5. Repeat with the vCenter Virtual Appliance

Build Nested ESXi servers

This section defines the steps to deploy ESXi servers running as virtual machines. Although not designed to run production workloads, this will enable simulation of ESXi functionality with test workloads. Learning the installation process, configuration options, and core hypervisor settings can provide the foundation for building a solid foundation of your vSphere Infrastructure.

For an additional details on Nested ESXi hosts, see William Lam's guide on his website: http://www.virtuallyghetto.com/nested-virtualization

1. Install ESXi using your documentation
2. Configure Management Network
3. Configure SATP/PSP defaults
4. Configure ESXi Dump
5. Configure NTP
6. Configure CPU Power Management Policy
7. Configure Memory Compression Cache
8. Configure Syslog
9. Configure Firewall
10. Configure Standard vSwitches
11. Add ESXi Host to Active Directory
12. Configure storage (NFS and/or iSCSI)

Use Update Manager to Upgrade ESXi servers

This section guides you through the upgrade process of ESXi hosts using the VMware Update Manager software. Understanding this process, how it works, and the choices provided during the application of an Update

Manager Baseline to a host/cluster, allow you to make appropriate choices when determining operational processes.

1. Build a cluster of ESXi servers at least one version old, so you can upgrade ESXi servers via Update Manager
2. Import new ESXi ISO into Update Manager
3. Create a Baseline for the Upgrade
4. Apply Baseline to cluster
   a. Create and apply an Upgrade baseline
   b. Create and apply a patch baseline
5. Upgrade ESXi server using Update Manager
6. Upgrade ESXi cluster using Update Manager

Add vShield Manager (vCloud Networking & Security)

Learn to deploy the vShield Manager (vCloud Networking & Security), as it is the foundation of the advanced features in vCloud Networking and Security, as well as vShield Endpoint. As vShield Endpoint is part of a vSphere license, learn the integration process of vShield Endpoint, how it affect update/upgrades, and how to prepare the environment for use with 3rd party tools that can take advantage of vShield Endpoint.

1. Import vShield Manager
2. Configure vShield Manager
3. Integrate vShield Endpoint to ESXi servers

Add vCenter Operations Manager

This section asks you to install and configure vCenter Operations Manager, in order to become familiar with the product. Installing requires configuration of IP Pools (or Network Protocol Profiles). Once installed, you should utilize the metrics and reporting in vCenter Operations Manager, and use this experience to help build upon your existing analytics and troubleshooting skills.

1. Verify IP Pools (Network Profiles)
2. Import vCenter Operations Manager
3. Configure vCenter Operations Manager

Configure VMware Clusters

Configuration of VMware Clusters is very straightforward. Configuration of the High Availability (HA) and Distributed Resource Scheduler (DRS) is not so cut and dry. There are many options to configure herein. Learning about these options, the different potential configuration and setting, and the impact that they have on your solution for normal operations. Explore what happens when maintenance windows occur. Do you take on risk during maintenance? Learning the implications of these settings can help you build solution that is tailored to your requirements.

1. Configure HA Settings
   a. Host Monitoring
   b. Admission Control
   c. Virtual Machine Monitoring
   d. Datastore Heartbeating
2. Configure DRS Settings
   a. DRS Automation Levels
   b. DRS Migration Thresholds
   c. Power Management Automation Levels
3. Tune DRS
   a. VM Affinity rules
   b. DRS Groups
   c. VM to Host Rules
4. Add ESXi host to existing VMware Cluster
5. Remove ESXi host from existing VMware Cluster

Build Virtual Machines Templates

This may sound like a trivial thing to focus your time on, but there are tremendous benefits you can gain from exploring the details of the operating system you are deploying as a template, as well as setting in a Virtual Machine that can be tuned. After 12 years of working with Virtual Machines, it is still possible to learn new settings that can benefit you as you role out hundreds of Virtual Machines from template. Learn to tune the Virtual Machine settings, keep the operating systems as lean as possible, and optimize as many settings as you can. Working hard one time (when developing a template VM) has a huge benefit as many Virtual Machines are deployed from the template you build.

1. Create a new Virtual Machine that will be used as a Template VM.
2. Determine sizing (less is more in a template, as you can always add CPUs, RAM, and HDD space)
3. Configure Network, and SCSI adapters accordingly
4. Tune the BIOS of the Virtual Machine
5. Install the OS
6. Install VMware Tools
7. Patch the OS
8. Clean up and prepare the OS for marking as template (such as uninstalling the NIC prior to shutdown)
9. Shut down OS
10. Mark as template
11. Test the deployment of the Virtual Machine

Working with Virtual Machines

Virtual Machines have made many things seem trivial when considering datacenter operations. The goal of this section is to let you explore some of the positive and negative things that can happen when taking advantage of the feature and functions of a vSphere Infrastructure. Learn how an arbitrary setting change (such as changing a vNIC) can have negative impacts on production workloads when done incorrectly. Learn to recognize the things that can go wrong, and learn what the Guest Operating System is capable of supporting. Building your skills in these areas provides you the experience to build better ongoing operations documentation. Play with the nuances of these settings to gain this experience.

1. Deploy from template
   a. Work with customization specifications
   b. Determine how to allocate IPs to Virtual Machines
   c. Integrate with business process
   d. Additional onboarding processes for the Guest OS
2. Working with Cloning
   a. Clone an existing Virtual Machine
   b. Power on both original and clone
3. Compute Resources
   a. Add RAM while Guest OS is online
   b. Add CPUs while Guest OS is online
   c. Removing compute resources from Guest OS
4. Work with Virtual Disks
   a. Add VMDK's to Virtual Machine
   b. Add RDM to Virtual Machines
   c. Add a VMDK on a new SCSI Adapter
   d. Grow a VMDK file, and the VM's file system
5. Changing vSCSI Adapters
   a. Do this for the OS volume
   b. Do this for data volumes
6. Changing vNIC Adapters
   a. Do this without proper cleanup
   b. Develop process to change vNIC for Virtual Machines
7. Remove from inventory
8. Add to inventory
9. Tuning the VM's BIOS

Use VMware Converter

Even after twelve years of working in Virtualization, it is still possible to find a need to perform a Physical to Virtual (P2V) operation. It may even be a Virtual to Virtual operation. Want to safely shrink an overprovisioned VMDK? Need to virtualize an Operating System that you lost the application expertise in? What about using VMware Converter to help you 'customize' a physical machine that was restored from backup to a Virtual Machine (and is having problems booting correctly)? Learning to utilize this feature can help you with ongoing operational problems, as well as consolidation initiatives that you will have working with Virtualization.

1. Convert Physical Machine to Virtual Machine
2. Use Converter to shrink VMDK Size of overprovisioned VM

Migrate vSwitch to Virtual Distributed vSwitch

Working with vSwitches on a single ESXi host is fairly easy to do, and with a bit of practice, you can learn about all the settings in a vSwitch. Working and taking advantage of Distributed vSwitches has its pros and cons. Learn the processes of migrating ESXi hosts, and their Virtual Machines into a vDS environment. Continue this exercise and learn about the processes and specifics about migrating from one vCenter (and its vDS) to another vCenter (and its vDS). Understanding the actions to accomplish these tasks can provide a solid operational foundation for managing and migrating Virtual Networking.

1. Add hosts to vDS
2. Migrate VMkernel Adapters to vDS
3. Migrate Virtual Machine Networks to vDS
4. Deploy a second vCenter Server
5. Migrate ESXi hosts, all VMkernels, and all Virtual Machine networking from one vCenter (and its vDS) to another vCenter Server (and its vDS)

Work with Host Profiles

This feature enables not only simplified configuration of ESXi hosts, but ongoing validation that configurations and setting remain intact during normal operations. Configuration of this feature and its setting may seem overwhelming at first glance, but when you look at the controls you have over all the potential options, you comfort with this configuration and compliance tool will grow, and you will wonder how you went without this feature before. That, and it is a required skillset for the next set of tasks (AutoDeploy)

1. Create a Host Profile from an ESXi host
2. Modify Host Profile
3. Attach Host Profile to Cluster
4. Scan for Host Profile Compliance
5. Apply Host Profile to ESXi servers
6. Configure Scheduled tasks to perform periodic and automated scans of Host Profile Compliance

Add vCenter Auto Deploy to existing vCenter

The ability to network boot an operating system has existed for quite some time, and the ESXi hypervisor has attained this ability recently. While this is no trivial task to undertake, it is not a task to be feared or avoided due to perception of complexity involved in managing and maintaining this solution. With Virtualized (or Nested) ESXi hosts, it is very simple to approach this skillset. Much documentation exists around this feature, but until you build and deploy your own Auto Deploy solution, you will not have full understanding of all the requirements involved. Once you have learned the mechanisms to manage and control Auto Deploy, you will be required to pull on the skill of Host Profiles (suggested earlier in this set of tasks), as this provides the final configuration of ESXi hosts in a network boot environment. As you master this skill, ask yourself if you even will need VMware Update Manager in the future....

1. Modify DHCP Scope for ESXi hosts
2. Install TFTP Server on vCenter Server (if Windows)
3. Install Auto Deploy on vCenter Server (if Windows)
4. Create Images
5. Create Profiles
6. Establish relationships of Profiles to Images
7. Test Deployment
8. Apply Host Profile to ESXi Servers
9. Test Full deployment via Auto Deploy
10. Configure Caching of Auto Deploy on local media of ESXi

Build a vCenter Authentication Proxy

The need for authentication, authorization, and access control does not stop at the vCenter Server. The need to extend these controls to ESXi servers is a business requirement for many organizations. Learn the methods available to you with this tool to abstract administrator credentials for Active Directory from vSphere Administrators, even if you do not see the need for it at the current time. Learn how to apply permissions to the ESXi hosts that have been configured for control via Authentication Proxy.

1. Build a new Virtual Machine for Authentication Proxy
2. Install Authentication Proxy
3. Configure ESXi server authentication using Authentication Proxy
4. Configure ESXi server, and specific Organizational Unit placement using Authentication Proxy
5. Test Authentication Proxy against ESXi hosts

Storage

Shared storage has been an integral part of a vSphere solution since ESXi 2. Consideration and management of shared storage is part of the normal tasks any vSphere administrator or architect must be aware of at all times. What are the limitations imposed by older versions of VMFS that you might encounter? How do those limitations change as VMFS versions change? How do the tools in vSphere (Storage Providers and Storage DRS) change the way you perform tasks, and how do you adjust operational processes to take advantage of these features? Exploring the different types of VMDK files, and the impact each type has on your operations, maintenance, and monitoring tasks is key to understanding which configurations and setting benefit the situation at hand. Once you have mastered these, take on additional storage related technologies, such as converged appliances that provide Software Defined Storage (SDS).

1. VMFS-3
   a. Deploy VMFS-3, 500-GB LUN
   b. Upgrade to VMFS-5
   c. Grow to 2.5-TB

2. VMFS-5
   a. Configure Path Selection Policy
   b. Grow LUN backing VMFS-5 Datastore
   c. Grow VMFS-5 Datastore
3. Configure Storage Providers
4. Configure VM Storage Profiles
   a. Create Storage Capabilities
   b. Apply Storage Profile Policy to existing VM
   c. Deploy new VM and apply Storage Profile during deployment
5. Storage DRS
   a. Configure Storage DRS
   b. Configure Thresholds
   c. Configure Scheduling
   d. Configure VMDK anti-affinity
   e. Configure VM anti-affinity
6. Tune Storage I/O Control
7. Thin Provisioning vs Thick Provisioning (Eager & Lazy Zeroed)
8. Explore Software Defined Storage, and its impact on your storage architecture (in a lab environment, you can utilize a VMX configuration: scsiN:N.virtualSSD = 1)

vSphere Data Protection

VMware has been providing mechanisms to address the backup, and more importantly the recovery of, Virtual Machines since ESX 3. Backup vendors have been working with VMware for the past decade to make their products have a better solution in a Virtualized Infrastructure, and different backup products provide different solutions, as well as new pain points for the vSphere Administrator. Learning to utilize the existing backup software you already have licenses for should be key to your ongoing operations, and SLAs regarding recovery of workloads. Learn about the tools you already have, and determine if they are appropriate for you to integrate into your operational processes, and if they can meet the SLAs you have for your applications.

1. Deploy vSphere Data Protection
2. Configure vSphere Data Protection

3. Backup Virtual Machine
4. Restore Virtual Machine
5. Restore files from Virtual Machine backup

vSphere Replication

vSphere Replication was once only available to Site Recovery Manager users. Today, it is part of most vSphere products (except the very basic Essentials edition). A tool that is part of the licenses you already own that can provide replication, above backup and recovery functions, per Virtual Machine can be very powerful when Business Continuity, Fault Tolerance, High Availability, and Disaster Recovery is concerned. You may still use SAN based replication, or 3rd party software replication, but you should be familiar with the tools you already own, and determine if they can meet your Recovery Time Objectives (RTOs) and Recovery Point Objectives (RPOs).

1. Deploy vSphere Replication
2. Configure vSphere Replication
3. Replicate Virtual Machine
4. Make changes to the Virtual Machine being replicated
   a. Change Network
   b. Add VMDK
   c. Grow existing VMDK
5. Switch to replicated VM

Management Tools

No automobile mechanic uses a single screwdriver to perform all his work. Neither should any vSphere Administrator. Using the graphical utilizes available to you may make your tasks seem easier, but not all things can be done through graphical management tools, nor are they always the most efficient. Learning these additional tools will provide you insights into which tools may be the most appropriate for the tasks you must perform.

Learning which tool is right for which job should be your takeaway as you explore these, and other, tools to managing your infrastructure.

1. Use the vSphere Client
2. Use the vSphere Web Client
3. Work with vSphere Management Assistant
   a. Deploy vSphere Management Assistant appliance
   b. Connect vSphere Management Assistant to hosts
   c. Run script against hosts (Suggested reference – vGhetto script repository - https://communities.vmware.com/docs/DOC-9852)
4. Use VMware CLI (esxcli, esxtop/resxtop, vmkfstools, etc.)
5. Use PowerCLI

VMware Horizon View

Installing a single VMware Horizon View instance, and configuring it to provide desktops is relatively straightforward. Building the solution so it has redundancy and fault tolerance is not always as easy as it seems. Notice the first task is to configure a load balancer, which allows for many VMware Horizon View servers to provide the function of connection broker behind the load balancer. Start small, with perhaps only one VMware Horizon View server behind the load balancer. Once you have the first View Server deployed, you can explore the configuration policies that are available in the VMware Horizon View software. Explore permissions, all the settings available, and most importantly, configuration of logging options.

1. Configure Load Balancer (Use Google to find an open source Virtual Appliance load balancer if needed)
2. Deploy first View Server
3. Configure VMware View
   a. Configure Global Policies
   b. Configure Licensing
   c. Configure Global Settings
   d. Configure Administrators (roles / permissions)
   e. Add a ThinApp Repository
   f. Events configuration of Database

g. Events configuration of Events Settings

h. Events configuration of Syslog (and log to file)

4. Add additional Connection Server

5. Test failover and operations with Load Balancer

6. Install VMware Horizon View Composer

7. Add vCenter Server

Create Active Directory OU Structures & Group Policy Objects

With a Virtual Desktop Infrastructure, management of computer objects in Active Directory can be performed in new ways. No longer are Organizational Units required to address variances in hardware, geography, or a selection of operating systems. You should review the requirements that you need to fulfill, and rethink how these requirements could be met. When building manual desktop pools, you may have a set of Group Policy Objects that provide configurations of those Virtual Desktops, very similar to your physical desktop strategy. When adding Linked-Clones to the conversation, simplifying the ongoing application of Group Policies could provide as few as one (1) Group Policy object to be applied to all Linked-Clone desktops. The goal of this section is to challenge you to consider ongoing operations processes, related to management of computer objects in Active Directory through Group Policy Objects. Starting with a new high level OU can assist in minimizing the effect of existing Group Polices you may have today.

1. Plan Active Directory OU Structure

   a. Create New high level OU for desktops

   b. Create new nested level for Linked-Clone Masters

   c. Create new nested level for linked clones

   d. Create new nested level for manually deployed desktops

2. Plan Group Policies Objects

   a. Leave Linked Clone Masters open for administrative users

   b. Lock down Linked Clones for end users

      i. No System Center Management

      ii. No Updates being pushed

      iii. No software being deployed

    iv. Disable sleep / hibernation

    v. Identify setting you need, and how to deploy / configure them

  c. Create Group Policy to manage manually deployed desktops

    i. This may mimic physical desktop management

    ii. May require many subgroups/sub-GPOs to do this appropriately

Create Virtual Machine(s) for View Consumption

There are a tremendous number of options in configuration, process, and strategy for deploying Virtual Desktops in any Virtual Desktop Infrastructure. Taking all the knowledge you have of Virtual Machines, and coupling that with in-depth knowledge about the Guest Operating Systems configuration, creates so many possible variables of configuration options, that this process never seems to stop. While these base images may constantly require tuning, you will find that some core settings are always tuned the same. Why would you need to have the Wireless LAN service configured on a Virtual Machine? Why would you run a defragmentation on a Linked-Clone Virtual Desktop that will be refreshed tomorrow? This is another exercise that asks you to rethink how you manage computer objects in Active Directory, though now, you will be working with the details of the Operating System. Each Operating System brings new features and challenges with it, and you should not limit yourself to deployment and understanding of only one Desktop OS.

1. Create Template Virtual Machine
2. Create 'Master' Virtual Machine for use via View
    a. Disable unnecessary services
    b. Disable unnecessary tasks in task scheduler
    c. Continue tuning for VDI
3. Create Virtual Machines for ThinApp Creation
    a. Windows XP
    b. Windows 7
    c. Windows 8 / 8.1

Initial Work with Desktop Pools

After you have created Virtual Machines specifically for a Virtual Desktop Infrastructure, it is time to start deploying them, and then consuming them. Using VMware Horizon View, there are quite a few options to choose from...explore them all. Some key considerations are provided in the list of tasks below. With each item, consider the impact each choice will have on the backend administrative teams. Most importantly, you must take a step back, and consider how each choice will affect the user who is consuming the Virtual Desktop. The goal should be to make the user experience better than a physical desktop, and no special knowledge required of the end user. As you build pools, start with small numbers (no more than five desktops per pool) to keep it manageable as you learn.

1. Create Manual Desktop Pool
   a. Make all virtual desktops manually (or use physical PC)
   b. Install View Agent
   c. Make desktop pool
      i. Floating Assignment
      ii. Dedicated Assignment
2. Configure Pool Policies
3. Create Automated Desktop Pool
   a. Floating Assignment
      i. Full VM vs. Composer Linked Clone
      ii. Understand Connection Server Tags
      iii. Understand Remote Desktop Power Policy
      iv. Understand Auto Logoff at Disconnect
      v. Understand Allow Users to reset
      vi. Understand Allow Multiple Sessions
      vii. Understand delete vs refresh vs never
      viii. Understand Provisioning Settings
         1. Naming Convention
         2. Sizing a dynamic pool
      ix. Disposable File Redirection
         1. Did you build so you can disable this
         2. Desktop refresh at logoff can accomplish some of this

          x. Replica vs Delta disk allocation
- b. Dedicated Assignment
  - i. Enable Automatic Assignment (repeat above exercise with this setting)
  - ii. Do not enable Automatic Assignment (repeat above exercise with this setting)
  - iii. Learn why you probably prefer Floating Assignment in most instances
4. Full VM vs Linked Clone
5. Pool Settings
6. Provisioning Settings
7. Storage Allocations

Updating Desktop Pools

Once you have desktop pools being provisioned, and have users that can consume a Virtual Desktop, your considerations do not end there. How do you plan to manage these desktops, patch them, update core business applications, and incorporate these processes so there is little to no impact to the end users? Performing these operations, and seeing the impact to the choices offered when performing any of these suggested tasks can familiarize you with what the impact to the end user could be. The goal would be that the users never know that maintenance has been performed on their Virtual Desktops. How do you accomplish this feat? By exploring, testing, and validating the processes. Learning the impact of these choices can help you make better decisions as you build and maintain a Virtual Desktop Infrastructure.

1. Rebalance
2. Update Master Virtual Machine (linked-clone master)
   a. Update pool to newest snapshot
   b. Recompose
   c. Recompose (and update newest image)
   d. Roll back to previous image in desktop pool
3. Change Desktop Pool settings
4. Change number of desktops in pool.

Create / Configure Security Servers

No Virtual Desktop Infrastructure would be complete if there was no way for a user outside the corporate network to access their Virtual Desktop. In VMware Horizon View, a security server role exists which can eliminate the need for VPN software requirements for many, if not all, the users. This may require some creative networking for you to test in a lab, and it may frustrate you. Once you have this working, and can see that the experience is just as good inside or outside the corporate network, you have succeeded.

1. Deploy Additional View Connection Server
2. Deploy Security Server (in DMZ)
3. Add Security Server to View
4. Test connectivity of VDI through the Security Server
5. Enforce tags to determine external access

Work with ThinApps

Working with the creation of a ThinApp can be a treat, or a nightmare. The goal of this is for you to understand some of the methods of capturing an application, and the available options in VMware Horizon View to push (or stream) an application to end users. Without applications, our Desktop Operating System is pretty much useless. Many of the applications required by users might be part of a Virtual Machine's base image. Creating a ThinApp is one way of capturing an application as a single EXE file. Selecting different options during the creation of a ThinApp will allow for different type of deployments, different manners in which updates to the application are managed, and provide you controls over how to maintain the data a user generates in a ThinApp captured application. Understanding how the nuances of how this could fit in your solution should be the result of your time spent with ThinApp. Work with simple applications, such as a PDF reader, or SSH tools like PuTTY (you are learning the process, and small applications are quicker to capture). This warrants a couple tips, to help you accelerate your learning curve.

1. Deploy a Virtual Machine that will be dedicated to creating ThinApp.
   a. Do not join a domain
   b. Do not install any applications
   c. Minimize the number of updates applied (the three above bullets keep the 'capture' machine clean, and forces you to understand all the requirements of any application you plan to capture)
   d. Shut down the Virtual Machine
   e. Take a snapshot (so you always have a Virtual Machine, in a known 'base' state, that you can turn on and create a ThinApp with)
2. Build ThinApps
3. Explore all combinations of options for MSI, EXE, and Entry Points
4. Work with other ThinApp options
   a. AppSync
   b. Relink
   c. SBmerge
   d. Explore all options available in Packages.ini
5. Add to ThinApp Repository
6. Scan ThinApp Repository
7. Publish via login script / thinreg.exe
8. Publish and manage via Desktop Pool.

REFERENCES

The following references have a value to both the authors and the readers. You will notice that we include several references that are not related to infrastructure design but provide an approach that crosses multiple disciplines.

Books

- Arrasjid, Balachandran, Conde, Lamb, Kaplan. *Deploying the VMware Infrastructure*. United States: USENIX Association, 2008.
- Arrasjid, Epping, and Kaplan. *Foundations for Cloud Computing with VMware vSphere 4*. United States: USENIX Association, 2010.
- Arrasjid, Lin, Veeramraju, Kaplan, Epping, and Haines. *Cloud Computing with VMware vCloud Director*. United States: USENIX Association, 2011.
- Arrasjid, Lin, Khalil, *VCDX Boot Camp, Preparing for the Panel Defense*, VMware Press, xtAxis Press, 2013.
- Arrasjid & vCAT Team, *vCloud Architecture Toolkit*, VMware Press, 2013.
- Burgess, In Search of Certainty, The Science of Our Information Infrastructure, O'Reilly, 2013.
- Burgess, Thinking in Promises, Designing Systems for Cooperation, O'Reilly, 2015.
- Dekker, *Drift Into Failure*. Ashgate Publishing Limited, 2011.
- Duarte, slide:ology: The Art and Science of Creating Great Presentations, 2008.
- Elbeyali, Narkier, *Business Demand Design*, Lulu Press, 2015.
- Erl, Principles of Service Design, Prentice Hall, 2008.
- Erl, *Design Patterns*, Prentice Hall, 2009.
- Gallo, The Presentation Secrets of Steve Jobs, McGraw Hill, 2010.

- Khalil, Storage Implementation in vSphere 5.0, Technology Deep Dive, VMware Press, 2012.
- Linthicum, Cloud Computing and SOA Convergence in Your Enterprise, Addison-Wesley, 2010.
- Quarterman, The Matrix: Computer Networks and Conferencing Systems Worldwide, 1989.
- Tieger & Barron, *Do What You Are*, Little, Brown and Company, 2007.
- Tufte, *Envisioning Information*, United States: Graphics Press, 1990.
- VMware vCAT Team, *vCloud Architecture Toolkit (vCAT)*, online and through VMware Press, 2011-2014.

Documents

- *Design and Delivery of Tactical Decision Games*, http://www.fireleadership.gov/toolbox/TDG_Library/references/TDGS_STEX_Workbook.pdf, TDGS/STEX Workbook, PMS 468, September 2011.
- VCDX Boot Camp presentation.
- *SRM Design Workshop*, VMware PEX architecture design workshop on VMware Site Recovery Manager solutions, Arrasjid, 2006.
- *vCloud Design Workshop*, VMware PEX architecture design workshop on vCloud solutions, Arrasjid, 2010.

Online

- The Open Group, *TOGAF® Version 9.1*, Online, 2011. See http://pubs.opengroup.org/architecture/togaf9-doc/arch/
- Tufte. Envisioning Information. United States: Graphics Press, 1990
- Zachman. *Conceptual, Logical, Physical: It Is Simple*. Online, 2000-2011. See http://www.zachman.com/ea-articles-reference/58-conceptual-logical-physical-it-is-simple-by-john-a-zachman.

- Gabryjelski. *How to Build a Home Lab for $2,000.* http://www.youtube.com/playlist?list=PLLQ3sn5-bIVgJ69HsGPm9-58E4hzjxtq2
- VMware vmbooks, A Practical Guide to Business Continuity & Disaster Recovery with VMware Infrastructure, 2008.
- vBrownbag series include VCAP Admin, VCAP Design, and VCDX boot camp session, http://professionalvmware.com/brownbags/.
- USENIX Association, www.usenix.org.

INDEX

19250255R00267

Printed in Great Britain
by Amazon